TANGO 190

PC DAVID RATHBAND TANGO 190

THE GATESHEAD SHOOTINGS AND THE HUNT FOR RAOUL MOAT

WITH TONY HORNE

\Bb\

Biteback Publishing

First published in Great Britain in 2011 by
Biteback Publishing Ltd
Westminster Tower
3 Albert Embankment
London
SE1 7SP

ISBN 978-1-84954-153-4

10 9 8 7 6 5 4 3 2 1

A CIP catalogue record for this book is available from the British Library.

Set in Garamond and Placard by Namkwan Cho
Cover design by Namkwan Cho
Printed and bound in Great Britain by CPI Mackays, Chatham ME5 8TD

To Kath, Ash and Mia

'Kindness makes the deaf hear and the blind see'
Katherine Rathband, *after Mark Twain*

BIRKHALL

9th August, 2010

Dear P.C. Rathband,

Although I fear this is dreadfully belated, I did so want to say how deeply concerned my wife and I were to hear about the very serious injuries you received during that frightful incident back in July. We are both much relieved to know that you have survived such a life threatening attack, but you can have no idea how much we sympathize with you over the appalling injuries you have sustained, particularly to your eyes.

I need hardly say that we have the most enormous admiration for the extraordinary resilience and courage you have displayed. The United Kingdom owes a huge debt of gratitude to policemen like yourself who are prepared to sacrifice so much for others in the line of duty.

This letter comes with our heartfelt good wishes and every possible healing thought, together with a small bottle of "medicine" which, we hope, may help you a bit through the coming months – should the medical people allow it!

Yours most sincerely

Charles

Letter from Prince Charles to PC Rathband

CONTENTS

ACKNOWLEDGEMENTS

I owe an incredible amount of people such a lifetime of debt that it is – as they say – impossible to thank them all here.

However, I would like to thank our agent Humfrey Hunter at Hunter Profiles who without reading a word of our manuscript said yes on instinct. Thanks also to Alan Shearer for putting us in touch with Humfrey.

At Biteback Publishing, I am hugely grateful to James Stephens in Marketing and Sam Carter our Editor for their vision, brilliance and ability to turn my story around at lightning speed, and for the sensitivity which they brought to the project.

Thanks too to Biteback MD Iain Dale and everybody in the team.

To all of the individuals who helped save my life on the 4 July 2010; without you there wouldn't be a story.

To my old band of friends who have stuck with me and to my precious new friends – you all know who you are; and thanks to the public for the many kind messages.

My sincerest thanks and appreciation to my Chief Constable Sue Sim QPM. A true leader!

Special thanks to the ghost Tony Horne for his dedication and compassion; now friends for life. He is keen for you to know he has written funnier books than this and you can find them at www.tonyhornebooks.com.

I would like to acknowledge my dearest sister Debbie, Rivers, Paul, Lei and my twin brother Darren and his rock Ange… thanks guys!

Finally, to my darling wife Katherine and my dear children, Ashley and Mia; without my vision of these three, I wouldn't have had the will to survive.

Never forgotten and always with me – Naomi x

PROLOGUE

On 1 July 2010, Raoul Moat was released from Durham Prison. Within forty-eight hours he had shot his ex-partner Samantha Stobbart and brutally murdered her new boyfriend, Chris Brown.

In the early hours of 4 July, Police Constable David Rathband was gunned down while sitting in his patrol car in East Denton, just outside Newcastle upon Tyne.

PC Rathband was blinded for life and one of the biggest manhunts in police history began, culminating in Moat's death six days later in the small Northumberland town of Rothbury.

For the first time, this is PC David Rathband's story in his own words…

PART ONE – SEVEN NIGHTS IN ROTHBURY

ONE WEEK LATER

'It's over. David, it's over.'

Kath was asleep in that same chair she had been in all week when the two armed guards from Merseyside Police knocked on the door.

It was 1.30 a.m. and I had been drifting in and out of deep sleep all day because of the morphine. Occasionally the whirr of the helicopters in Rothbury isolated themselves from the Sky News soundtrack and dragged me back to consciousness.

'It's over. David, it's over,' the guards said.

Barely capable of moving and scarcely able to talk after a week of life-saving operations, this was the moment I had been waiting for. My whole world filled with relief as I knew that I wouldn't have to face Moat with no eyesight at trial in the months ahead. And now there was no chance that he would get an early release, so Kath, Mia and Ash could walk safely down the street without running into him one day.

'Has he shot himself or been shot?' I asked, desperate for them to say he'd taken his own life.

And that was the answer.

All my birthdays had come at once. It was important for me that no Police Officer had pulled the trigger and would now be putting themselves and their family through months of investigation and rigmarole that would inevitably follow.

I was at ease for the first time since it happened.

The helicopters wouldn't wake me again.

With the morphine now in full control and no longer any need to resist, I slipped into the deepest and most peaceful sleep that I've ever had.

Only when I woke in the morning would I begin to make sense of the previous week of my life.

SATURDAY 3 JULY 2010

The day my world changed forever.

I couldn't wait to get to work but I shouldn't have been there at all that late in the evening. I was meant to be on a 2 p.m. to midnight shift.

Yesterday I'd spent the day at Wansbeck Hospital in Northumberland representing the Washington family as a family liaison officer (FLO) at a child death review meeting after a double fatal collision out at Chollerford.

Consequently, my shifts had changed. It had been my plan to take *today* off. In the end I just decided to do a late shift.

I'd come home tired and emotional last night after the draining day, did nothing more than have a meal with Kath and go to bed. I hadn't seen the news at all.

Tonight was also my daughter Mia's birthday party. She'd turned twelve on the 1st but this evening was the big one. Did I want to be at home with a house full of giggling girls all night? No, thank you. Give me traffic patrol any day of the week.

I was up at 7 a.m. for an early round of golf – a little bit of me-time before the chaos began! My friend Peter Holleran and I were taking part in a competition day at Warkworth Golf Club and I'd bagged second place with a two below par score of seventy. Not quite the Ryder Cup but a good start to the day with £28 in prize money – not that I would see any of it!

Kath had ordered £100 worth of party goodies for Mia. The cash went in one pocket and out the other. By 1 p.m. she had me nailing screws into the ceiling and stuffing piñatas with sweets and surprises for the girls. God only knows what state I could expect to find the house in when I clocked off in the early hours of tomorrow morning. My mind was already thinking about how quickly I could fill the holes back in. Work couldn't come quick enough.

Just after 3 p.m. I got chatting to my then-neighbour, Jim, as I was about to head out for a 4 p.m. start. I had been so wrapped up in the case yesterday and Mia's party today that I didn't have a clue what had gone on.

'Have you heard about the shooting?' asked Jim, assuming that a copper like me would know everything about it at this point.

He wasn't really asking me if I had heard about it. Of course I had. He was really saying 'Tell me about the shooting'.

Except, I had nothing to tell.

I hadn't heard.

Only now, thinking back, do I realise the significance of that conversation. It was just neighbourly chat. Jim would often ask me about work. We had had this type of conversation hundreds of times over the years. Little did I realise that I would never *see* Jim again.

At the time, it just gave me an extra impetus to get to work and to find out what was going on. Nothing in my immediate behaviour changed – I kissed Kath at the door, told her I loved her and would see her later, tucked my cartoon sandwich box under my arm like a good, honest, hard-working, hen-pecked husband, and drove off to my headquarters at Etal Lane in Westerhope. It could have been any Saturday.

I took great pride and satisfaction in sending bad people down, proud of the fact that, in five years, I had one of the best records as a traffic cop in the entire Northumbria police force. I wasn't nasty or over-zealous. For as long as I can remember, I've had a profound sense of right and wrong and this was the job that I lived for.

At 3.40 p.m. I wandered into the Parade Room to check the force computers. In my mind, I thought that if a gunman were on the loose, a vehicle chase was highly probable. It could come at a moment's notice and at any time of day or night. I had to be ready, although the screens were showing me nothing at this point. Within the hour I'd received a text from Jon Masterman, a shift colleague of mine who was currently on leave. 'Have you seen who they are looking for on that murder? It's Moat.' I couldn't believe it. A chill ran down my spine. We had previous.

I won't say that you never forget a face or a name as a serving police officer – that's not true – but you do carry around a portfolio in locked compartments of your brain of certain individuals whom you never want to see again. Moat had a whole compartment all to himself in mine.

In March 2009, I was assigned to Operation Absolute. I know what you're thinking. 'Who came up with that shit?'

You've not heard of Operation Absolute, I assume. That's because it was top secret – 'need to know' basis only. This was the top drawer stuff for which I had trained – classified material with a big stamp on it that only the chief of all chiefs could authorise.

In reality, that's not how it was at all, but given the significant role that Absolute plays in my personal story, I am now releasing this document as though the statute of limitations had just expired.

The fact is that you could only do the job you were assigned, and over occasional fortnightly periods in 2009, this was the gig. Reading it back now, it seems trivial, but you don't work like that as an officer. Someone else makes those decisions and you enact them.

In the North East a sudden 'invisible industry' had cropped up. It was quietly gathering steam but probably didn't merit much attention in the grand scheme of things. Operation Absolute had been put together to detect and deter metal theft. It was the big thing of the time and I had arrested people for stealing cables from the Tyne and Wear Metro, street manholes, and even bus stops. Oh yes, I enjoyed that CCTV footage in court – a man casually leaving the scene of the crime with an X10 bus stop.

These people weren't mindless idiots though – far from it. They were calculating crooks and metal was the new currency. It was making people a lot of money.

There had already been a massive theft at Pelaw in Tyne and Wear. £50,000 worth of copper was fleeced from the Metro. We found length after length of it stored in two skips around six miles away at Walker, stripped, cut and clean in two-foot sections and already sold on for £4,000. The yard was closed down for the day, and we had to lock up half the staff.

We were stopping all types of vehicle, sometimes on gut feeling, sometimes on intelligence.

And this was how I first met Raoul Moat.

I remember it as a pleasant sunny day – 2 March 2009 – around 3 p.m. Jon and I were coming to the end of our shift. We were just on the road into Blaydon, about a couple of miles from the Metro Centre, and hovering around EMR Limited, the local scrap metal place.

I'd seen Moat's pickup and was suspicious. There wasn't much scrap in it for the naked eye to see but my instinct as a trained plumber-turned-copper was that he was full of shit and his van full of stolen metal. When I pulled him over I saw the copper pipe and an old radiator hidden underneath a load of garden waste. I knew that copper goes dull quickly and I could see that *this* was fresh copper, so I wasn't buying it when he said that he'd removed the remnants of the central heating as part of a job.

He had been a doorman, I've since learned, but was claiming to be starting afresh as a tree surgeon. He told me without batting an eyelid that he had been cleaning out a garden in Morpeth, just a few miles up the A1.

I didn't even need to ring the old lady in Morpeth where he claimed to have been. There was no point even trying since he was so vague on the detail – couldn't remember her name, couldn't remember the street.

We did him just outside the scrap yard under section 165 of the Road Traffic Act. This is how we nailed the uninsured and unlicensed – I'd seen the destruction that these people cause, clocking millions of pounds worth of damage. What would have happened, for example, if he'd gone flying off up the road uninsured, and the boiler he was carrying had flown off the back and killed someone?

His insurer's certificate was with a company that I had dealt with time and time again in relation to metal theft. I knew they wouldn't insure you to carry scrap metal.

I was working quickly while Jon was working Moat. We'd done well to get him back onto the road rather than in the yard itself where he could have destroyed all the evidence. Normally, we'd take it in turns to nail our target, but this time I felt I'd done enough for the day and Jon hadn't.

Moat was horrible, absolutely vile. He was that massive that he took up two seats in the car with his little round head, bulging eyes and steroid-induced body. He started off reasonable enough, telling us about working as a landscaper – to the point that Jon was going to let him off with a producer – but then Moat cottoned onto the fact that the longer this was going on, the more checks I was able to run on him.

I was on the phone to the Motor Insurance Bureau. They had told me straight that he wasn't covered to carry scrap metal. Jon was of the mind not to seize the vehicle but I rang my supervisor, Phil Patterson, to check.

I'd taken an instant dislike to Moat, but that was also copper's instinct. If you like, he failed the 'attitude test', but I felt uncomfortable with him in a way that I have only ever felt with one other member of the public previously, who just happened to be a psychotic schizophrenic. Moat was that bad and intimidating and his casual opening posture of a landscaper soon turned into a bitter diatribe against anybody and everybody in authority, from Social Services to probation officers.

I was clear in my mind and Phil backed me up: we had to take the vehicle off him. Jon doesn't like confrontation, whereas I rise to the challenge of it. I knew I couldn't beat Moat in a fight but in law there was no contest. He was three times bigger than me but I could defeat him in other ways, by taking his car. I knew I was right.

Now I wish I had never set eyes on him but I'd take his car off him again tomorrow, because that's the kind of policeman I am.

In the end, I convinced *Jon* to take it off him. To this day it's Jon's name on the paperwork.

Moat was Jekyll and Hyde, blowing hot and cold all the time in the car. Jon didn't want to book him but I couldn't stand Moat. He intimidated me.

I have had criminals in the back of my car hundreds of times but I felt then that he was going to come for me and he made it quite clear that he hated anyone in authority. All I had as a safety blanket was to attribute the decision to the supervisor. It was *my* decision but I didn't sell it to him like that.

We interviewed him under caution in the back of our car and called the recovery truck to seize his on our behalf and remove it to the pound. He had seven days to produce his documents. He was looking at a £150 release fee and around £12 per day storage. That would probably send him nuts too. He was also screaming that his missus would go mad if he lost the vehicle. I'm not sure if that was Sam Stobbart, the mother of his other kids, or someone else.

After about an hour, another big, steroid-looking bloke came to fetch him. Looking back it might have been Karl Ness, who was also to reappear in my life but I can't be sure. I just remember a huge, repulsive Moat wandering off in one of those naff gym tops with a picture of a weightlifter on it. That image is imprinted in my mind.

We drove off, safe in the knowledge that he could pump all the iron in the world but he wouldn't be lifting any more metal.

Something wasn't right though. Of course, on many occasions you clock off and your head is still buzzing. Being a policeman is so often all about 'unfinished business'. You often leave loose ends for the guys on the next shift to tidy up after you've gone home, but this job lingered ominously in my mind. I couldn't shake Moat off. He'd got to me. I'd try and think about something else but he'd keep cropping up in my thoughts.

I drove home that night to my old house near Blyth, up the Northumberland coast. I couldn't get him out of my mind. He was irritating me big time. Of course, your last job of the night can sometimes do this to you. You can't legislate for being moments from clocking off and a big one coming in that sends you home late and pumped with adrenalin. Yet this was different. I was always proud to do my job and difficult members of the public and tasks overrunning were just part of it but he had got under my skin.

I couldn't get rid of his image, driving home in a preoccupied daze. He had frightened me but also really wound me up. It didn't matter what anybody said to me at home that night, I was only half listening. I just couldn't get that huge, bitter, issue-fuelled monster out of my head.

The next day I awoke and he was still there, bugging me. This went on for a couple of days. This usually only happened if I'd locked somebody up and then they had got bailed so that I would have to go and get more evidence while they wriggled on a technicality. I'd get aggravated by the system then.

This time I was irritated by the man.

At the back of my mind was just one common thought – he'll come again.

‡

Once I knew that Moat *was* back, I had to get up to speed and quick. I learned that he had been in Durham Prison, serving eighteen weeks for assault on a minor. He'd been released a few days earlier, on Mia's actual birthday. In the early hours of this morning, he'd gone to Birtley, near the County Durham border, to the house of his former girlfriend Samantha Stobbart, under the impression that her new partner Chris Brown was a policeman. That's where the vendetta began. Brown was, in fact, a 29-year-old karate instructor.

Samantha Stobbart and Chris Brown had been out for the evening. They had then gone on to a friend's house where they continued to drink, unaware that Moat had been crouched under the open window of the living room for a good ninety minutes, listening to a group of them mocking him. At around 2.40 a.m. Brown left the house, clutching an iron bar, with Sam Stobbart in tow.

They were his last steps.

Armed with a sawn-off shotgun, Moat shot Chris Brown from less than a metre away, straight through the right side of his chest. This was the first of the three shots that would prove fatal. While Stobbart's mother was dialling 999, Moat fired through the window. Sam Stobbart was hit in the arm and abdomen and was taken to hospital for emergency liver surgery and placed under armed guard.

How had I missed this?

It's my job to know everything and, in this day and age, it sometimes seems like it's impossible not to, especially when you have a professional interest in something. Yet my neighbour Jim had known more than me.

After Jon's text I went straight to the computer at the station and banged in Moat's name. There wasn't much on there but what I found left me reeling.

He had come in to the station last year to remonstrate and Jon, who had taken over the investigation, had issued an NFA – no further action.

I couldn't believe it.

He had faced no summons for the insurance, though he had had to pay the release and storage fees which sent him ballistic. I hadn't been there and hadn't seen him since but I was devastated, always having been convinced that we had done him for being uninsured.

He had got under my skin so much that I thought that I had that moral high ground over him but he had wriggled free. There had been something not right about him last year, which had frustrated me. I had spent an hour at the scrap yard, satisfied that I had enough to nail him. Technically you could look up anything on the police computers, though you weren't supposed to. I could get his address, of course, and see things like previous arrests. I could also see that he'd been charged with conspiracy to murder – something to do with a knuckle duster which had then been confiscated in 2000 and, later, an incident with a samurai sword in 2005.

In all he had been arrested fourteen times but had only done time recently. He had had so many scrapes, including relative nonsense like driving off without paying for fuel, but he'd never been sent down until now. My instinct had been right all along.

Of course, I attach huge significance to this now. I'm proud that my sixth sense was correct but all I could think at the time was why we had let him squirm his way out.

‡

At around 4.50 p.m., my colleague Chris Dodds and I were given a job to head out to The Keelman pub near Newburn Leisure Centre. The caller was in a silver Vectra and had been drinking with Moat all day.

'This sounds like a bloody crock of shit this does. Why are we going down? We're bloody traffic cops and we're not armed,' I said to Chris.

But we agreed to go.

We couldn't even be sure who we were looking for. I could see Moat in my head, but the computer was pulling up no contemporary shot of him. He hadn't been photographed on his exit from Durham Prison.

I drove around the pub car park a couple of times, even following the nearby old farm track to speak to the farmer but there was nothing. He hadn't been here and wasn't here now.

It had been a hoax call from a regular hoaxer – a guy with all sorts of baggage and rubbish against his name. His entry registered every type of police warning on the system from 'no female officer to approach him' to 'heavy drugs user' – and this wasn't even Moat. This was one of those other sick fame-hungry nutters who waste police time to have their fifteen minutes of fame.

So we were none the wiser. I parked up by the substation on Newburn Road, on the lookout for Moat.

Around 8 p.m. I went back to headquarters for some bait. You call it tea, we call it bait! I remember Chris finishing off my banana and yoghurt. My bait is your bait and if you don't eat it, someone else will. That's just the rules of the jungle.

I'd been texting Kath too to see how Mia's party was going.

'Be careful,' Kath had replied. 'I'm going to hide under the stairs in the shoe cupboard! The house is so noisy with the girls dancing and the music blaring, it's the best place for me!'

'Move over, I'll get in with you,' I had sent back.

We didn't hang around long on break though. Only last month I'd been sitting on the A69 scanning cars in the wake of the Cumbria shootings, when a nutter called Derrick Bird had killed twelve people.

I was back on the A1, off up the West Road, on to Stamfordham Road in West Denton, back down the A1 again. Nothing was happening. No sightings, nothing on the radio, no new intelligence.

I rang home at half nine. The shoe cupboard was clearly the place to be. Mia had fallen out with the girls! I wasn't surprised. It was always going to end that way. I told Kath to send them all home if they were misbehaving. We carried on texting after I'd put the phone down.

My shift had done a group picture and we'd run it through the *Fat My Face* app.

'You should send that to Darren in Australia,' Kath texted.

'You read my mind,' I replied. I had just pressed send to my twin brother, completely oblivious to the fact I would next hear his voice in hospital.

I could never have known that texting such a stupid picture would be one of the last things I did before my life changed forever.

I popped back to the station briefly at 10.40 p.m. but nobody was there, so I went straight back out. I had put Moat out of my mind for a moment, when word came on the radio about a possible drunk driver being followed from Whitley Bay to Newcastle. I hit the A1 southbound and snuck in as the back marker police car just up the Westerhope slip road. It was nothing though. The driver was just drowsy and the moment passed.

By 11 p.m. I'd left the A1 at the West Road and parked up on the drop kerb at the edge of the pavement at the top of the slip road. If you think like a criminal, you've a good chance of catching them.

At the back of my mind were two major armed robberies that had happened on my watch with Northumbria Police, carried out by proper hardcore crooks linked into really evil networks of crime. On both occasions they had their getaway sorted. They took the A1 to the A69 junction, fled down past Hexham about an hour down the road through country terrain to the M6 and then tore down the motorway back to Liverpool and Manchester. If you wanted to get out of the region by car this was the number one option for the relative discretion you got on the narrow roads on the high ground past Haydon Bridge. Heading the other way, straight down the A1 and onto the M62, left you much more exposed. Beyond Hexham, you'd be lucky to see a police car. That's the way I'd go anyway. That's why I made the crucial decision to park up here.

That was a key decision in what followed. This thought process changed everything – for me, for my family and in the hunt for Moat. Talk to my friends and colleagues, Paul Turner and Chris Dodds, and they know it could have been them. It could have been any of us. My pride tells me that I stopped one of my mates getting shot and who knows how many members of the public. He could have gone into the city centre, pretending to ask for directions and blown any cop's face off when they wound down the window. Or turned up at the police station and done the same. Imagine that happening to a female colleague of yours in her twenties and having to explain it to her parents or her young baby. I have to believe that I took one for my colleagues.

I know that what happened next forced him out and enabled the police to narrow down the focal point of the manhunt. We always say that if you have a field with a rabbit in it and there's only one hole, then descend on that hole, the rabbit will pop up at some point. But that was still to come…

SUNDAY 4 JULY 2010

I remember every moment of what followed, and there's hardly an hour that goes by when I haven't replayed it my head since. The detail doesn't change – the sound is just as loud in memory as it was when it happened. The desperate moments of reaching for help are still just as exhausting. You can play it back in slow motion however many times you like but the outcome remains the same. It doesn't get easier over time. You just learn to live with it, as much as you can. There are bad days, and there are less bad days. Simple as that.

I decided to give it until quarter to one and then I'd go back to Etal Lane and call it a night. We'd see what tomorrow would bring. I had done all I could, without doing much at all. As Saturday nights in Newcastle go, it had been incident-free, with just one suspected drunk-driver the main focus of attention.

It was pretty quiet out there. I'd had a sneaky fag inside the car, put my phone and cigarettes in the door so as not to be distracted and waved to a passing paramedic as he passed. That was just something we did in the fraternity. I thought nothing of it at the time. I'd done it a million times on shift before, as everyone in the emergency services had.

And then, it happened. I felt a presence.

I couldn't be sure what it was but I knew I wasn't alone. However, I didn't register that it was him. Although I never froze, my brain didn't work quickly enough. I just sat there and watched.

Moat had driven off the A1 northbound at Denton and come round the corner onto the off-slip road. He got out of the car and crawled round the corner of the barrier. I'd backed my patrol vehicle against the concrete screen so there could be no way anybody could park behind me. I'd made sure of that.

He must've been doing everything possible to stop me seeing him, squeezing his big figure down to the ground. It would have taken him just a few steps to get alongside my car.

There was a metallic tink on the glass.

I didn't know what that sound was at this point. It was such an unusual sound but one that now stays with me forever. I'd never be able to replicate it exactly because of the connotations, but it was that hollow noise that drew me in. He had found me.

Drawn by the sound, I leant over the passenger seat and looked up.

'Oh fuck, it's him,' I remember thinking.

Jesus, I'd been sold a dud.

It didn't look anything like the steroid-driven, pasty-faced, orange monster, whose truck we'd taken sixteen months ago but I knew it was him from his profile and his stupid 1980s Mohican haircut. This was a meaner, leaner beast. Prison life had shed him a few pounds and the pictures stored on the police system – that the whole of Northumbria Police were working from – bore no relation to the guy in front of me now.

I know now that we were also looking for the wrong car. We'd been told to look for a blue BMW but he was driving a black Lexus. Wrong profile, wrong vehicle and, for me, wrong set of senses tuned in. I had seen that black Lexus drive round the roundabout where I was stationary but not really clocked the fact that it had one of those dodgy exhausts which automatically draws attention to itself. On any other day, at this time of night, any copper would say 'I'll have a look at that'. Normally it might be some kids who had pinched a car and were just being kids, nothing sinister, but as a traffic cop, you don't usually miss stuff like that.

Moat had taken full advantage of the bad info out there. Once he had spotted me, he had his target. Before parking up himself, he'd gone down a junction southbound on the A1 – he travelled to the junction at Scotswood, turned around and returned northbound towards my location, some moments later.

And that was when I came face to face with him, literally looking down the barrel.

My instinct just hadn't kicked in.

I don't know what I was expecting – perhaps that a car would drive past me. I had been mentally preparing for a chase not a showdown. He had come for what he wanted and there was no stopping him. I was alone in the line of fire staring at the spike at the end of what I thought looked like a 4-10 shotgun – the kind a farmer would use.

In the seconds that followed, I looked into his eyes, a focus of ice-cold white, from which any warmth had long since passed. This man was a father to three children but had long-since shunned regular society. He was alone – his eyes told me that story. He never blinked and he never quivered. There wasn't a moment of doubt in his actions, nor an ounce of emotion. In his warped mind, he mistakenly believed that Sam Stobbart was dating a copper and he had taken him out last night. I was next and the more trophies he could get, the better, with no thought of consequence or exit strategy. This was a calculating killer who was angry and determined to hand out his own justice before society got him again.

His face didn't move. He knew what he was doing.

There was a white flash of light from the barrel and that was the last thing I saw. My lights went out, I would never see true daylight again.

He'd got me right between the eyes. My cousin Stuart later told me that he'd seen five shotgun shootings in the army and none had survived. Number six just got lucky.

It is extraordinary to think that I remained conscious throughout the moments that followed. The pain of the noise rather than my injuries was the worst. The shot didn't bother me. The sound in my head had become isolated from every-thing else. It was all I could make out because it was so pierc-ing. I was aware that blood was spraying everywhere but all I could concentrate on was the sound within my skull. It was as though I'd put my head in a big silver drum and someone was rasping my face from the forehead down to my throat with an angle grinder. The noise was relentless and it was that which, in my surprisingly rational thought process at the time, I believed was causing me the pain.

I knew he was still there lurking. The thunder in my head wouldn't let up but I knew I had to carry on fighting, and act quick. I was thinking as logically as possible against the metal-lic drumming bashing the inside of my head. Some miracle had kept me conscious, and in the few seconds that followed I knew I had to save my skin.

I thought that I could see the touchscreen of the Automatic Number Plate Recognition System (ANPR) which was record-ing in front of me. Of course I couldn't but I didn't yet realise this. I had a good sense of where everything was in the patrol car which could explain why I thought I was still seeing it. I'd been driving it for years after all. I was trying to hit the little red triangle on the ANPR – emergency button. My brain was telling me I could see it but my fingers couldn't locate it. I believed I was pushing to call for help. In reality I was probably completing the same motion over and over again like a drunk putting his key in the door and ultimately getting nowhere near. I was now in serious trouble and worse was to follow.

As I was trying to push the screen, my lapel mic to the radio rolled off down my chest and hit my knee, nestling onto my right foot. I remember thinking 'Fuck, it's gone,' and with it my last chance of getting a message out. I could feel it near my foot but I was unable to reach for it, not paralysed in the literal sense of the word, but momentarily slumped motionless.

Nothing was slowing down. There were no movie cliché slow-motion sequences, stretching out time. Between being aware of Moat outside the car to contacting control to say I had been shot and needed assistance took in all about twenty seconds. With the reverberations of the gunshot still splintering my head, the only sound I could hear other than that was my blood spraying out and splashing against the dashboard; I could feel the warmth of the blood soaking through my clothing. I had no idea how much I was losing but that wasn't my priority.

I know I was still thinking straight and still fighting this noise.

'You've got to get the door open,' I told myself.

The car was locked and Moat couldn't get in, making my next action seem pretty stupid but the voice in my head was making me do this. I had to take this risk given that I couldn't operate the radio. My only other hope was for someone to see me.

I quickly opened the door so that the interior light would come on and I put my right foot between it and the A-frame of the car, ramming it in there so that the door couldn't shut itself and Moat couldn't shut it either.

People have since said to me that this was my training kicking in but nobody teaches you how to deal with a madman carrying a gun, other than telling you to avoid him. The body is an amazing thing though. Half of my face was hanging out but I still understood that my overriding objective was to get a message out on the radio, or to get the interior light on.

The impact of the shot had forced me into the footwell.

'Fuck, I've just been shot in the face.'

I could feel the blood spraying out of my face again and I knew I had to sit up.

Then he came for me once more.

He had been waiting to see if I was dead.

I don't think he really expected me to sit up again, but he'd reloaded. For some reason, and I don't know why, as I was hitting the ANPR, something made me raise my left arm to cover my face. While some of my other actions were rational, I have no explanation for this – but it was one that would save my life.

He fired a second time, aiming at my throat as soon as I sat up. The flesh underneath my left shoulder took all the blows. If I hadn't made that uncalculated movement to screen my face when, consciously, I had been trying to press the red triangle, then that would have been it.

The second shot, straight through the glass, meant that I was probably looking at minutes left rather than hours. Moat would have been convinced I was finished. I had slumped back into the same position he would have seen me in after the first shot. The patrol car door remained open with my right foot in it.

'I've got to find the gear lever,' I told myself. How I was having clear thoughts, I do not know. Perhaps it *was* my train- ing kicking in, it may have been human instinct, or maybe I was clinging to the last drops of good fortune. I needed to find the little red or yellow push-to-talk button velcroed on the side of the stalk. This would activate the radio. Other than being discovered, this was my last chance. I was play- ing dead; I knew that if he saw me move he would shoot again. That second shot left me in no doubt – he wanted me dead.

My left hand inched slowly towards the lever and pressed hopefully into the darkness. The sound of my blood pouring everywhere and the incessant pounding in my skull was inter- rupted only by the radio jumping into my life. My joy turned to agony instantly. I couldn't get on the damn thing.

'Why don't you just get off the radio 'cos I need to get on?' I despaired.

A late night Dog Cop was booking off and in no particular hurry to do so. This could not be happening. I couldn't go down because one of my colleagues was nonchalantly signing off his canine friend.

'Why don't you just shut the fuck up?' I said to myself.

By the time he'd finished I had little left to give. I went to press the mic again, waiting for the carrier signal which you get before you go live. The carrier signal picked my key mic up but I dropped off the radio because the dog guy came back on.

'Why don't you just shut your mouth?' I tried to shout.

I was furious. I knew I was dying and had summoned the maximum amount of effort with little left to give, just to even press the damn thing in the first place.

Finally he wrapped up and I just had to go for it.

'Bollocks to it,' I thought.

I could feel myself slipping away but somehow found the strength to press the mic and keep my thumb on it. Eventually it went live but even then I was still in trouble because the mic in the Volvo is situated by the interior light in the roof of the car. I knew I had to turn my face to be heard, or I'd be talking to the foot well.

I had to think systematically – do this, then do that – whilst all the time groggy with the pain and the noise and not sure if Moat was still there or not.

'I've been shot. I need urgent assistance,' I whispered.

There was nothing.

Exhausted, I let go of the button.

The radio fell deadly quiet. Everything up to now had passed in the blink of an eye. But this was the moment which never ended.

Still, there was nothing on the radio.

This was the lowest moment of my life. I had been shot twice but was still trying my best to think like a cop and follow any kind of procedure I might have been taught to deal with circumstances like this. I had given my all.

I lay there, lonely and alone.

No longer a cop, just me, abandoned and helpless. This was my darkest hour.

‡

'Did he just say he's been shot?' one of my traffic colleagues broke the silence, which had felt eternal.

I didn't recognise the voice and they didn't recognise me. Given my position in relation to that of the microphone, my muffled voice hadn't carried, despite the fact that I had tried my best to be heard.

I was broken.

Just making contact, after waiting for the space on the radio, had taken every last drop of will from me. I couldn't do it again. I knew I couldn't do it twice.

'Did he just say he'd been shot?'

The words made me angry, replaying them in my battered head. I had made all this effort to get a message out and the disbelieving tone and slow reactions of my colleagues seemed to slam the door in my face. I couldn't come back from this.

'Please don't think I didn't say it because I can't do it again,' I said to myself.

What happens next in these situations is either luck or genius and I needed either. I was out of options.

Nothing happened for about fifteen seconds.

Then the radio picked up again.

'LB, he's just said he's been shot. Find out where David is on his SatNav. Do a GPS on him,' I heard.

It was Andy Nicholson.

He'd recognised me through the distortion and faint speech. Not only did he know my voice, but every time you fire a message on the radio, each device transmits its own individual number. He will have associated my voice with my number if he'd had time to look at both.

My loneliness lifted and I knew it was only a matter of time. If I could hang on, they would come and find me and capture Moat.

I was at a crossroads.

Moments before I had used my last shot of energy to hit the radio and the despair of rejection had sent me spiralling.

I could have gone either way but silence had condemned me. Now hearing Andy reinvigorated me to find strength and fight. Where I had been slipping away moments ago, now I was rationalising again.

'Hang on,' I thought, 'don't do a GPS on me.'

There wasn't time to wait for them to do anything other than to get back on the radio and say 'Yes, he's here, we've located him'. I knew if they took much longer than that I would bleed to death.

Hearing Andy's voice gave me focus. *I* had to get back on the radio.

'I'm on the A1 roundabout at the junction of the A69, Stamfordham Road,' I managed.

But I wasn't on the Stamfy Road at all.

Despite having been a traffic cop for five years, I'd always got it confused with the West Road as they both looked the same.

I'd given out the wrong location.

It was to be the last thing I did. There was no going back on the radio a third time. The exhilaration of hearing Andy's voice coupled with the short-term energy-burst it gave me to radio my position had exhausted me.

This time I faded, and there was no coming back.

My world turned to blackness.

I was gone.

But at least now they would know.

It was Tango 190.

‡

Sirens woke me, merging in to my consciousness and getting louder as they got closer and as I came round.

I had died in that car.

While I lay there Steve Winn had got back on his radio. I was oblivious to this. He knew I wasn't where I had said I was because he was only half a mile away up the A1. He was in fact at the junction where I had said I was. He had then come straight to me.

Meanwhile, an ambulance had passed me on the other side of the road and driven on into Lemington Road End. This time I hadn't waved. That resonates with anyone in the emergency services. They had seen me hanging out of the car and must have assumed that I was being sick on duty, as they had seen what they thought was vomit running down the open car door. Consequently they had driven off.

But something had bugged them and they, too, returned.

I can only recall this:

Kath, Mia and my son Ash appeared before me. There was no sound, no wind, no bright lights, no heavenly gates, no police car. Nothing. Just peace and darkness – the metallic drumming in my head had gone. All pain had ceased.

Kath was standing far away to the left of the kids. Mia seemed small, about half the size of Ash who was huge. He drifted his six-foot figure from left to right and began to pull at me using his right hand.

I've tried to make sense of it since, but how can you? How can you be certain of your own thoughts in these moments and who can you sit down with and ask if it has ever happened to them? We're in the department of limited knowledge and very little shared experience.

I've asked myself if it is the circle of life. My son Ashley had been born at thirty-one weeks weighing a mere two pounds, fourteen ounces. He measured just forty-four centimetres. Kath and I spent months in the hospital, back and forth, not knowing if he would live or die. To this day, some eighteen years later, we attribute his survival to a miracle, aided by a special course of steroids with potentially serious side effects.

I attach no religious significance to any of this but I can't help but wonder if Ash came back for me in some sort of parallel moment.

I don't think I was dead for long.

When Ash pulled me I sat bolt upright and some pain returned. The sirens entered my consciousness. I wouldn't have heard them at all, through the double-thickness of the windows, if I hadn't half-opened the doors previously.

Was I in some sort of departure lounge from this world to another, all but gone but with a minuscule chance? Did Ashley yanking me pull me round or is that of no significance at all and will everybody ultimately have similar experiences when their number is up, or did the penetrating wailing of the sirens from the A1 southbound bring me back to life? As my colleagues from Etal Lane hurtled towards me from the north, I heard another siren coming from the right, up the West Road.

It was Nathan Crain and Paul Beavis from the night shift. They had been out with two other traffic cops and arrived to find Steve Winn at the scene.

Paul then ran all the way back from the roundabout up onto the West Road where an ambulance was parked up about 400 metres away, in a similar position to my car. The guys were resting there to cut down on travelling times, given the pressure they face to meet targets nowadays.

As well as Nathan and Steve, I also heard another voice. I now know that it was Shaun Wright, the paramedic.

'Keep still, I'm trying to put something on your face,' Steve was urging me frantically.

I could feel my head being pushed. I knew blood was everywhere.

'I can't get his fucking seat belt off,' Nathan was frustrated as I was doubled over on the seat after talking on the radio.

'What's his name, what's his name?' shouted Shaun.

'It's David, it's David,' said Nathan, exasperated.

'I can't keep pushing his face. I'm scared of putting my fingers in his brain,' said Steve.

Nathan put his head past my chest and unclipped my seat belt. I heard a massive click and felt the pressure released off my waist. In the same moment, I could hear the ambulance trolley being wheeled closer to the car.

'We can't get him out the car. We're going to struggle to get him out of the car,' I could clearly hear from the road.

I remember thinking that there was no way I was going to die in this car, having survived this far. I could never leave Kath and the kids with the knowledge that their dad was left dead in the car for as much as two days, while the investigating team were doing their scene preservation.

'I am not dying in this car. I am not dying in this car,' I kept telling myself.

Whilst they were arguing about what to do with me, I found some mental strength to manoeuvre my right leg, which had been trapped in the door, onto the tarmac. Shaun was holding my left shoulder from underneath my armpit and as he pulled me I stepped up out of the car towards the stretcher some four feet away.

'He's getting out of that himself,' I heard a disbelieving Nathan say.

I could hear everything now. Crystal clear.

There was no pain, all I felt was the power in my legs. Nothing else in my body worked but I knew I had the ability and I wanted to walk. The top half of my body was gone. I was like a dangly string puppet, like somebody fainting. As soon as I hit the stretcher I let go of the power in my legs. My body relaxed as I fell onto the trolley, holding both of Shaun's arms tightly.

'Please don't let me die,' I begged him. 'Tell my wife I love her.'

When he had lifted my head moments ago he had thought I was dead. He was talking to me all the time but was gobsmacked to get a response. He'd dealt with dead people before but in the emergency services we were a fraternity so this cut right though him. All *I* could do was moan about my shoulder!

I don't know where I found the words, let alone the strength of character. I had always been determined but how I passed those messages and moved myself I don't know.

If we had been having a hypothetical conversation about my chances in this situation, then they would have been zero. If you had said to me that the human body – my human body – would respond like this I wouldn't have believed you. It just shows, you don't really know anything until you've experienced it and actually been there.

My focus remained. I remember seeing the ambulance with the lights on while Shaun was talking to me.

Ahead, slightly to the left but in the centre of the roundabout in front of my traffic car, I could make out two coppers. I assumed that they were supervisors. I couldn't tell who they were but I just assumed that one was *my* supervisor Ian Dey.

I don't know where that came from. I just assumed. My brain was probably just pulling from the obvious all those things that it could at this point, snatching at familiarities without any particular foundation.

My car was visible to me. Nathan and Paul were visible to the right of the stretcher. And then, I was taken into the ambulance and I can't remember seeing anything after that.

I was blind from the moment I was shot but I recall all of this. This is the disparity between mind and time. My brain is offering me the last picture of where I had come from – that's the only conclusion I can draw. I'd died in the car, passed those messages and had come out of the vehicle without sight – medics will confirm that – but these moments are so clear to me. Is this my out-of-body experience which is crystal clear to *me*… and I am seeing where I *knew* I was but, I can't physically see any more? I can see where it all happened but I am outside of where I was in reality.

Of course, it was now a crime scene too. This is the fine line that any officer has to tread between working to preserve human life and preserving the scene. Normally, Northumbria Police would never go to a firearm crime scene. It may still be active after all. They would leave it cordoned off and normally the radio would be full of 'Attend RV (rendez-vous) point, do not approach the scene'.

Chris and Paul had already decided to come to me, even if they had been told not to. If anything had gone wrong, they would have been slaughtered both internally and in the public but they are to be commended in my eyes. Instinct and fraternity kicked in – from my point of view, thank God they did. Steve Winn was a dog handler – that was his speciality – but he didn't hesitate for a moment at this specialist firearm scene.

It's important to mention Steve here because, as more and more officers turned up, they divided into those dealing with the 'victim' and those with the 'crime scene'. You've got guys like Steve who saw me in isolation, a fellow man and colleague, who could easily see himself in my place. *He* was only concerned about getting me out of the car.

I know for a fact that tempers would have been frayed.

And still there was a mad gunman on the loose.

‡

I don't remember the ambulance doors shutting, nor much of the journey.

'There'll be a sharp scratch on your arm,' Shaun kept saying.

It seemed an irrelevant detail. One more scratch wasn't going to make much difference.

'David, talk to me. Don't go to sleep,' he pestered relentlessly, whilst trying to get the fluids in me.

I like my sleep. If I'd had the energy, I know exactly what I would have said to him.

They were running tests on me even though it was just a short journey to hospital. I found out later that I got a thirteen on the Glasgow Coma Scale, which is good apparently. My blood pressure was also ridiculously normal at 130 over 70. I have no idea how.

When the ambulance stopped I knew we were at The General. I could just tell.

The trolley went flying out of the back of the ambulance and up the ramp into the corridor – they started getting me out as it was stopping but I felt nothing. I was past hurting, the morphine took care of that.

They took me into a room on the left. I recognised this was bed number one in the Resus Room. I had been here many times before for work and the short distance from the ramp to the room told me just how poorly I was.

This was the room where people came to die.

I didn't feel I was there. All was quiet and calm within, if not around me. I didn't care. This was no out-of-body experience – I just had nothing left to give. All my energies had been spent on staying alive. I had known I was dying and mentally that finished me. Physically, my legs had felt like lead, and getting from the car to the stretcher had left my tank empty. There was no sense in me that because I was here now, and had gone through that, the worst was over.

'We need an urgent CT scan,' I heard a male doctor to my left say.

I knew that was so that they could look at my brain. Everything I then heard in that room related to all my experience as a traffic cop, dealing with road collision victims. I couldn't speak to tell them there was nothing wrong with my brain. I knew that was fine. All I could do was lie and listen, detached from the moment.

'The fluids aren't going in quick enough. Can we get them pushed through?' a female nurse behind my head asked.

I was still losing a lot of blood.

'I am going to cut your clothes off,' another male addressed me directly.

Normally, I wouldn't stand for that! I don't like people going there. Uncharacteristically, I couldn't give a shit this time.

They cut from left to right and when they got to my shoulder, it was that sodden with blood that my uniform hit the hospital floor with the thud of wet clothing.

I knew I was in the best and safest place. It was warm and I'd stopped hurting.

I was happy.

To have died in that car and have my family know that I'd been blown to bits would have devastated me. Now I had survived that, I drifted contented into sleep, not knowing if I would ever wake.

All that night I drifted in and out of consciousness. The bright white lights in the ceiling and the white walls of the Resus Room were clear to me, but this wasn't me hanging onto the last drops of sight. This time I knew I was just visualising from memories of many previous visits here. My brain was replacing true images with what I imagined was there.

I could see Kath to my right, with her blonde permed hair.

God, I don't think Kath has had blonde permed hair since we first met in Annabel's in Stafford as teenagers. This severe time dislocation gave me my first realisation that I was blind. Of course, I had never been here before so I don't know if this is normal. Shouldn't my new perceptions be based on the last images that I saw or was this the morphine? Maybe, in my new lonely world, this was pathetic melancholy for more innocent times, a mental equivalent of the foetal position.

The image of Kath was defined, though. It's almost as though I was seventeen again and it was that night back in my flat in Stone, Staffordshire, surrounded by all the furniture from my previous relationship. I had known Kath Moore through schools, though we hadn't been at the same one, and just recently got it together at the expense of my ex.

That night the ex had rung and I wondered if I'd made the wrong decision in Kath. She could see I was troubled. This amazing woman told me to go round to my ex. If I decided I wanted her in the morning, she would come and get me.

There are only three significant details from that night with the ex: great sex, a soundtrack of Michael Bolton, and ringing Kath first thing the next morning.

We were married six months later.

I was woken by a rubbing sensation on my chest. Kath was to my right and I could hear the temporary Chief Constable, Sue Sim, to my left.

'I'm sorry,' I cried to Kath.

I thought I could see them.

I knew my right eye was gone. I had felt it being sucked out, like a balloon filled with water being squeezed through your hands. I was sure I had protected my left one by moving my head quickly away from the white flash; all of those years playing in goal should have paid off, my team mates always said that I had fantastic reactions, that's why my nickname had been 'The Cat'. Thinking back now, this was one of my nine lives.

'You've got nothing to be sorry for, it's not your fault,' she replied.

I could barely reply – so many tubes were in and out of me.

I knew the implications of what had happened. It was clear what this would do to our life. That's the only reason I said what I said. I wasn't apologising because I had done anything wrong.

She had arrived at 1.40 a.m. Paul Turner and Chris Dodds had gone to the house within half an hour of me being shot and by all accounts must have bombed it at about 140mph to get her to the hospital. They didn't tell her I had been shot, though she did ask them.

From a family liaison point of view, I would have done the same. At most, I would have offered 'badly injured'. You never lie to a family in these situations. But you do protect them. It wouldn't have been right to tell Kath in the car – plus they would have been focusing on tanking that car up the A1.

She *knew* though.

Before Kath entered the room, two nurses had gestured that they were cleaning me by making a circular motion with the hand around the face. That's a poor way for Kath to find out.

She was holding it together better than I was, drawing on her experience as a nursing manager to get through this. She will have wanted to pick up the clipboard at the end of the bed but wouldn't have done so, as that would be unprofessional in her eyes. Anyway, she didn't need to. She could see how bad I was.

The staff knew too. They had cleared out one side of A&E, sealed both ends just for me and placed armed guards on the door. One late night drink-fuelled youth that you find in hospitals in the early hours of a Sunday morning in a city centre even had the audacity to heckle one of the Firearms Unit. I know that's crazy, but that's drink, drugs, and possibly poor upbringing for you.

However, the real problem – Moat – was still out there.

Everybody else in casualty was moved. Some of this is procedure. But it was also partly because they didn't know if I had been specifically targeted and if he was coming back.

'Don't worry. We'll get him. He won't hurt anyone else,' Sue reassured me. I was pleased to hear her voice. The support from my Chief meant a lot to me.

But only Sergeant Bell had actually asked who had shot me. There had been a student officer called Daniel placed in the ambulance to see if I made any 'dying declarations' to use later as evidence. Ian Bell had actually come up to me in the Resus Bay to see who had shot me, much to the annoyance of the nurses since every time I spoke, blood was spraying everywhere. I was the only person who could confirm it was Moat.

Nobody else saw him.

Ashley arrived at 3.30 a.m. Mia came much later. One of our neighbours had to babysit my little girl's sleepover. No twelve-year-old deserves to remember her birthday party like that.

Ash tells me he was burning rubber, flying over the humps in the road behind the ambulance as I was transferred from The General under armed escort. I didn't even realise that I had been moved to the RVI Hospital, a couple of miles across the city, where all the key specialists work. I have no recollection other than leaving my room for a CT scan.

At 7 a.m. Kath rang her good friend Dani to tell her what had happened. Her daughter Kim is one of Mia's best friends and was at the sleepover so Dani went to ours, rang all the other parents and took Mia back to their house, keeping her away from the TV. We both regret that Mia had to find out that I was 'badly injured' this way. Given our time again, we would have done things differently. By 8 a.m. my sister Debbie had turned up from Stafford and Kath's mum Sandra, who lives in Spain, was heading to the airport. I have little memory of this either. It annoys me not really knowing how and when things happened.

I am used to being the master of my own fate but I was so away with the fairies that all these other people were making decisions about my life. I had no control. I have no idea if Kath and the doctors were having conversations about organ donation or indeed anything.

Although the doctors were very non-committal, Kath is adamant that at no point did *she* think I was going to die. Knowing how poorly I was, I find that warming. It wasn't based on any medical assessment or on having read my medical notes, because she hadn't. She just knew me better than anyone. There was no way I was dying here. That's why I had fought so hard in the car.

I know the doctors would have told her that they were concerned but I don't think anyone ever said they were struggling to keep me alive. In the ambulance I was quite stable, all things considered, but I had deteriorated in the hospital. I felt poorly too, much worse. I wouldn't have been in the Intensive Therapy Unit (ITU) otherwise.

Things were so bad that at one point one of the nurses came in and went to put her medical gloves in the bin in the corner. In the NHS, you are always trained to use the foot pedal and not touch the bins. She banged the lid down so hard that I almost began to levitate, screaming, thinking it was the sound of the gun again.

By mid morning Kath had been introduced to the family liaison officers. This is normal procedure, of course, if 'normal' still exists in these circumstances. Kath, however, would have been terrified because she only associates a FLO with death. She'd seen me come home time after time, crying with my head in my hands at the breakfast bar in our house, because death was a constant presence in that job.

I never took anything else home from work, but death was all that crossed the front door from Etal Lane into our house, and every time I brought it home, a little piece of me died too.

Kath would have been thinking that FLOs only deal with dead people.

We had been assigned Alison Brown and Chris Clarke. I had first come across Chris a couple of years back at a FLO training day and thought he was a jumped-up tosser. My first impressions are nearly always right but I got this one totally wrong. He's a fantastic bloke. As for Alison – I knew of her during my time at Sunderland when I first joined the force back in 2000 but not more than that. They have proven themselves to be invaluable support and total professionals.

After I had been seen by MaxFax (maxillofacial consultants), plastic surgeons and ophthalmic consultants, Mia came by at around 2 p.m. Dani had kindly brought her in.

Kath left the ITU to find her shaking like a leaf, with all the colour drained out of her. Kath had warned her, of course, that I was really poorly and not to be frightened.

'Daddy, it's Mia,' she said, holding my hand for twenty minutes.

I didn't even know my little girl was there.

By 3 p.m., Sandra had turned up from Spain and Kath had gone home to fetch some essentials and freshen up. She had my blood on her clothes. I know she hated to leave me and as soon as she got home, her mind was set on coming straight back, even though I would be in theatre for the next seven hours. She felt like she was deserting me and barely said a word as Ash drove her home. Nobody could really know what lay ahead at that point. It was in this moment, away from all the drama in the hospital, that she knew nothing would ever be the same again.

MONDAY 5 JULY 2010

I had been violently sick in the bed last night after the operation. I was still alive though, which I guess is something. My face was so swollen after surgery that I could hardly talk. They had given me a syringe driver filled with morphine to control the pain.

At one point I had wanted to go to the loo and had tried to climb out of the bed against medical advice. I tried peeing in a bottle but couldn't go.

'You're going to have to have a catheter,' Kath said.

'Not on my bloody life,' I replied.

My bladder was like a lump in my stomach and would have had to burst all over the floor before I asked for one, on grounds of dignity, but Kath called the nurse.

'Don't pull that out,' I was told when they put it in. 'You'll do yourself all sorts of damage.'

There was a medical balloon on the end of it.

I hadn't peed since the night I was shot, and I really didn't give a toss about the balloon. As the urine drained away it was like having an orgasm, the relief was so great. But after that I wanted the catheter out, which of course they wouldn't do.

All sorts of people were now coming and going around me. It frustrated me hearing the voices and not knowing their names. I felt out of control. Following the frightening experience of the bin lid slamming down, Kath had taken it upon herself to tell me every time someone entered or left the room and exactly what it was that they wanted from me.

An important visitor was Mr Shafique, the consultant ophthalmologist who arrived early on. I was unlikely to forget this.

He shone a pen torch in my eye and there was no reaction.

'I'm afraid you've lost your right eye, and we're very concerned about your left,' came the crushing blow.

It was official. That eye was gone.

I couldn't see but I could feel the heat radiating from the torch into my left eye.

I still had pictures in my mind of course, but beyond that there was only darkness. The images of the shot and of Moat had gone, though I have replayed them many times since.

Now, instead, the morphine was destroying me with hallucinations.

It was like something out of *Pirates of the Caribbean* where the boats clash, they start fighting, and all these skeletons start jumping out, and their skin is water… dead eels and fish jumping out of them at every opportunity. This went on for hours and hours, and even when I was talking to people, they still tormented me.

I was in a big cave, with huge vines hanging off the ceilings. Everybody was looking at me but when I stared back, all I could see were bones. I didn't recognise any of the people because when I tried to, all their skin turned to bone.

'Thank you,' I would say.

'Who are you talking to?' Kath would reply.

'There are people in here,' I'd argue back.

The only way I could get them to go away was to talk to them. And then they would come back again and again.

I don't know if this is standard post-traumatic stress disorder (PTSD); a natural effect of morphine; or if I did, in fact, have some sort of subconscious control over my mind and my inability to see faces reflected my fear of what people were seeing when they looked back at me. I had an idea of how my head looked but I couldn't know for sure. All I do know is that I was within a whisker of losing it.

The doctors told me that I was on high alert. Every time I was drifting and my body was about to surrender to sleep,

I would jump again. They said this would probably continue until I could finally accept that I was in a safe place. The pirates in my head were doing everything they could to stop that from happening.

I associate the pirates with Moat and his henchmen. They frightened me and when sleep would release me from these daydream-nightmares, Moat would appear, returning me to what had happened over and over again. I could still see his left eye looking at me.

‡

Around six in the evening, Kath and I were talking when the door opened.

'How are you doing?' came the voice.

'Why are *you* here?' I replied.

Kath had rung everyone – from my sisters, to her work. Just over twenty-four hours ago, my twin, Darren, had been in his house, just outside Adelaide, when he got the call. He came straight away.

Yes, we were both policemen. Yes, when I broke my leg in 1984 he had inevitably broken his arm a year later. Sometimes we had even shared girlfriends but that was as close as we had got to having a special twin bond. I had always felt that Darren had got lucky in life but still wasn't really happy, whereas I hadn't been fortunate and had worked my butt off for everything. He had made his way up to senior constable without really breaking a sweat; I had been turned down by both West Midlands and the Metropolitan Police, before joining Northumbria Police in 2000. He just seemed to sail through; I had grafted non-stop.

The memory of seeing my dad still working seven days a week out in the cold, at the age of fifty-seven, while mum was out gambling at the bingo in Stafford, where she worked, created a blueprint for me of how I was not going to live my life. I owe much of that to my nan, who practically brought us kids up.

I didn't realise half of this until it was too late academically. My school reports said I was a distraction and didn't try hard enough – my dad had already promised that I could follow him to take an apprenticeship as a plumber so I had a job waiting for me once I turned sixteen and therefore little motivation. Apart from Nan, I had looked up to my sisters Debbie, Julie and Karen but they were all older than me and had all had kids by the age of nineteen.

Only when trying to get into the police did I realise how short-sighted I had been at school and I regret that hugely.

Darren followed a similar path, starting a job in the building trade which my dad had arranged. He lasted about twelve months and joined the police in 1997, following a couple of years in the army serving in the tank regiment from which he was medically discharged after an accident. He had filled out the police applications and sailed through selection, but only after I had mentioned that I was going to apply, disillusioned and unhappy as I was during my two years with the Territorial Army.

West Midlands Police had told me to get some experience as a special constable.

I'd always felt that I was the black sheep of the family, especially when our parents couldn't have been prouder at his passing out parade for the army at Catterick, North Yorkshire.

But mostly I remember that the time I spent as a kid with my mother was largely in the bingo hall, watching her pump her wages into the slot machines. It seemed to me she was fixated by money.

In 1985, my first wage packet was £35 but mum wanted £10 for board. It annoyed me that I was working hard and that she wanted rent, which I knew she was frittering away at the bingo.

One time during an argument she grabbed some loose panelling from around the door and started attacking me with it. She would be locked up for that nowadays.

The first time I had been suspended from school, I must have been around ten or eleven. Afterwards she took me home, pulled my trousers down and beat me black and blue with cable shaped in a figure of eight. I had welt marks from buttock to heel.

So, when I was suspended for a second time after a fight, I just ran away and hid in an old air raid shelter until evening, before heading to my sister's. She rang my dad, who drove me home in silence. Mum was at bingo when I got home and nothing was ever mentioned the next day.

These weren't isolated incidents. Clog-beatings were the norm and she would only stop when I cried.

Darren didn't get any of this. That's not his fault. That's just the way the egg split, but whilst he raced to Adelaide Airport on instinct and without hesitation, I suspect he came out of guilt too.

And what a journey he had to make, knowing little other than that his brother had been shot, halfway across the world finding a newspaper on board the plane with my blood-stained face splattered across the front page.

I was glad he was there. My sister Debbie had come too. I believe she too had additional reasons for coming.

In November 2002, her daughter Naomi had been found dead in the Blackpool flat that she shared with her new boyfriend. The coroner returned an open verdict; the police had treated it as suicide as she was found beside a bottle of wine and empty pill packets. There was no evidence of crushed pills around the house or in her stomach though, and just two weeks previously, Naomi had gone home to Stafford and told Debbie that she would be coming back for good.

The night before Naomi died she had rung me. I missed her call. She had also sent a text to another family member saying 'Help me'. Nobody ever did and I've struggled with that ever since.

At 2 a.m. that night dad had called to tell me she was dead. All I could think of to say was 'Are you joking?'

It just came out.

I got straight in the car and drove to Stafford, arriving two hours later to find mum hysterical.

I couldn't cope with that.

For the next two weeks I sat in a room all by myself drafting the eulogy and planning the funeral. I never spoke to mum.

I don't know why I felt this was my role except that I had done the same when Kath's dad, Mick, had died from lung cancer at the age of 51 and I had found it cathartic. I was also very close to Naomi.

All three of my sisters had lived in the same street and worked at the same nursing home. When Kath and I married it was expected that we would fall into the same trap and ultimately that is one of the reasons that we moved away. The dynamic of all three sisters, always in each other's houses meant that if two met up, the third was always the odd one out. In the years since, affairs, divorces and fallings-out ripped them apart.

Since Naomi died I had withdrawn from my family by choice. I didn't have the energy to placate them all. I've worked hard and joined the police – something which I am very proud of and my parents rarely come by. Kath is my life and her love for me has no boundaries. Her mum is my mum. I have two amazing kids and I live for them now. The distance I keep between myself and my family is deliberate. For me, there was no turning back the clock. Yet, as Debbie rushed to *my* bedside, it seemed obvious why.

Symmetry.

TUESDAY 6 JULY 2010

'Fuck, this is warm,' I moaned.

I had been transferred to ward 47. The far corridor of the ward was cleared for me, and I was placed in a side room. There were armed guards in the room opposite and only the staff knew I was there. No other patients had a clue.

I could only sense that I had been moved because of the heat.

'Can we buy a fan?' said Darren.

It was warm and humid. I've never known a place like it in my life. I was on the plastics ward and they have to keep the skin moist. What a faff.

Whilst I still had no sense of time, I was starting to recognise the nurses by their voices. That at least was some comfort.

Despite this, Kath wanted to wash me, knowing how funny I am about my dignity, even in these circumstances. She'd brought me some boxer shorts too as I was naked in the bed. Very soon, she was using the swabs to wash my mouth. She knew that's what I wanted.

I was on first-name terms with my armed guards too. Paul, Lei, Bob, Elliot and many others whose names are lost to the morphine! Every time a shift changed, they would pop their head round and ask if I minded if they said hello. There was such kindness and goodwill shown by everyone.

I was amongst my own.

But that meant nothing when I found out about the letter.

I was so angry and upset that it set my recovery right back. I wanted to go home. Suddenly I wasn't just a police officer who had been targeted *because* I was a policeman. Now, I knew it was personal.

There had been an armed robbery at the chip shop on Astley Road, Seaton Delaval. I knew exactly where that was – right near our house. What was Moat doing up there? He lived in Fenham, just a couple of miles outside Newcastle city centre, and Sam Stobbart was the other way down the A1 towards County Durham.

Assistant Chief Constable Jim Campbell came to see me, though I'd have preferred my boss Sue Sim. Still, I had met Campbell about eighteen months before and thought he was quite level-headed, a decent guy, and one for the troops. I had no reason to doubt him.

'I want an armed guard outside my house,' I told him.

Alison, the family liaison officer, had already told me that it wouldn't happen, but that was no comfort to me.

He tried to placate me, saying they didn't have the resources. He couldn't put an armed guard outside the house, because they had to put everything into hunting Moat, though, of course, with him just a few miles from my house, I felt the best place to start looking for him was there. The FLO had told me he'd been all around Blyth, Bedlington and the McDonald's in Ashington – that's just four miles from the house. If I had been the FLO, I would have disclosed this too. Golden rule of family liaison is always to make sure that the family hear it from you and not the press. There was no way I *wouldn't* find out.

I was more adamant than Kath about this, and she had seen a page of Moat's letter. She kept out of this conversation. In her eyes, this was police work and she would just listen.

'I'll make sure some cars cruise past the house,' Campbell had said.

That was the best he could offer.

'If I can't protect my family, I want you to,' I begged, sobbing.

The letter, in clumsy Moat scrawl, poorly written and in barely punctuated English, named my collar number. And I wasn't the only one. He listed the collar numbers of other officers who he thought had fitted him up too. Some of us were just traffic cops but he blamed us all for hindering his business and preventing him from seeing his kids. I was no longer just any figure of authority to be hated by him. He'd made it personal and was collecting trophies. The alarm bells were ringing. I had been here before.

In August 2009, we had been away when Ash rang me in the middle of the night to say that my car had been blown up. Sometimes you can live too close to the people you send down. That always stood there in my mind as a reminder.

Overcome with emotion and fear for my family with just Kath's mum back at the house looking after Mia, I begged Campbell one more time.

'Leave it with me, I'll get it done when I leave,' he said.

WEDNESDAY 7 JULY 2010

'Get me the Chief,' I shouted to Alison.

None of us deserved to be lied to.

The hallucinations were back too.

I was living two lives. I was gutted that Campbell hadn't delivered, *but* at least Moat's pirate henchmen were gone from my head.

It's ironic that at the moment in which I was the most angry and upset in hospital, I was also at the most serene in my morphine-laced mind. The pain had gone. No snakes or pirates were torturing me any longer. There were just three or four children, a girl with a white jumper and white trousers holding our Yorkshire terrier from home and a boy. They may have been Ashley and Mia. I don't know.

I was grateful for the tranquillity. Sinister had gone and peace had replaced it. I would talk to the children all the time. If I stroked them or looked at them, they would turn and go away. But they would come back too. I was in a better place now the pirates had gone, until the tranquillity would wear off and I realised that some of the bad people were those I was working for.

'Get me the Chief,' I said to Alison again.

I had phoned home this morning and had been told there were no armed guards. I felt I had been sold down the river like I didn't count. That left me furious.

In the cold light of day, anybody impartial could understand if, due to lack of resources, they had moved my family to a safe house, rather than provide an armed guard. That's fair enough, I guess. But then I wasn't in the cold light of day, and I thought I deserved better than a fob-off.

When Sue Sim arrived at the hospital, Alison intercepted her as she walked up the corridor.

'Can I speak to you before you go in there,' Ali asked Sue.

She told her that I was not in the best mood after being promised that the cavalry would be posted outside our house, only to discover this morning that nothing of the sort had happened.

'Somebody has lied to me,' Sue was heard to say.

Kath could hear her shouting outside on her phone at the other end of the corridor. Eventually she came in the room apologising, assuring me it was now sorted.

That was typical Sue and meant a lot, giving me reassurance I hadn't felt before. I could trust her. Sue was tearful.

'He won't hurt anyone else. We'll get him.' she'd said, referring to Moat.

It was like having your big sister next to your bed, though ironically my big sister was there too, just showing that companionship found in life, whether through a professional capacity or otherwise, can override a family scenario. I felt good with Sue by my side. Crucially, of all the cops who came to see me, Sue was one of a handful to express genuine emotion and show her human side.

For many others, I was just a job. Something they had read about in a manual. Sue was different, doing the best for the public and doing the best for those who served them. Her dignity and humanity were outside of some political ladder she was trying to climb. She stood by me 100 per cent.

Regular media briefings had now thrust her into the spotlight and were coming thick and fast on the news channels. Whilst I had become desperate for constant updates since finding out about the letter, I could see now where this was heading. Every inch of this would be played out in public but the public wouldn't necessarily understand the game.

'The net is closing,' Detective Chief Superintendent Neil Adamson had said yesterday live on Sky.

Today he was getting slaughtered for it.

I didn't think much of the backlash because I had been briefed by the Chief. I knew too from experience that what Neil Adamson was saying wasn't really for the public or the media's consumption, despite obvious safety concerns for everyone with Moat still out there.

They were now getting dozens of sightings around Rothbury. Two accomplices claiming to be hostages had been picked up by the side of the road in this little Northumberland town, around twenty-five miles to the north of Newcastle. Hardly anyone had ever heard of it. There was also a £10,000 reward, which was bound to attract both a selection of nutters and some important information.

However, the net wasn't really closing at all, although his words gave some expectation to the public that an arrest was imminent. But Neil Adamson used those words looking down the camera so that they got back to Moat. That was the sole purpose of the phrase: it was meant for my attacker. My colleagues knew he was getting information and people were feeding him snippets off the news, so they were trying to intimidate him. If they could play tricks on his mind and flush him out, he would have to move. That was the plan.

Moat *was* on the move though. They had found an abandoned tent and another letter. This one was only eight pages long compared to the nearly fifty he had written at the weekend for Sam Stobbart. He was still adamant that Chris Brown had been one of us, which the Chief Superintendent denied.

FLO Alison was starting to get concerned that, when I wasn't getting official word from Sue Sim, increasingly I was starting to learn other nuggets through the media. Sam Stobbart's father, Paul, had been on TV telling Moat to give himself up and asking what kind of legacy he was leaving to the daughter he shared with Stobbart.

'You know I won't lie if she asks about her dad, how good a dad you have been and how bad it has turned out,' he said.

We could have done without that. It would probably make Moat flip just a little bit more.

The press wanted every drop of it and were descending on Rothbury en masse. At times I had to pinch myself at what I could hear. The media was clearly the most helpful tool in getting to Moat and were being drip-fed little morsels at a speed which suited Northumbria Police. And then, every now and then, something strange would fill those half-hours between developments.

Not for the first time this week would I find myself turning to Kath and saying:

'You couldn't make it up? Did they just say what I thought they did?'

I found out that Moat had changed his Facebook status to read 'Just got out of jail, I've lost everything… watch and see what happens'. What a decent man he clearly was, holding his own cyberspace press conference to give us all a head start!

And I couldn't believe it when I heard that they were interviewing a guy called Barry Lister from the Rothbury Cadets live on the telly.

'If I was him [Moat] I wouldn't use one [an abandoned house] because once you're in, you can't get out without getting seen. As long as you stay within the woodland area you are not going to be seen.'

He was now giving Sky News survival tips for any mad gunmen who just happened to be camping out in the hills of Rothbury.

THURSDAY 8 JULY 2010

'Do you suffer from motion sickness?' the anaesthetist asked me.

He wanted to know why the anaesthetic during Sunday's operation had left a trail of vomit in my bed.

The fact that I did seemed an incidental detail back then given the state of the rest of me, but we couldn't risk me throwing up again. I was due in theatre for a long day to apply fixation to my face as I now had what is known as a 'floating face'. All of the bones had been smashed with the impact of the shots but my face was so swollen that the bones weren't moving. If I even slightly sneezed, coughed, or broke wind, I was on that much of a medical knife edge that the bones could move and penetrate the brain. They had to get me in there quickly to apply the fixation before the swelling reduced.

I was scared to death. And this time for completely different reasons.

To come this far so quickly and then to cause further permanent damage if I needed to clear my throat or some dust got up my nose would be just more bad luck. Death was once again a real possibility.

'Don't worry, I will see you at the other end of it,' Nurse Lindsey said, rubbing my hand as they led me once again to theatre. Armed guards accompanied me, not for the first time.

I would be gone for ten hours – probably a good thing when I learned what had gone on in my absence.

Darren had been on telly, much to Kath's annoyance. I can only assume that since Moat's mother, his Uncle Charlie and Stobbart's dad had all had their say, something had kicked in within my twin brother who felt that *his* silence had been deaf-ening. It also gave him some purpose having flown halfway round the world, only to find himself helpless by my hospital bed as I disappeared once again into theatre.

'I feel like he hasn't been my son since he was nineteen years old. He now has a totally different character, attitude and manner. Now when I see him I don't recognise him at all. He would be better off dead. If I was to make an appeal I would say he would be better dead,' Moat's estranged mother Josephine Healey had said, not having seen him in eighteen years.

Clearly, my brother felt that the wrong people were getting too much airtime.

Kath was annoyed at Darren facing the media though, because she hadn't felt it was right to be going public at this point. Her focus was all about me. She always said that when she went to the canteen or occasionally back home, she was staggered to see me on the front pages, or people looking at her differently. She had no idea that whilst the manhunt for this monster was raging across the North East countryside, her husband was the centre of so much attention. For her, I wasn't a story. I was just David, the man who, for some reason, she loved, father to her two beautiful children.

As Darren said those words about my long road to recov-ery, I was under the knife and pumped up with medication but I know he spoke well, bringing some dignity to some of the chaos that seemed to have been filling the airwaves and rolling news channels.

Things were getting tense out there.

Neil Adamson had to call for a second press blackout in an off-the-record briefing. It was now believed that Moat was going mental at some of the stuff that had been written about him.

Perhaps in an indication that Moat wouldn't be taken alive and was already worried about his legacy, the Detective Chief Superintendent asked the media to tread very carefully in what they wrote. They had found a Dictaphone with more ramblings on it and Moat had moved the goalposts. Now, for the first time the wider public were at risk too.

Further media briefings were delayed then cancelled but the police were still sure Moat was in Rothbury. Rolling news filled its time with whatever it could. Worryingly, one expert had said that there was more chance that 'Moat would win the lottery than be shot up there in the hills'.

I was very groggy when I came round and learnt this, aghast that such 'experts' were even allowed on the news.

'God, I hurt,' was just about all I could muster as every part of my body was banging.

'Push the syringe driver. Keep pushing it,' one of the nurses said.

I was now inseparable from the PCA (patient-controlled analgesia) pumping me with morphine – the pain was *that* bad again. The only consolation was that I knew it was my last big operation, other than for my eyes themselves. To that degree at least, the worst was over and that was a huge relief as it meant I could finally start to mend.

Death by smelly trump was no longer an option.

They had managed to stabilise my face and Kath explained to me how it looked. My forehead was distorted, swollen like a football. I had had no bruising on Sunday but now was black and blue, and yellow in places from all the stitching.

I had no vanity issues at this point though I hoped my face hadn't been blown away. At the back of *my* drug-fuelled mind, I managed to compose my worst fear – that my head now looked like this drug dealer I had come across in Byker who I knew was a bad sort. I didn't want to look like him with his big, fat, heroin-ravaged face. Staying intact was all I wanted. Afford me a small amount of dignity, at least. For now too, I would tolerate the fact that I could only eat jelly and ice cream.

Things had been moving at pace while I was under the knife. It felt, from the snippets I could get my head around, like we were hurtling to some conclusion but when that would come and what the consequences would be for whichever of my colleagues were involved was anybody's guess.

Clearly, things were tense on the ground in Rothbury.

Sue had been fronting up to the media, going on walk-about through the high street. Some of the media had said Neil looked 'uncomfortable' and had snapped back at some journalists' questions.

This was clearly a change of tactics from my superiors given the threat to the 'wider public'. Sue wasn't hiding behind a desk. Just as she had sat at my bedside and assured me of my job and that there would be armed guards, now she was making every effort to be seen in Rothbury, up and down the streets, saying that there was no way Moat was going to wander down the high street brandishing a gun – or words to that effect.

Meant to reassure that wider public, these seemed danger-ous predictions, or was she goading him to move again? I knew there were enough firearms units on the scene that he wouldn't get far but, equally, it would only take one more moment of Moat madness and I would have somebody in the next door bed to me, assuming they got as 'lucky' as I had.

There had been reports of vegetables being stolen from allotments and rummaging in back gardens. Even people claiming they had walked past him. Some of these would be nutters or glory hunters, others would be mistaken and one or two probably got it right. Either way, the Chief's words meant he would have to move again, which is smart given that a special drone helicopter had been flying at 10,000 feet above the hills with all the latest gear on board. It was that good that if a patch of earth was moved, they had it caught on camera. The only thing short of intelligence was the monster they were hunting.

It was typical Sue not to think of her career or herself and she put everything on the line that evening. In an unprecedented move, residents of Rothbury were invited to a public meeting in the town. It was broadcast live on TV.

Chief Superintendent Mark Dennett urged people to keep their windows and doors locked and not to make any unnecessary trips out into the countryside. 'We are saying be vigilant,' he said. 'Do not put yourselves at unnecessary risk. We are in a country area here. It is common for people to leave their doors and windows open. What we are saying is to close your doors, close your windows. If you want to go out then go about your business but do so with vigilance.'

Further arrests had been made; new information had come to light; Moat's circumstances had changed but Sue hadn't said how, though press were told that he would kill one person for every inaccurate piece of information published about him. That was actually good to know because it showed he was cracking.

She kicked the whole thing off as the doors were locked by pointing out the emergency exits like an air hostess. This was taken in the spirit in which it was meant by those in the hall but was slaughtered by the watching media.

That was minor compared to what happened next.

In what was clearly meant to be a warm, light-hearted moment to show the strength of the relationship between the community and hordes of police from forces up and down the country, officer Sue Peart stupidly read out a card from goodwill wishers saying how appreciated the efforts of the police were.

Second only to Moat storming the building live on Sky, this was the worst thing that could have happened in this brave but high-risk strategy in a week in which brilliant work was being done behind the scenes but in public we were being made to look ragged.

The card came from two children.

It called Moat a nutter.

My first reaction to this was 'Well done, you read my mind', but it went out live around the world and so did the nervous giggling which turned to uncomfortable silence on the thunderous faces of those involved.

Moat would definitely move now. And probably flip tomorrow.

FRIDAY 9 JULY 2010

'Text in Kath, I want you to text in,' I said.

I'd been listening to the *Tony Horne in the Morning* radio show on Metro Radio as I had done for years. Tony always said what people were thinking. As I lay there in drowsy recovery, all I could hear was that Raoul Moat was a hero.

It just didn't ring true. I had no doubt that Moat was no hero at all but it didn't seem right that the guy to whom I had listened for years was in his camp. I kept hearing 'Moat is a hero' and I just couldn't believe it.

I was lying there, out of my head and back on the brink again after yesterday's long day in theatre and I was getting Kath to text a stupid radio show.

And then I got what he was saying.

'Raoul Moat is a hero, say his fans on Facebook. Let these idiots have their say. Their arguments will unravel themselves and the right-minded, fair-thinking man in the street will be even more disgusted with this vile scum. Who posts on the internet that this Moat is some kind of legendary character? These people are as bad as him and shouldn't be allowed a vote, let alone an internet connection,' Tony ranted.

Thank God for that.

For a moment, I'd thought I had lost the moral high ground. I woke up and suddenly thought that I, little David Rathband, was the bad guy and I was hearing it from a guy that I trusted. I was mortified and incensed until I saw the light. Today was meant to be a recovery day. It had begun with me agitated.

My Sky TV was back which was good news. I had lost it for a bit but now it was on all the time. You just got that sense that everything was going down today but I was struggling to keep up – my thumb constantly pressing for more morphine.

Mark Dennett had said that the decision to keep schools open in Rothbury was down to individual head teachers.

'There is no specific threat against the schools, children, or anybody else in the Rothbury area,' he said, at odds with the discussion of the threat to the 'wider public' and indeed everything that had happened in Hungerford and Dunblane in the 1980s and 90s.

I would have been watching non-stop if I'd had the eyes and the strength but I was just fading in and out. I would hear a snippet of information and that would be enough to send me back calmly to the land of nod. Kath didn't want to know, other than to hear those words 'It's over'. Nor did she want me to ask questions for fear of damaging my face and every time I woke I had a fresh batch of questions.

Her only concern was me.

I was now back in ward 47 and with all my operations over except those on my eyes, Kath knew that she was now looking at my future, and that started here. The worst was over but there was still more to come.

She was totally singular in her dedication to me, while the rest of the world was wrapped up in events outside. She didn't care for the details about Moat. She just needed things to be over and she needed me better.

Yet the whole planet seemed gripped. I could pick up those vibes from the armed guards outside my room.

We had had a change of personnel with officers from Merseyside replacing the guys from Yorkshire, such was the range of the expertise being called upon nationwide. They always came to say hello but today was different. I really got a sense that they wanted to be in Rothbury. This told me it was ending.

They had trained to kill where necessary and again had that fraternal spirit towards me but you knew they were dying to be where the action was. Their brothers were in Rothbury protecting people. From time to time they would tell me stuff just to perk me up but it is the natural instinct of any officer to have wanted to be there. I knew that.

The police feed was coming thick and fast now with Neil seemingly sidelined. At 10 a.m. they released images of equipment that Moat had used while hiding in Rothbury. That seemed to quash any rumour that he *wasn't* in Rothbury.

I suspect that this information was largely useless other than to confirm that he was still there and that the police *did* have intelligence when really we hadn't said much of any depth all week since announcing that the net was closing.

Sometimes you have to release any old information just to keep the story moving. The game is as much with the journalists as it is with the madman.

By midday it came out that three mobiles used by Moat since he came out of prison had been recovered and, an hour later, the National Trust closed the stately home Cragside House while armed police descended on the property looking for him. It is incredible how many abandoned or disused farmhouses in Rothbury there actually were.

Moat clearly knew the landscape.

The media was full of waffle, reporters delighting in police cars flashing past them with their 'blues and twos on' yet still unable to pronounce Ponteland as anything other than Pontyland. Survival experts seemed to litter the channels. Whose side were they on? Not for the first time this week their sense of drama seemed to override their sense of justice. Did they actually care if Moat was caught or did they just want ex-coppers-turned-TV-pundits and scout leaders who thought they were the SAS filling their airtime before the next big breaking news?

Ironically, even I got sucked in.

Word had got back to me that Northumbria Police had shipped in Ray Mears, the survival expert! What was going on?

He had been smuggled in wearing a sergeant's uniform on a bus carrying extra troops! My life was becoming a movie. Ray Mears was now hunting Raoul Moat.

I was supposed to be getting better but I was in a bloody TV show. It was ridiculous.

Of course I still needed care, lots of care. My left eye had become more and more important as the week had gone on. The doctors kept coming in, saying they had done lots of scans and the ultrasounds weren't very positive. They told me that they would leave it a couple of weeks and they would then attempt another exploratory operation.

I don't know if they knew it was all kicking off and they were sensitively giving me some space. Everything seemed to be happening out there. As professional as they were, they must have known.

I was flicking the channels as much as I could. I would hear the odd thing and then I was gone again.

At one point I heard a holidaymaker, caravanning in Northumberland, complain to the TV that they hadn't been warned that the area was dangerous. Well, what can you do? I apologise now in writing for wrecking their summer break.

Northumbria Police seemed to know that a conclusion was near. If Moat did indeed have a TV, he would be getting edgy too. The drama was coming thick and fast. At half four, it was confirmed that the RAF Tornado with hi-tech imaging equipment was being used. That would have told Moat to move because we were tracking him but it would have also told him that if he did it was over. Drains were being searched and homed in on all over the news. He had supposedly been living in one at the end of the town. There was a lot of fact that frankly wasn't anything of the sort. Either way, Neil Adamson's net seemed to finally come good on its promise.

We were still flicking the TV from Sky to the BBC News channel, to the local show, *Look North*. Then, at the moment when the media went home for the weekend and the local shows were off air, at 7 p.m. it all went mental.

Moat was on the banks of the River Coquet.

Patrol cars were tearing through Rothbury and police cordons were going up. Two vehicles actually collided and that tells you the tension on the ground.

'It won't be long. It'll be over soon,' one of the armed guards popped his head round the door to say.

The helicopter was whirring on Sky. That was the constant in the background and every now and then this was the only sensation that could bring me back to consciousness. It was like a *News at Ten* bong going off. Every time someone or something wanted to update me, the chopper would drag me momentarily back to life. It wouldn't last but I would get the headlines. And then I would be gone again.

I'm sure if I had been able to watch, this would have been the best night's telly of my life.

Locals were gathering at the end of the street, piling out of the pubs like the circus had come to town.

'It won't be long,' I said repeatedly to Kath in the moments when I came round.

He was either going to get rifled by bullets from the police or shoot himself.

Lying in my bed, I knew everyone felt it would be over sooner rather than later but I realised there would be a stand-off and the trained negotiator would be in as the key player. The negotiator takes the pressure off my colleagues. Taking out Moat would probably mean you would be removed from your job for twelve months or so while an inquiry ran its course and you would be displaced from what you had specifically trained for and were defined to do.

I was sure a bullet was being fired at some point tonight.

A man so concerned about his pathetic hardman image wasn't going to walk away crying in the arms of one of my female colleagues. Either way, someone else would come out of this with Moat baggage.

Despite the morphine, I could picture the scene. I just had no idea of how long things were taking.

I remember the rain. It was soaking wet.

Who can forget, too, Sky's crime correspondent Martin Brunt reporting around 7 or 8 p.m. that a police car had pegged it past him at the police HQ, nearly hitting a bollard, only to return moments later. The driver had come back to pick up a press officer, the reporter claimed. Well, that's modern policing and I knew already that this case would never go away. There wouldn't be a day without a scar, there wouldn't be a moment without a repercussion. Reputations and careers would depend on what followed. That, as I now know only too well, is the lottery of life. It seems ridiculous to go back for a press officer but then the press had been all over the force all week and what was clearly about to happen was the end game – the moment we would probably get slaughtered for forever as we were asked to justify the 'seven nights in Rothbury'.

It was full-on now.

Ash tells me it was mental online. Kath's mum Sandra was watching at home, doing everything she could to keep Mia away from the TV. Mia was the only person in the country *not* watching by all accounts. More and more people were tuning in at the prospect of a live shoot out. Extraordinary really, that TV and the world had come to this – that the best entertainment was real life. This actually was reality TV.

But it was happening too on the doorsteps of unknown Rothbury. One local dignitary misguidedly went as far as to say that it had put Rothbury on the map.

'I've had an enormous amount of friend requests on Facebook,' he said.

I'm sorry – was I now part of some 'brand Rothbury' marketing strategy? And why was it all about Facebook again?

People piling out of the pub late on Friday night were circling at the edge of the police cordon. Those gathering will never forget that evening, but standing there waiting for a gunshot? How did we get to this dark place?

And they were all queuing up for their media moment.

One of Moat's friends, Tony Laidler, arrived. One bouncer to another – how beautiful! This wouldn't change the ultimate outcome, I knew that, but it might mean one of my colleagues wouldn't have to face the inevitable career destruction for doing the right thing.

The strange thing is that I didn't need the morphine to see that there were real life hallucinations too – stuff that belonged in dreams was playing out in public. What happened next was just a drug-fuelled world away from my life as a traffic officer who had come back, one week ago today, from attending that review into the fatal at Chollerford. The regular guy who couldn't wait to come second in the golf the next morning; the proud dad who loved his little girl Mia but frankly didn't want to be around when the sleepover was going down. That was me and that was my life and no amount of drugs could produce the vision that followed.

'You can't make it up Kath,' I said again. 'Am I in a fucking movie?'

Paul Gascoigne had turned up.

I think I need to say that twice.

Gazza had turned up.

I just didn't know what to say.

What was he thinking? How was this to end? Were Gazza and Moaty to walk arm-in-arm down the high street of Rothbury to rapturous applause with the end credits rolling and the theme music playing?

Had everyone got lost in the Geordie moment? Had I heard Tony correctly after all this morning? Was the man who shot me some kind of working-class hero who people looked up to? Here we were at a very strange moment; a footballing hero around the world – but especially so in this region, even though he did very little professionally here – had just turned up to save the day. Overlook the wife-beating, the alcohol and the absolute rubbish that his life had become, people still laughed him off fondly as 'Gazza' so it was alright. And here he was, turning up on the doorstep of Northumbria Police's most tense moment ever, thinking that it was the World Cup semi-final in 1990. What a fucking dickhead.

As if my story with Moat didn't have enough circles already, I had previous dealings with Gascoigne too. In 2004 I had pulled him over for driving in an unfit manner.

He was on Osborne Road in Jesmond, the affluent part of town and home to much of Newcastle's student population.

In the boot of his car was £16,500 in brown Versace bags. Incredibly he claimed it was from a book signing in Birmingham.

Because, of course, the author always takes the cash in person from an established retail store! I confiscated it on 'suss'.

He ultimately got the money back because nobody could prove anything, He told me everything – he sounded lonelier than I was when I was shot, saying that his lifelong mate Jimmy 'Five Bellies' Gardner would only go out with him for five hundred quid and that many of his mates would always rip him off and sell stories to the press.

Ridiculously, when he left the police station uncharged, he signed my green diary 'Fair Cop, Paul Gascoigne' and went on his way. I thought *then* you couldn't make it up.

And now, you couldn't make it up again.

It was 11 p.m. and Gazza was back, carrying chicken livers, lager and fishing rods.

What?

Had he been sent a different ending to this movie script to everyone else? What was he thinking? This was not the time for a supposed national treasure to think he was still a country's hero.

'You couldn't make it up,' I repeated to Kath.

Something as funny as this for the watching public couldn't have been more depressing to anyone living it. I would have laughed too if I had been at home. But I wasn't – I was lying on my hospital bed, barely alive and when I was conscious, I was making no sense at all because of the morphine. Somebody who had five good years with a ball at his feet had suddenly thought he was a trained negotiator who could rewrite history.

Thankfully – and I'm sure that half of the guys on the ground would have been delighted to see Gazza in his heyday – he didn't get very far. The professionals in position were in the zone, dug deep for the night and no amount of star-struckness was going to allow Gazza within the cordon.

If Rothbury were the castle, there was a Moat all around it, and he wouldn't be allowed to cross it. My boys had it covered on all sides.

‡

I would receive snippets of information like this and then the morphine would take me back to sleep. I knew I hadn't dreamt this, though.

The circus had come to town on the most difficult night in Northumbria Police's history. Rothbury is quite a drive – what on earth was Gazza expecting would happen? Was he really that lonely that this was his Friday night out? And at what point did he appoint himself media manager for the North East's underworld, slurring his way through one radio interview after another? I wasn't well because of what had happened to me and the morphine that followed; Moat wasn't in a good place because he was a mess with a million issues; but Gazza, whose life would continue after this night in the normality to which he had now become accustomed, well, to me he was the most messed up of the three of us.

I tried to imagine the police cordon in Rothbury. I had heard the journalists right up against the 'Police Do Not Cross' tape. I had a sense of the rain and just metres past that cordon Moat was holed up on the banks of the river, snipers all around him in places he couldn't imagine, as trained negotiators played it long.

But at the other end of the town with locals still piling out of the pub, Gazza's appearance put smiles on their faces. How can that be? This was a situation that was beyond serious and would have consequences for years. Gazza delivered his most irresponsible behaviour yet. He turned up for his walk-on part in a panto.

What worries me about that is that I am sure he probably thought he was doing the right thing. He couldn't have been further from the truth.

'It won't be long. It'll be over soon,' I said to Kath once more in the occasional moments when the whirr of the helicopters would pull me back to the land of consciousness.

'We're live in Rothbury,' I would hear the reporters say, and then I would slip away again, my hand never leaving the PCA pumping me with morphine.

Some of the press had got beyond the cordon from another direction, and one was reporting from a neighbour's bedroom. They were constantly being told to move on. There couldn't be a shoot out live on TV.

Moat just lay there with his own shotgun to his head, the guns of the police pointing all around. He had nowhere left to run.

'I haven't got a dad,' the pathetic words of a coward rang out to the police negotiators.

Weren't we way past that now? He was a dad himself and surely you don't need half a brain to work out that when you have your own kids you must rectify the errors of your own upbringing. He had three children, whose lives he had now wrecked. Google wouldn't hide this from them in the future.

What a childlike whinge from a man who knew the game was up.

Every time I woke to learn a little bit more, I would soon drop off again. Staying awake was one fight I knew I couldn't win. I was shattered by events, exhausted by operations and events had now become so surreal that it was a constant battle between the helicopters waking me in the background on Sky and nodding off again after receiving the latest snippet.

'I have mixed feelings, he's a victim,' one resident in Rothbury told reporters. Interesting perspective. What does that make me?

And then I was gone again. It was as though the helicopter was my alarm clock. Every time it came back overhead I would know more news was coming. In reality, there was only one piece of news which was going to count. Everything else was just part of a TV show.

I got word that some bloke called Billy had been on *BBC News* earlier. He had seen a man on the riverbank when he was out walking. *He* genuinely was an eye-witness in amongst all the waffle, speculation, vigilantism, crazy theories and star guests.

'We turned away when my partner realised it might be Mr Moat and about five seconds after that two police vehicles came on to the scene. Armed officers exited the vehicles, told Mr Moat to lower the weapon, which he refused to do, but he did kneel down and point the weapon at his head. The officers then quite sensibly stood back pointing their weapons at Mr Moat, until they received back-up from other officers. Since then, Mr Moat has remained kneeling, pointing the weapon at his head, whilst a group of about ten police officers have been negotiating with him,' he described the moment perfectly to the reporter.

And then I predictably passed out. Kath wasn't too far behind.

Back would come the helicopters. I learned that they had taken Moat food and water. I don't think for one moment there was anything sincere in that gesture. This is standard in a hostage situation. He would have human rights and we would have to be seen to have tried everything to talk him down and find a peaceful resolution.

The armed guards outside my room wanted to be in Rothbury tonight rather than at my door. Raoul Moat had gone on the rampage, causing death and destruction. The consequences of the last week would remain forever. Any of those guys about to fire that gun in Rothbury were firing it for me, for the fraternity and for every officer who has ever been injured or killed in the line of duty, because on the rare occasion when an unarmed policeman is shot in an unprovoked attack, it hits home with everybody. There isn't one of them who didn't wake up last Sunday morning and turn to their partner to say that I could have been them.

‡

And then it happened.

The whirr of the police helicopter collided with the sound of a knock at the door.

It was 1.30 a.m. and poor beautiful Kath and I had both long since surrendered our souls. I had been asleep, this time for around forty-five minutes and couldn't stay awake any longer. Kath had done nothing more all week than grab moments of rest here and there in between my operations, police visits and looking after Mia and Ashley to give them as much sense of normality as possible.

Then there was the circus – the constant media, the drip-feed of information, the killer still on the loose. At times emotion turned to auto-pilot, at others it just overflowed. She was where she wanted to be – by my side. Despite the fact that our life as we knew it was over, I was still all that counted in her eyes and, within the four walls of the RVI Hospital, we avoided absolutely everything else which accompanied this crazy story. She hadn't yet had time to grieve or adjust but that's not my Kath. Whilst the eyes of the world had been watching the seven nights in Rothbury, she knew she was sacrificing the rest of her life as she sat hour after hour by my bedside.

'It's over. David, it's over,' the armed guys from Merseyside confirmed, just fifteen minutes after a gunshot and furious shouting were heard by the river.

But it wasn't over at all.

It was only just beginning.

PART TWO – THE AFTERMATH

SATURDAY 10 JULY 2010

'It's not all soot and terraced houses, you know,' I rang Kath from Newcastle to tell her the news.

A lot of time, love and tenderness had passed since Kath had come to fetch me from my ex's. Eight years to be precise.

Within six months of my shunning a life with Michael Bolton whining on in the background, Kath was pregnant. Having children meant having a wife to me. Suddenly we were on the wedding conveyor belt.

Whenever Kath has made one of her regular visits to a fortune teller in the years since, our three children are always highlighted. Sadly, Ash and Mia had a brother or sister who never made it.

Despite my sisters telling me Kath was not good enough for me, the wedding went ahead all the same. Not falling into that predictable Rathband future was one major factor when I rang Kath after my first visit to the North East of England.

I had to break the cycle.

'You'll have to come back and we'll talk about it,' Kath said when I told her I had finally got into the police.

There was no well done – just a lot to discuss.

By March 2000, I had finally been accepted. Kath would also have to give up her job as a cancer nurse at New Cross Hospital in Wolverhampton. This was our big moment to get a better stand-ard of living away from the humble beginnings of our £35,000 house, in a sorry old state after repossession and which, to this day, Kath's mum still shudders that I made her live in.

Unlike Darren it had been the hardest thing in my life to get into the police. I wasn't going to blow it now. Since 1997, I had been a special constable by night – on expenses only – learning my trade, and a plumber by day.

I wanted it that badly.

Previously, I had attended a recruitment weekend with West Midlands Police and was rated at 9/10. I was urged to apply but failed to get selected. Seeking reassurance that I should try again, I was tipped off.

'Re-submit your application, you'll be fine.'

They didn't say that to *me*, but had done to certain individuals whose numbers I had kept from the recruitment weekend.

In 1998, I applied to Thames Valley Police. I screwed up the spelling test. As part of the exams, you have to sit in a hall and transcribe a tape but you get a second chance if you fail so I practised for six weeks non-stop, night after night with Kath, mastering 'intuition' and 'necessary' and anything else that I might come a cropper on.

Finally, I passed.

People have often asked me since if I always wanted to be a cop, but in actual fact, I just wanted a career. At last I thought I was good enough.

I had reached the final interview stage.

It still wasn't to be.

At the age of eleven, Darren and two of his mates stole a bunch of Cornettos from a Co-Op, while I stood and watched at the door. They all came running past me a few minutes later shouting 'run'.

I hadn't been quick enough when the security officer nabbed me.

I dobbed everybody in at the time but failed to declare during selection the world famous 'theft of the Cornetto incident' of 1979.

Unbelievably this was still on file.

I'll never forget the sergeant ringing me up to tell me I hadn't made it and asking me why on earth I hadn't mentioned it. They had done their homework.

By the time I applied to Northumbria Police this was no longer my only conviction. I had a second for trespassing with an airgun on land.

Well, how else are you supposed to go rabbit shooting?

I had wandered onto a public highway after being given permission to shoot on a farmer's land. I had now been booked twice.

I had learnt my lesson early, despite these two minor offences. Some of my childhood friends were now doing fifteen years for armed robbery or ten for drugs smuggling. As a teen, I would keep myself apart but I always knew where the front line was.

By the time I had seen sense in my life, these incidents had left an impression on me.

To this day, I know that fighting crime saved me from life as a criminal.

That's why that phone call to Kath became the pivotal moment in our life where everything changed.

I had been the only one of nine people to make it on the day. There were people there with degrees, more deserving than I but this time I had made it. I walked from the recruiting house at headquarters and I watched the other eight all kick the same tree in frustration.

'What would you do if you were on duty and one of your colleagues nicked a Mars Bar,' I had been asked.

'I'd tell him to put it back and if he didn't, I'd tell a supervisor,' I answered.

I had also learnt my lesson and put all my cards on the table – they knew about the Cornetto and the rabbit shooting this time.

'I shall watch your career with interest,' the interviewing Chief Inspector replied.

Today, as I woke that phrase haunted me.

I don't know why he said it. Maybe he used this phrase to conclude every interview or maybe it was copper's instinct.

I had tried so very very hard to get in and now this is where it ended. That Chief Inspector would be watching now for sure.

When I raced the three and a half hours back home to discuss the move with Kath just over a decade ago, I knew it was my destiny and that I was moving to the North East to take this job whether she and Ash were coming or not. If you asked Kath on 3 July this year whether she would do the same again now, she would have said yes for all the ways our lives have been enriched. Ask again, twenty-four hours later and the answer, of course, would have been no, so as to avoid what has happened to me. For *me*, you could rewind that tape to the moment where I pulled up at the junction and it would play the same way every time for the rest of my life.

I was always going to take this job because I had to be a policeman. But, I'd give the world for five minutes of daylight this morning.

As I said, it was over, but it was also just beginning.

SUNDAY 11 JULY 2010

Moat had been pronounced dead in the early hours of yesterday morning. Originally it seemed that he had shot himself, then it was announced that we had fired a shot, or possibly shots. Initially it was unclear. It later emerged that Tasers were fired. The announcements came in stages which is always a worry. The more times bits of the same story were announced – when essentially all that mattered was that it was over – the more questions the public, the press and the families would have.

Sue Sim had acknowledged to the media that this was a very difficult time for many people still coming to terms with the events of the last week and thanked the people of Rothbury which remained a town torn in two. Normal life was at one end; a crime scene at the other. Just as when I was shot they would leave no stone unturned. It was clear that this last week would never be forgotten.

Eye-witnesses had begun piling in, murky videos were up on YouTube and rumour and nonsense were rife. It seems everybody had an opinion and a different story to tell.

Moat's Uncle Charlie had said 'he could have went down' to talk to him. His brother Angus said he had undergone a 'public execution'. Stories were circulating that Moat had been a police informer and that was why no previous charges had stuck on him. I begged to differ.

In fact, I would have bet my mortgage that he wasn't. We would have never worked with anyone like that. What on earth was he in a position to inform on? This would be the norm from now on – a minority in possession of the facts, the majority churning innuendo and rumour they had read on the net.

It had been confirmed that Northumbria Police had received a call from Durham Prison around the time of Moat's release but that didn't bother me either. There hadn't been a specific threat to any individual at that stage.

You will probably remember this day for other reasons.

It was World Cup Final Day.

I awoke to make sense of this, calm that it was all over, though tearful too. I didn't have many words left in me or much energy to consume anybody else's. As for the football, I had been following avidly until everything happened. Now it hit home. I would never see another game at all.

As the day wore on I felt the news slowing down. It was a Sunday and it was natural evolution for the cycle to move on from me to the big match ahead. The public probably craved that too. That just left us picking up the pieces. We would soon be seen as yesterday's news and we needed that time as a family.

'Has my face been blown away?' I kept saying.

I couldn't feel it.

'What does it look like?' I would ask different people at regular intervals.

It was that swollen and I was so at the mercy of the morphine that I couldn't shape it with my own hands. In fact, it didn't even seem to feel part of me. My face was just some abstract concept and if Kath hadn't kept on reassuring me, I would have assumed it had gone.

I had to get my nasopharyngeal airway tube removed. This had been sewn in during theatre and was killing me. I didn't even realise that a tube about the size of my little finger had been stitched to my left nostril going down through the back of my throat and into my lungs.

My face was so swollen that if I didn't have it in, my airway could have been compromised. Eating was almost impossible – like shoving a bent spoon to the back of your mouth and having to get the food over that. If I coughed it would dig in at the back of my throat.

I had been banging on for the past three days.

I wanted them to take it out.

Finally I could breathe and cough by myself. Every little detail like this was progress and a small step on the journey to the new me. But there was a hell of a long way to go and I had little energy to get there.

Time and time again I dropped off, only to wake to Kath reading me more of the cards that were arriving all the time, even though it was Sunday. The table was full, there was no room to move on the window sill and then more would arrive. Then I'd nod off again so I didn't have to think about it all. Many were simply addressed to 'The policeman who was shot – Newcastle Hospital' and they were all so kind and supportive.

Then there were all the cards from compassionate people who had just seen the whole thing on the news but for whom I had suddenly become a recognisable figure. I was uneasy with this too, though it wasn't lost on me that they sent words with real, heartfelt emotion.

They didn't know me from Adam but for some reason felt that they could channel their life stories into the small space that a card allows. I wasn't used to this, nor was I expecting it. It was one thing for the last week to be international news but people had quickly made up their minds to send me good wishes and I assume that when they began to find the words, they could only be seeing me in the context of their own lives.

Steven, a prisoner from Leeds, in and out of a cell for most of his life, had written to announce that he was now going to turn his life around because of what had happened to me. He too had followed it on the news and thanked me, now determined to spend his life with his family and not his fellow inmates.

Another young girl sent a crystal. Her parents owned a craft shop so she had picked a piece especially with a fossil in it, knowing that I could still feel if not see. I loved that thoughtful consideration.

Others enclosed money; a few had cancer; many had Kath in tears.

They came from all parts with thousands of different stories.

'Stop bloody crying,' I said to her.

'I can't,' she replied. 'I can't stop reading them.'

You would never know there were so many unhappy people out there, upon whom circumstance had thrust tragedy. Suddenly, now their lot didn't seem quite as bad.

The majority were hugely touching – people were re-evaluating their lives because of what had happened. The sheer horror of this gunman, coupled with the hugely negative way he had portrayed himself, had united people's compassion. I sensed too that this wasn't another bomb going off in a place they didn't know, nor an aid appeal for a cause they didn't care about. The randomness of the brutality was the key. It could have been anyone and yet no one deserved it.

There is no better example than the message I received about baby Jonah. His parents had also taken him to see Mr Shafique who was dealing with my eyes. They had seen my name on the white vinyl board at the entrance to ward 21 just before they took their son in to be examined.

Jonah had been born with one eye significantly smaller than the other. Seeing my name up in lights turned this moment around for them as they learned that their little lad had a deformity and was blind in one eye. He too would need count-less operations and would probably need it removed or to have a prosthesis. Their words came from deep inside their hearts as they described how they were at a place that they didn't want to be with their son but, on seeing my name on the board, they realised that it didn't matter what was wrong with Jonah, he could still have a very good life if he was looked after. And their little lad was just starting out. That moment had become a point for them to re-evaluate their own lives too.

I hadn't seen any of this coming and I hardly knew any of the people writing to me. I had been too busy being ill.

Kath's phone was also going into meltdown. You could access all my personal information on the police computer and the guys at Etal Lane had attached a note saying to ring Kath's mobile rather than mine. I wouldn't be answering in the foreseeable future.

At around 6 p.m., just as the world was settling down to watch Holland v. Spain, Chris, Paul, Jon and Glen from work all turned up.

Paul was the grandad of our shift. Always dead straight and monotone, he was struggling not to be emotional. He had a sombre, respectful outer calmness but I knew he was churning inside because occasionally there was a nervous joviality in his tone and that wasn't Paul. We had a great relationship and were studying together to go for a sergeant's job next year but he just wasn't the kind of guy you had warmth with. This was unknown territory for all of us.

'Alright soft bollocks,' Chris Dodds piled in.

This was the least I expected from the joker in the pack. Whatever the circumstances, Chris would always have a line. This time it helped him through too. He was a great cop as well.

When I first joined the force, he was untouchable for traffic figures and year after year we used to slug it out to be the best but I knew he was also struggling seeing me. I knew this time his banter was a cover for his emotions.

Jon was more complex by nature.

Even though I couldn't see him, I knew he was shaking. I could tell because his voice was wobbling. He told me that when he heard what had happened he thought he would never see me again – and I had been about to train him up to be a family liaison officer.

He was the most emotional of the four. This was a Jon I just hadn't expected.

Then there was Glen, an exceptionally good cop and far better than me. He lives and breathes traffic, and when he arrived in the force I saw myself in him and took him under my wing.

I loved him to bits.

I was so grateful to see those guys. I was desperate to talk to somebody who had been at the scene.

'Were you there? Where were you?' I asked them.

My last memories were of Paul and Chris but I needed to be sure it was exactly as I had 'seen' it.

The lads told me they had been waiting for the call on the radio to attend an RV point and *not* the scene but had already decided that they were going to come anyway. They had said it to each other simultaneously, knowing that it was me who had been shot.

They had both come over to the car but didn't want to get in the way of Steve Winn and Nathan Crane who were trying to get me out of it so, on instinct, Paul turned to Chris.

'We'll go and get Kath. She needs to get to the hospital.'

They both walked up to Sergeant Ian Dey at the roundabout to tell him what they were doing.

'Do you think that David will want her there?' Dey replied.

'She needs to be here now,' Paul answered back and they both left without waiting for authority, amazed that their stance had even been questioned.

They left before they were told not to.

'Tell me what it was like at the scene,' I asked Paul and Chris.

'It's exactly as you described it,' they confirmed.

I needed to know that, but I can't explain it either.

I seemed to have visualised the crime scene exactly as it was even though my eyes were gone. It was important to me that it was as I thought it had been but I didn't understand how I seemed to have had a fading level of vision even though my sight had well and truly gone out on the impact of the shot.

This was all so different from the Chief, the ACC, or the FLO coming in. These were brothers. I knew without asking that each of them was twisting and turning inside with the same thought.

They could have been lying here instead of me.

Chris and Paul had already had some time to deal with how I looked and what had happened, having been straight on the scene. But they were on duty then, and even though I was a brother, work is work.

This, though, was a different, private moment, where grown men cried and cried like they had never cried before. One would start and another would follow. Nothing in life prepared any of us for this incident and for this moment.

For Glen Robson, seeing me for the first time cut like a knife. He had been on holiday with his girlfriend Jess on the night Moat shot me and didn't need telling that if he hadn't been on annual leave, he would have been in the passenger seat that I leant over to.

Glen knew he would be dead.

But instead the fates dealt their hand my way and it was knowing that I would never work with these four again that made me emotional. I was so poorly and so tired but this was the professional curtain coming down.

I knew this was the end of an era.

MONDAY 12 JULY 2010

'One tenth of the entire armed forces in the country were working in Rothbury,' I was told.

I couldn't believe it. I thought they were all outside guarding me!

Thirteen forces had been operating.

It was reassuring, but ultimately it didn't matter.

Seeing the boys last night helped me fit the jigsaw and now, as I reflected on their visit, I began to get my first understanding of the sense of expectation in the outside world.

'Are you OK?' I asked Kath a hundred times.

If she left the room for even a second, it left me anxious she wasn't coming back. I know they thought I was like a patient in *One Flew Over The Cuckoo's Nest*. I was borderline breakdown material and all I had was Kath.

'Are you OK?' I would ask again.

But I wasn't asking for her well-being. I was asking for me. I was scared.

I'd lost my powers, my Superman cloak had gone and all I could see was that at the time I needed Kath the most, she had more reason than ever to call time on us.

Every time she said she was fine I believed it less and less. All I knew was that the dark future was even darker without Kath.

She wouldn't leave me now at this moment but I knew all this could pave a way out for her in time.

I was at the bottom of a mountain and couldn't go any lower. For the first time the burden of the future felt like it would crush me. I couldn't be more scared. Amidst these aching, soul-searching moments, the pressure was on to go public.

'I think I should contact Max Clifford,' my twin Darren advised.

'I'm not interested,' I replied.

I couldn't care less about any of that. Too ill and too drained, all I cared about was my left eye and any chance it might still come back to life.

'I'm just thinking about what's best for you,' Darren tried again.

I couldn't be bothered, nor did I want to talk to anyone.

But then something changed.

I was hearing rumours that other people involved in all of this were doing six-figure deals to sell their story which just appalled me. Max Clifford didn't want a penny to represent us and all of a sudden it became a priority for me to have the loudest voice in what I could sense was going to be a media free-for-all. Chris and Ali also confirmed that Sally, Chris Brown's mother, had said she would never speak to the press and when I knew *that* I became empowered, on behalf of dignity and reason. I had to be the one to talk sense and it had to be my interview that people would remember.

Not for ego, but for justice.

I told Darren to do the deed.

TUESDAY 13 JULY 2010

By 9 a.m. the cameras were setting up for my interviews. But this didn't have Max Clifford's fingerprints all over it. This was my witness statement.

I felt like there was a stranger in my bed.

I wasn't ready to face the world's media, nor was I in a fit state to give evidence.

This was my 'Ade' interview, as it was known – for people who were considered vulnerable because of their age or the violent crime against them. This was standard practice.

'Hello David,' the unnamed man said.

'I'm just setting up the cameras,' he elaborated.

And then he said no more. That was it.

One camera was on me, the other on the two interviewers so the whole room was visible, meaning that at trial the jury could see that there was no coercion going on. This was textbook. But in total, I was only asked three questions and it lasted about the same number of hours.

This was the first time I had told my story in full, start to finish, warts and all.

It was harrowing.

I was back on the roundabout.

I knew I had to narrate as a victim but I wanted to behave like a policeman. It was impossible.

I couldn't get off that roundabout and I couldn't stop sobbing.

It had hit me, and as the words came out of my mouth with one side of my brain operating systematically like a cop, the victim in me heard them half a second later and that was all it took to set me off. If I had been in any denial up to this point, this was the wake up call.

And when it was over Chris and Ali who conducted the interviews packed up the cameras in forty-five seconds and left the room.

I was devastated.

Never have I felt treated more like a piece of meat. I clung to Kath like a tearful baby.

I felt empty, abandoned and alone.

They had taken me to places that I didn't want to go but worse, they had left me there. Once again, I was hanging out of the car on the roundabout, bleeding and in blackness wondering if they heard the call for Tango 190.

I had undergone cognitive interviewing, as we call it. As a FLO, I had also asked victims to do this in the past. I never left any of them at their roundabout.

It couldn't have been more clinical or more damaging.

And then I found out why they had left so quickly.

The process of natural justice had to wait.

The Sun newspaper was at the door.

It was all so wrong. I was still sobbing when they came in the room and they started setting up for interview with *their* cameras. It was exactly the same process except the target audience was different.

I was still on the roundabout but Kath was seething inside. We had agreed to do a written interview but suddenly Hollywood had showed up.

'Are you alright to do this?' Robin Perrie from the paper at least had the decency to ask, though I suspect my answer didn't matter.

'Yeah, let's just get it done,' I replied, knowing that in reality I just had to repeat what I had told the official investigation.

There was one difference.

I didn't understand my role during the police interview.

Trying to be a policeman, I merged into victim. For the newspaper, the parameters were different. The paper wanted victim and I was happy to be there. They got me off the roundabout whereas my colleagues could only leave me there. Clearly something was massively wrong in that process.

I had permission to talk about Moat and I found myself saying I bore him no malice. I don't know where that came from but I do know that nothing will change the facts. It was only afterwards that I found out that there were now ten people who had been arrested and two were hostages.

What?

Ten?

How could hostages have been arrested?

Something – or rather lots of things – just didn't add up, and I was playing catch-up while the rest of the world was living every minute of this. Then I heard again that Tasers had been fired at Moat.

God, had they really pulled in ten accomplices? That nagged away at me. Moat looked so random in his actions. The thought was gathering momentum within me again that there was nothing random about this at all. He knew who he was looking for. Everything that had happened must have been premeditated.

I was tense and tired, confused by the parallel interview experience, dismayed that professionally the process left me abandoned but personally *The Sun* set me free. This new information didn't help and to top it all off, the people who were meant to be close to me were making it all so much worse.

Kath had gone out to fetch herself a chicken sandwich. This was the only occasion I had sent her away deliberately and could bear to see her go. I had to lay down the law to my own brother and sister. With no sight my senses were sharpening to know on instinct that there was an atmosphere in the room.

Kath had only just recovered from a back operation herself yet Debbie would take the comfy leather chair. Whenever the two of them would come in, they were all very nice and kissy-kissy to me but there would be an awkward pause before they even acknowledged Kath. That's Kath, the woman who, if she didn't rightly decide to bugger off, was going to be picking up the pieces when Darren and Debbie had long gone.

I could sense it now and I also knew from history how my family worked.

Just yesterday Kath had been upset and didn't want to cause a fuss but I got it out of her. The pair of them were shits to her.

'I might be blind but I'm not stupid. Please stop treating Kath like this,' I said.

'I don't know what you're talking about,' Debbie tried to fob me off.

'You made her sit on a plastic chair all day with her back, and when you come in the room you don't even say hello to her,' I explained.

'No, it's not like you think it was,' they protested.

But it bloody well was.

They were treating this like some holiday. Debbie would go shopping in Newcastle before coming to visit me. See the landmarks, have a spot of lunch, and get a new outfit before popping in to see the invalid? That was how it was, I knew it and it was going to stop.

They were my family but, going forward, I only had one family that mattered. This was when that became crystal clear. All the years I was told Kath was no good for me, this was the line in the sand where they showed their true colours. They hadn't taken Kath under their wing, and caught up in their own worlds, they missed the one chance they would get to show that actions were louder than words. I felt let down.

This was all too much for one day.

Little did I know that when I woke in the morning, I would have kicked Tiger Woods off the front page of the newspaper.

And the rest of the media too.

WEDNESDAY 14 JULY 2010

I wasn't the only one with problems. Tiger Woods had been fronting up in a cosy press conference ahead of the British Open. I had shoved the world's greatest golfer way down the news agenda.

It felt like I had achieved what I intended to but I was cross because *The Sun* had given the video of me to Sky when that hadn't been the deal. That tape wasn't for broadcast.

As if that weren't surreal enough, the new Prime Minister David Cameron was looking down the barrel at Prime Minister's Questions as suddenly Facebook was brought up in the House.

I couldn't give a toss that I was now parliamentary fodder, except that it wasn't about me at all. It was about Moat being a hero again after the disgusting Siobhan O'Dowd admitted setting up the tribute pages.

It didn't matter to me except when I momentarily misunderstood that the world was against me as I had done on the Friday of Moat's death. I was just fighting for my future. Why would I care about any of that?

They had their own agenda and I had mine: with the physio. Yes, every leak and every new soundbite depresses you but when the medical professionals are checking you for a chest infection all that becomes bullshit. My thirst for news last week had been replaced by my fatigue with it. Constantly tired, being less poorly was all I had to aim for. Equally, when I heard that Tyne Tees Television had been given hours of tapes that Moat had recorded *himself* with social workers I couldn't give a stuff.

It was all Moat this and Moat that. My curiosity extended no further than wondering if Moat had taped us when I nicked him on the scrap metal charge, so paranoid was he but I didn't want to listen to his self-pity droning on for hours in these recordings made in the previous August, in which he asked for psychiatric help.

If he was well enough to know that he needed it himself, he probably didn't need to ask for it. He also said he was on the edge, though it may have been a ploy to be reconciled with his children and he talked of his own childhood memories of Rothbury.

God, the clues had all been there nearly a year ago.

Any drop of Moat news and the press were all over it. And it wouldn't stop there. If they had pulled in so many people for questioning, there was a hell of lot more to come. This wasn't going away quickly.

Meanwhile, I was sitting here in bed hanging on to the last signs of life in my left eye.

And today I had to walk unaided for the first time.

Wasn't that the story?

Imagine blindfolding yourself and walking into a room full of razor blades and having to negotiate by feeling them. This was what I faced.

I thought it would be easy but nothing could have frightened me more as I attempted my first steps.

The ever-courteous guards wished me good morning as I passed. That was the last location I had a sense for. Beyond that I was groping into the wilderness.

The nurses kept telling me to stand up straight.

I couldn't do it.

I was facing a twelve-foot corridor with two rooms to the right, which had been emptied. The end of the corridor hadn't been cordoned off so I wasn't allowed past, nor did I want to go there. Twelve feet was twelve feet too far. I was a prisoner. Yes, I was free to roam but there was nowhere I wanted to go. Nor did I know how to get there.

I had spent so much time in bed that I hadn't given any thought to how small my room was but when I stepped into that corridor, I felt like I was facing a marathon.

It took me fifteen minutes to reach the other end. I couldn't go through this for the rest of my life.

'Oh well done!' everyone said.

I felt about three years old, angry that they had to help me and that I could no longer do anything on my own.

I was terrified too, not so much at the never-ending darkness, because I was still seeing bright lights in my head, but of the reality that I had a lifetime of dependency ahead of me.

And then came the bombshell.

'We're going to move you to ward 21 tomorrow,' one of the nurses said.

'I'm not going anywhere unless it's home,' the cantankerous David Rathband who always knows best replied.

No, I was staying exactly where I was.

I had a relationship with the nurses and I couldn't face starting again.

Deprived of sight, trust was king. I had just about built a rapport with the people who were looking after me and this was further abandonment. The intensive care nurses continued to visit me when I first arrived in hospital and I was still hoping that I could fill all the pieces in my memory back in. No, I could just about understand the parameters of my new world up to now and I wasn't about to trust afresh.

For twenty minutes we argued the toss.

And then the doctor walked out.

He just left.

'I'm not going anywhere,' I told Kath.

I was too vulnerable to contemplate change and Kath was the best person to sit between my medical and emotional needs. She had been here before and she would tell them straight.

But clearly there were conversations going on behind my back and someone had seen something in me which indicated that I was coping a hell of a lot better than I felt.

Later in the day Julie the ward sister came down from ward 21.

She was trying to assure me it was the best place to be.

'I don't like it. I'm not coming,' I said firmly.

Wendy the staff nurse then came down too to assure me it was the best place to get the treatment I needed. This was gathering an uncomfortable momentum.

I didn't really know what was going on. I was front page news, the discussion of Parliament, being tricked by the media and taking my first proper steps. I wasn't ready for this emotional curveball and, stubborn as I am, I couldn't see that these two nurses would have any concept of what was best for me.

They weren't me nor had they been shot. What could they offer?

'Please try it. We really want to work with you for preparing to go home,' they said.

They had just mentioned the home word for the first time.

I wasn't in a hotel where I could choose my room.

This was happening with or without my say so.

'If I don't like it I'm either coming back here or I am going home,' I laid my terms on the table.

They probably knew that if I had moved from no to giving *them* a choice then they had beaten me.

How bloody stupid was I?

THURSDAY 15 JULY 2010

It turned out to be the best thing I could have done.

Once again I was in a side room; guards were still on watch.

But the goalposts had moved.

Julie and Wendy were amazing, communicating with me in a completely different way. They were used to caring for individuals with visual impairment. Everybody else had just been trying to get me better.

As we entered ward 21 and I went in my new room, they made me map the room out. I stood with my back against the door, and was left to walk around on my own to find everything. This was it. This was how it was going to be.

'I'll try it for three days, and if I don't like it I'm going home,' I told them, recoiling into my defence mechanism.

'Well we'll revisit it in three days then,' Julie said.

She knew if she could get me to tomorrow, I would have no options.

Julie and Wendy were also confident as they were experts in their field and I wasn't, always touching me when they spoke, never failing to give an explanation for what they were about to do. Even so, as they explained the layout of the room to me and where the furniture was, every time I bumped into something, I just broke down.

I wasn't the kind of person to put faith in other people and I couldn't see where this would end. All I could make out was the next obstacle and that would set me off again. I couldn't shape a better tomorrow when I struggled to get through today.

To add insult to injury, Mr Shafique reviewed my left eye, asking for it to be cleansed and dressed and drops to be added.

This was now happening several times a day and things were so touch and go that I had to wear an eye shield to protect my cornea. If the eye wasn't clean, then infection would finish me off.

'Can you see any light or dark?' he said, shining the torch in my eye.

'No,' I replied.

That meant one thing.

I was officially blind.

He would return tomorrow with a specialist in gunshot wounds to the eye.

'How many cases had there been in the North East over the years?' I wondered.

Apparently one case twenty years previously made him an expert.

Regardless of what they could or couldn't do for my eye, there was another agenda at play and I was slow to catch on. So reluctant had I been to move wards that I didn't see that my rehabilitation began here. I was struggling enough without being encouraged to move on. The staff had advanced their mindset from repairing me to adjusting me for a new life and when I cottoned on that this was the plan, I burst into tears.

I wanted to be mollycoddled but that wasn't an option. Wendy and Julie told me they were in it for the long haul and would be with me every step of the way but the tears weren't for six months from now and how far I might come, they were for this moment when my new reality began.

Up to this point, I hadn't really lifted a finger, but now suddenly they were telling me what we would do today and tomorrow. Their plan filled me with fear, and the physical fatigue of concentrating on my first unguided steps was matched pound for pound by the mental drain it was placing on me too.

And still there were requests from the media, sacks of cards were arriving all the time and a cast of hundreds were still calling by, from a change of guards, to staff who had treated me in my first moments in hospital.

But this was the first time I had met Bridie Grant.

'You have Charles Bonnet Syndrome,' she said.

'Fucking hell, who's he?' I replied.

Charles Bonnet Syndrome was the name for the hallucinations that people with poor sight or no vision at all come to be tormented or comforted by. In the eighteenth century they used to throw you in a mental institution until Bonnet figured it all out. And I thought I had been clever trying to rationalise it all.

Simple patterns, straight lines, or detailed pictures of people and buildings would be with me for eighteen months or so, I was told. It gave me little reassurance that I would have to live with these images for so long but at least it told me I hadn't gone completely mad, though of course, now that I knew such a condition existed, I probably would lose the plot completely.

Kath also spent time with Bridie but it was the worst possible moment for her because of the tension with Debbie and Darren. She never showed it in front of me but I know she was distraught about this. Wendy and Julie also took her aside to say that I needed structure.

If it meant telling my family they only come at a given hour, then so be it. My life needed discipline and they all had to be told. Today marked a change, and Kath knew from her NHS work that when they needed to move you on, there was no time to wallow.

In the same way that I had delivered my evidence as a witness to the police investigation but then told exactly the same to *The Sun* as a victim, I knew Kath the nurse was dealing with it all methodically and was coping by taking control, but when she left the room she too crossed that frontier and became victim.

She wouldn't let me see but I knew that when she went out *her* cloak of invincibility came off too. Comfortable and trusting in her colleagues on the NHS, she found confidantes in Wendy and Julie that she never found in Debbie and Darren, and that's hard to swallow.

As for *The Sun*, I was cross and relieved all in one.

I naively thought that my interview would be the end of everything but since they had given the video to Sky News it had led to further media requests.

I had opened the floodgates.

I also learned that David Cameron had labelled Moat a 'callous murderer', which he was of course. It was early days for the Coalition government and he could say what he wanted. I just didn't want to be the tool he used to look tough on crime.

Siobhan O'Dowd, meanwhile, has pulled her Facebook page down after being slaughtered by Ian Collins on *Talksport*. The fact that she was from the North West and not even someone in Moat's circle is very worrying. Heaven knows how many nutters will turn up for his funeral, whenever that may be. In amongst them, of course, will be several of my colleagues infiltrating this anti-establishment subculture for whom this monster became a hero.

On the other side of the coin, I was grateful for *The Sun* piece because I felt I had done a good job and held the moral high ground. The paper had written it up sympathetically, though let's face it, O'Dowd did half the work for me. But never mind all that, they had got me off the roundabout, and only I understood the significance of that mentally whilst all around me everyone else was moving on.

Charles Bonnet had helped too, not that he will ever know.

Bridie's words made sense and her accent took me back to happier childhood times in Paignton, Devon. She had a gentle West Country burr and that, together with her words, gave us a bond. Of course, now I was making all sorts of decisions based on sound alone. I'd decided that Bridie was five foot six, blonde, with a small face. It didn't matter that she wasn't at all.

She, and Charlie Bon-Bons, had made me realise that I just couldn't do it all on my own. People like Sally Bayliss, from the RNIB, were also helping me move forward. She was the eye clinic liaison officer and couldn't have been more lovely over the phone. Again, I fell in love with her from her voice alone.

Within a day, I had gone from mapping out my room to talking through an order book for gadgets to make life easier at home with Kath.

'This is to help you not get lost in your kitchen,' Sally explained.

It hadn't even crossed my mind.

She was detailing 'Bump Ons' to attach to items so I wouldn't get lost.

'How the fuck can you get lost in your own kitchen?' I thought.

'What good is a stupid little sticker going to do?'

In my naivety, I had so far to go.

But that's because yesterday I wasn't even thinking about this.

And today I was having Penfriend – a device that reads out labels – described to me from the catalogue.

I would now be able to attach and read audio labels.

So fucking what.

Nor did I have any idea of who was paying for it. I'd just grunt 'Yeah whatever' as Kath window-shopped for the blind. They were moving me on fast but it was the least of my priorities. I told Kath just to get everything. I wasn't interested. I just wanted home.

I needed this kick up the arse because otherwise I would never get out of hospital, but I had gone from being molly coddled to making big decisions in a matter of moments, while around me Darren and Debbie were becoming more and more out of tune. Every time I spoke to them my face would swell up and set my recovery back even further. One step forward, two back – all because of stupid family politics.

Kath wanted me to stand on my own two feet, literally and metaphorically, because she understood what the future had in store. She took her lead from her NHS colleagues who were moving me into the next stage of rehab. My family seemed to want to sit there and stroke my hand. I knew, even in the state I was in, that it was some sort of play for family reunification after years of unspoken tension.

Darren was also doing his own thing. He had been to court for the remand hearing of two individuals who had assisted Moat and then given a short statement on the steps of Newcastle Magistrates Court.

We only found out about them from the telly.

I just sat there, mouth open, aghast that this meant Moat *had* been helped. Suddenly the parameters had changed. Nobody had told me this officially.

I knew there had been several arrests but I didn't know that Darren knew so much more than me and that there had been three people in the car that night.

Six months from now I would be a witness at the trial of Moat's accomplices.

There was no such thing as 'It's over'.

FRIDAY 16 JULY 2010

I had lost two stone.

The dietician came to see me last night, concerned. All I had been eating was liquidised food – soup and ice cream.

I hated it.

Kath's mum had been bringing me in child's portions of fish pie and trifles but I could barely stomach that. Nor did I have a sense of smell to appreciate any of it. Food was now functional and I wasn't functioning. I was using so much energy trying to heal that there was no way I was able to replace all the calories being used. I was becoming the skeleton from the pirate world of hallucinations which had tormented me in the hours after the shooting.

And today Moat t-shirts went on sale. Obviously I ripped out all my tubes, and rushed out to buy one for all the family.

Goodness, what was going on?

I had to stand up to this nonsense.

Just as I'd learn to deal with one thing, something like this would leave me reeling. I didn't crave the limelight other than to counter all the publicity this monster was getting, but the real story was not that some chavs were adorning themselves with Moat merchandise but that he had left a trail of destruction from which many people would never recover.

Who would buy and then wear a Moat t-shirt if they knew how I was spending my day? Did it not occur to them that at the moment of purchase, I was mapping out my room again and taking my first shower for thirteen days?

Yes, nearly two weeks. This was my first proper wash since I came second in the golf – a lifetime ago, both in how it felt and in how my world had changed.

And my God, you can't know how that felt in so many ways.

I loved it, partly because I wasn't blind in the shower. Well, of course, I *was* blind, but you don't think about it as the water rushes over you with your eyes closed. It's just the shower experience, isn't it?

This was the first moment that I forgot the inevitable.

And it felt great.

The nurses were obsessed with getting me to use a shower stool. It would be easier for me to sit down, they claimed. It was their holy grail to get PC Rathband to shower with a stool, but I wasn't having any of it though I didn't want to offend them. I wasn't spending the rest of my life sitting in the shower, as unsteady as I was right now.

Fuck that.

I threw the thing out to Kath as soon as the nurses had gone.

I knew every shower valve in the world from my years as a plumber but now I had no idea what I was turning. Kath had pre-set the temperature and if I twiddled it to the right, it came on. That was all I knew.

But it was wonderful, and being blind wasn't on my radar, so much so that, knowing I no longer had eyes to speak of, I put the soap where my eyes used to be.

My left eye was completely bloodshot and my right was just pink flesh – an empty space had been sewn down. In my bid to eradicate the terrible, never-ending stench of blood still on my body, I rubbed soap into my 'eyes' and stung myself senseless.

'You haven't brought the right shower gel,' I said to Kath.

Except she had but I had no sense of smell.

These were the same gels that I had used for years but now I couldn't recognise them. I went to open my eyes to look and that's when the soap penetrated the flesh and left me in further agony.

I was in there for forty minutes – the longest shower of my life. But I had got out of bed to achieve something on my own, washing that filth away – and momentarily, I ceased to be blind.

It couldn't last for long though and that's why I stayed in there for such an age. Asking for my towel and clothes when I got out just reminded me that this moment was temporary.

My head felt deformed too.

It was now on two levels with a pair of holes in it. I had a scar from ear to ear and hundreds of staples pieced together like a Hornby train set, locking into one unit across my head. Wendy and Julie wanted to get to work immediately on removing alternate staples.

That was the next job and I couldn't wait.

It felt like a cheese grater. I knew instinctively that staples out meant home was closer. Also, as much as this really hurt, it was just more pain on a body that could probably now endure anything.

Or so I thought.

Some of the staples were bent in my skull. The bloody NHS was saving me on the cheap. If I could see, I'd be looking for a 'Made in Taiwan' label. It just seemed like they were operating on me with the cheapest gear going. It felt, sounded and acted like a regular staple-remover for paper.

'Can you not just go down to Rymans?' I said to Kath.

My tubes were coming out too and my morphine addiction was on the wane! Now, I realised what was going on and it had been a whirlwind twenty-four hours from refusing to move to knowing that in the nicest way possible I was about to be kicked out of hospital.

I didn't feel ill anymore.

Mr Barclay the dental surgeon came by. I don't suppose he had seen anything like me before. Seven of my teeth had been blown out, he confirmed. Temporary fillings had to go in. My voice whistled when I spoke.

But now home was all that was on my mind, especially as they had upped the ante in the last day, preparing me for what lay ahead. An attitude of sympathy had been replaced by a 'pull your socks up' mentality and that suited me fine. I have never relied on anyone in life and my two feet are the only ones I like to stand on. Give me home any day and send me there now.

But still there were surprises coming thick and fast. Suddenly Paul Johnson showed up.

'You cheeky bastard, I haven't seen you for ten years,' I thought.

I had been his best man and he mine. Darren had somehow found him in his bid to fill the void of long, empty hospital hours, so far away from Adelaide.

But I was cross too.

We had been really close friends and it had taken this.

Perhaps like my family he saw this as the moment to make up for lost time. Yes, these were extreme circumstances but true friends and true family love should have borne fruit regardless of what happened because true love is unconditional. You don't suddenly love someone because you found out they were on the brink. You love them all the time, don't you?

But at least Paul came.

All the way from Hong Kong too. I think he felt some guilt that all the years had passed without contact and that was good enough for me. Whatever had passed was water under the bridge once my initial shock subsided.

'I know I haven't been around for a long time but I've wanted to find you for a few years. I'm here to stay and if you ever need anything, all you have to do is ask,' he said.

And I think, with those words, we wiped the empty years clean and both realised that it was right for him to be there.

He offered me the best eye consultant in the country to come up from Birmingham at his expense but, most importantly, he was the first to ask how Kath was. How were we as a family? Were we coping? And that told me I had been quick to judge and wrong to do so. I think seeing me and knowing that I couldn't see him knocked him for six.

I didn't feel this about everyone and his visit after all these years set everything else into context.

Hundreds of cards had arrived today. Amongst them, one from my sisters Karen and Julie, and one from my mum.

'If she thinks she's coming here she can forget it,' I told my sister Debbie.

I may have been groggy and permanently drowsy but I knew who was showboating in my family. This was not going to be a moment to right all those wrongs and suddenly to pretend that everything was fine again. I had Kath and the kids and they were my family. I wasn't allowing my mother a way back in or showing an open door to my sisters. They should remember that they'd said Kath was no good for me and look at her now. She was right by my side every moment of the day, and she would continue to be long after they had fucked off. It wasn't about gestures now. It was about what had gone on before and the long road ahead. Could I count on them in a month, in a year, in a couple of decades?

Could I fuck!

'Just put it in the bin,' I told Kath.

She had flown over from Cyprus where she now lived.

'She's waiting to come and see you,' Debbie told me, clearly in on it.

'You tell the nursing staff,' I instructed Kath. 'She's not to come anywhere near me.'

'That's fine,' she understood and it suited her too.

I could see that a deal had been done behind my back and nothing irritated me more.

Darren had done this before, throwing a family reunion to try to get everyone back together. I don't know why he would do this from time to time. He would say otherwise but he has always been bloody lucky and seemed to be living the dream in Australia. It could have been testimony to some sort of guilt he was feeling at being so far away.

No doubt in my mind Darren saw this as a great opportunity to get everyone talking to each other.

'I wouldn't see my mum if she was the only eye specialist who could save my eyesight,' I said to Kath.

I had no respect for her.

Yet, I was desperate for my dad to come.

I respected my father and craved his love now, but I knew this was the trade-off. There was no way my dad was coming without my mum, even though I had been shot and it was about me. I needed the love and I needed my dad.

They didn't get that though. They were trying to cut deals, and no mum meant no dad either.

I knew that and it tore me to pieces. I was devastated my dad didn't have the courage to tell my mum I didn't want to see *her* but I did him and that he would come. He didn't ultimately have the guts to say that.

While others were seeing this as a moment to correct a lifetime of wrongs, I would have opened the door to my dad despite years of silence. His work ethic for the family left its mark on me.

My mother had only told me twice that she was proud of me. Once was at Kath's dad's funeral and the second at Naomi's funeral and both meant nothing to me.

They were the wrong words at the wrong time.

I found her words mistimed and hollow.

I may have been ill and ploughed with morphine whilst adjusting to this life-changing moment but I wasn't about to allow people back in to whom I had meant little over a lifetime.

There had clearly been more conversations behind my back than I was aware of. And it didn't stop there.

'Hello?' I said.

Debbie was handing me the handset.

My sister Julie was really upset and the next thing I knew Debbie had engineered ringing her.

I didn't want to talk to her either.

We hadn't really fallen out but I had stopped talking to her because she was so close to mum.

The phone call was as empty as ordering a cab.

I felt nothing. I wanted it over but I didn't have the ability to say no, nor did I want to offend Debbie who believed she was doing the right thing putting Julie on. Also, at the back of my mind was the thought that Kath might not hang around.

I didn't know who I would need in the long term.

But there were too many petty games going on; for heaven's sake, this wasn't about any of them. In reality nor was it about me. It was about what was left behind for Kath.

Only Wendy and Julie seemed to get that. Their kindness was limitless.

After nearly a fortnight they brought in an extra bed so Kath and I could sleep together. It was bliss and felt like a hotel as we pushed the beds together. It was also another hurdle overcome because every night previously I used to reach for her hand at the side of the bed, so scared was I that she would leave the room. The nurses knew she wasn't going home and that she was clearly way past tired. I was grateful for their gesture. They understood my needs more than my own family.

But I was restless. I held Kath tight all night long as there was no real sleep for me. I flinched and woke. I dropped off again and then suddenly was bolt upright.

SATURDAY 17 JULY 2010

Something was making sure I was awake towards Moat hour. Morphine had taken me to a deep, dark place, out for the count and with no chance of staying awake. But there I was, my body shaking with fear. Involuntary jumping movements shot through my arms and legs making the drugs redundant. Beyond any control that I could exert, my limbs took on a life of their own, leaving me wide awake. One press of my new talking watch confirmed the time. It was 'Moat hour'.

At the moment when I was shot in my patrol car, my body released a massive amount of adrenalin. It had two options, the specialists had told me.

Fight or flight.

I chose the former.

Because of the amount of energy released into my body to keep me fighting, my brain clock refused to allow me to return to the state of relaxation I had experienced in the police car, doing my job without fear, exercising drills as I had done for many years, and breaking it up with the odd text home or message on the radio.

My brain was telling my body one simple message.

As the night-time morphine kicked in, I was being warned. Last time I relaxed this much, I had released a massive amount of adrenalin.

This was simply my body telling me to fight again. I couldn't get past this point in time and into a calmer state. My body remained on high alert. This now seemed to be my normal bedtime routine.

And there I stayed until 5 a.m. this morning, barely able to catch more than a few snatches of sleep at a time.

When I woke at dawn I was frightened.

Something had changed.

Until this moment my perceptions had been of bright white light. This was what I had been 'seeing' and had told myself it was light filtering in. It felt like a winter's sun glaring off a snowy landscape, magnified to the power of a hundred. That's how clear, strong and penetrative the colour of white had been.

Now, for the first time, it was pitch black.

I didn't know what it meant but I was petrified – more scared than when Moat shot me. Here I was, over the worst and being shown a new life mapping out rooms and buying gadgets that speak to you and gradually tubes were being removed from me, when from nowhere the much more frightening prospect of a life of total darkness replaced the already dim outlook of a life of blindness with moments of light.

I lay there distraught, sobbing to Kath, still always by my side.

I tried to get out of bed only to fail.

'I'm scared,' I said as I woke her. 'It's gone black.'

There didn't seem any escape. Just ahead, another realisation of what was to come. I would learn to deal with one thing and then something else would replace it. This was how it was now.

I had arrived at officially the worst moment of my life and it *was* worse than the shots because that was a temporary situation from which some sort of recovery was possible. The pain would always be there but would lessen over time. The noise of the shots would come and go; the flinching fight or flight body would surely pass in time.

But as the light went out for the last time, so did any glimmer of hope. This was permanent.

There was no way back and as the day wore on, everything I did confirmed that.

I was delighted that my uncles and aunts had come from Birmingham but at one point there were nine people in the room including Darren and Debbie and it left me shattered. The only difference was that this side of the family could see what Kath was doing, trying to minimise disruption to me. Colin, Stephen, Thelma, Yvette, Sonia, Justine and Kerry knew exactly when to leave and I respected that. They came all that way for an hour without an agenda, just doing what proper families do.

They were there for me.

Once they were gone I was claustrophobic and needed to get out. There were still press swarming around the building – some had even got inside, plus I was still largely kept away from the public though people knew I was there. My name wasn't on the white board here.

There was no way I could get out the front entrance for air.

Supported by Kath and my police guard, I stumbled and fumbled my way to the hospital's roof-top garden.

I should never have bothered.

I lit up my first cigarette for the best part of three weeks and it hit me hard. There I was pumped on medication and I had gone off for a sneaky cigarette without even considering the consequences.

It went straight to my head, leaving me dizzy.

That, combined with the exhaustion of the visit, set my personal journey back another step and hammered home the new black-blind sensation as a permanent status.

Walking through the garden I had no idea how it looked except that I passed through two doors and a walkway into a circular opening, past a raised wall with flowers.

'That's a brick wall,' I said to Kath. 'What's in there?

'That's a garden,' she replied.

I put my hand in and touched some foliage.

And then broke down.

I couldn't feel sunlight or fresh air. It was another nail.

Waking up in total darkness was one thing this morning. Feeling your way through the everyday and ticking off all the things you could no longer see was harsher. Getting better, mapping out the room, taking first steps and ordering the equipment were huge strides and every time I put a sequence of these together, someone would smash me over the head with a huge concrete brick.

I was never an Alan Titchmarsh but I knew that the sight of flowers, trees and grass were beyond me. I had learnt to deal with the big stuff; the incidental was killing me all over again.

There was no need to discuss it with Sue, Wendy or Bridie. Kath and I dealt with this privately. Only she could help me now. This was the future and she would be dealing with it when we headed home. The only way to cope was to put it in a box and close the lid. This was me the family liaison officer liaising with myself.

As I did with Charles Bonnet, which I calculated in between the morphine was post-traumatic stress, I rationalised this latest setback there and then as it happened at 5 a.m.

Then I shut the box.

Who could possibly explain it to me better than myself? If anyone professionally were wiser, then they would have warned me this was coming. That never happened.

Only I was in a position to know.

So we dealt with it. We cried. Then I locked it away.

My only rationale was that this was it.

And when I got over my fear, I felt strangely better. The bright whiteness had kept me awake for hours on end up to now. Now the darkness was luring me back to slumber. It told me it was night time, and it told me it was night time forever.

It would never be morning again.

SUNDAY 18 JULY 2010

There it was again: Moat hour. My brain was out on loan, and my limbs were controlled as if at the whim of a puppeteer.

It was worse now we were forewarned. We knew Moat time was coming.

And Kath was awake too.

So much for all the new-fangled gadgets to help me through blindness. The talking watch had become the bane of our lives. Every twenty minutes I would press it and every twenty minutes the robotic voice would announce the time.

I never once pressed it during the day but the nights were long and the fear of Moat hour seriously affected my quality of sleep. So instead we did what everybody else does in hospital.

We drank tea.

Through all these sleepless nights, I was starting to miss home more and more.

Home was the only place I was heading.

'You can go tonight,' Nurse Julie suggested.

'I'm sorry?'

'You can go tonight.'

I was desperate to get out of there, just for a few hours, to be around the only true family I had.

Together, Kath and I began preparations to head home.

And then it hit me.

'Shit, how am I going to do that?'

Press were still everywhere outside. Yes, I had 'courted' the media with *The Sun* interview but that wasn't meant to fuel the need for more, it was meant to counteract the Moat band-wagon and restore police confidence.

We didn't want anybody at home except the kids. Poor Ash had been trooping in every morning and afternoon. We deserved to be alone together.

It took two hours to organise the logistics.

Kath drove the car to the side entrance of the hospital, and I was taken down there by one of the nurses and a policeman.

It was horrific.

This was now the first time in my life I was forced into a passenger seat. Kath would never normally drive unless I had had a drink, which in itself was rare.

I felt crippled.

I was in slow-mo, unable to move my limbs at all, an officer supporting my shoulder, turning my leg around and getting me into the car. I was dependent.

Blind, I still followed every inch of that journey. I felt each manhole and knew each junction. I had driven this route a thousand times. Kath would say where we were but I already knew.

I just knew.

And then the engine stopped.

It had been twenty long minutes up Grandstand Road, past Haddricks Mill and onto the Spine Road. Nobody knew the A-Z of the North East better than I.

But I had long since seen these places for the last time.

Kath got out of the car and came round to the passenger seat.

She picked her handbag up and opened the door as I pulled myself up.

'Let go,' I told her as she tried to help me out.

I had to make those steps on my own.

Thankfully there were no press on the drive because nobody knew that we had left hospital.

Kath's mum was in the kitchen but the only two people who mattered to me were Ash and Mia. I could have had the eyes of a football stadium on me but all I cared about was that my two children see me walk to our front door.

I was adamant that Kath wouldn't hold me.

There were just seven steps to the door. I wanted my children to see me without being held and without being blind.

It took more out of me than getting on the radio, or getting out of the car and onto the stretcher, or anything I had experienced since.

Ash greeted me first and my instinct was to kiss him.

The dogs were going berserk with a sixth sense that I now had to develop myself.

I walked straight into the kitchen and crash bang into the island in the centre.

I was determined that nobody would help me.

This was my home and I knew it on instinct, even though, only a few hours before, the concept of mapping out a room had been explained to me.

I wandered to the window and couldn't see anything.

That's obvious, I know, but it hadn't occurred to me. The houses to the right weren't visible, nor was the sea coming in from Blyth on the left.

I knew these landmarks well but would never see them again.

Being in hospital and having a theory lesson, if you like, was one thing but this was daily life in practice.

The familiarity of home and family that I'd been longing for had been a dream. The alien surroundings of the hospital and my home were now one and the same.

Darkness, frustration, dependency and fear now reigned supreme.

MONDAY 19 JULY 2010

'**M**um's going to *The Sun*,' Darren broke the news.

Wait a minute. This was way out of control now.

'I've told her not to,' he added.

God knows how but the paper had tracked her down in Cyprus a few days ago and my refusal to see her had, in her eyes, left her no option.

I was livid.

Why was this 'thing' always about other people?

I was staggered.

I really didn't want much more of this.

In my view Darren was also doing too much media and it wasn't something we ever wanted. I knew he was doing it for the right reasons but why did I feel it was about him not me?

I had tried to control the media by doing the one interview and releasing one picture. Northumbria Police wanted a bog-standard shot of me in my uniform to encourage people to come forward with new information but we suspected that those with whom Moat was associated all hated the police and weren't about to sprint to Etal Lane Police Station queuing up to testify. Kath was adamant that people should see me as a normal person and not as a policeman. As a dad to Mia and Ash.

She wanted everyone to see the pictures and to be angry about what had had happened to me. She deliberately chose the stills from when I came in that night and was taken straight to the Resus Room. We were both only now starting to realise that people were shocked, moved and angry like we were. But I also didn't want any skeletons coming out of the closet.

As if coming home hadn't been tough enough. Last night had been both a dream and a nightmare. To be home was heaven, but hell too. It had been fifteen long nights since I had felt my own bed, and smelt the Rathband aroma. Drinking tea from my mugs, stroking my dogs, sinking into my own bed – it had been an eternity.

But the reality loomed large. It was clear that I had a lot to learn and fast. The impact of mapping out rooms had taken its toll on me in the hospital, but they were, in truth, nothing more than a couple of simple annexes off the wards. I had no idea about my own house and all the other obstacles that lay ahead. Plus the doctors still had to look at my eye again. There remained a very tiny chance that they could do something but the odds were long. I had to hold out the tiniest hope. So back to hospital I went.

From the calmness and paradoxical insecurity of home, my surreal story continued.

The Under Secretary of State James Brokenshire MP from the new Coalition had come to see me. I had never heard of him and knew that I was part of some political posturing. I wanted home again. My mind was a yo-yo.

Last night we were told he was coming. Then he wasn't.

Finally he turned up on his way to Rothbury with the Chief.

It pissed me off that he was coming and then he wasn't when equally I didn't understand why he was coming at all.

Then I remembered Soham, and Selby and all the others. They would want to show solidarity to the people of Rothbury even though an officer serving Queen and country and an innocent were brutally wounded and killed 45 minutes from there.

Rothbury was where the coward ended it all. The lives which were really affected were miles away.

Somebody important always turns up on these occasions.

To be honest, I couldn't have given a toss if the Queen had showed up. This was mine and Kath's life – our story – and we didn't want to be part of some media frenzy. *The Sun* interview hadn't killed the story as I'd naively hoped, it had only fuelled it. Neither of us could understand the cameras outside the hospital and the constant media requests.

I knew people would say we were open season because we had allowed one piece of access but we had never experienced anything like this before. We couldn't possibly have imagined pictures being beamed to Australia, David Cameron mentioning us in Parliament or Theresa May, the Home Secretary, writing to us.

They all said the same things although their efforts were noted. None of them was mechanical in their language but if people I never knew were 'humbled' and told me about my 'great dignity' and that I had 'risen above' the call of duty, well fine. But they were just words that would mean little tomorrow.

Theresa May said that she recognised 'the dangerous job that you do' but Kath struggled to read her scruffy writing. If it had been typed we would have said it was cold but because it was handwritten it looked clumsy. They meant well, I'm sure, but they really didn't understand the big challenges I was facing.

James Brokenshire, to his credit, was sincere, sweet and funny but also left me wondering who the bloody hell would turn up next.

'You must come to London and I'll treat you to some cream cakes at the House of Commons,' he said.

I knew what that was about.

Sue Sim had tipped him off!

It was always the joke on shift that if you were late, your duty was to repay it with a visit to the baker.

When the Chief started, I had said to her that gaffers never get out often enough. So typical Sue, she wasn't having any of that and joined me on traffic duty.

'Don't you dare mention the cream cakes,' one of the guys had warned after she was running ridiculously late.

I couldn't resist.

'By the way Ma'am, you're late,' I said.

The following day we were in hospital in a family liaison capacity after a terrible fatal. Wonderful Sue waited for her moment and then turned up off-shift to deliver the goods.

If the rules of traffic duty meant Mr Kipling got rich, then they were rules and she was playing by them.

She had obviously told Brokenshire this story!

I enjoyed his company but what irritated me was the RVI standing on ceremony. They had been brilliant to me but there was no need to give the wards an extra clean or have the head of the hospital come down just because some MP was passing by.

And I don't think he wanted that either.

That was further evidence that there was a circus developing. I hated it.

I was also still waking up at the same time every night. I had rationalised this as PTSD, but I couldn't account for the smell of blood which never left me, nor the hallucinations of gothic buildings and cartoon characters.

I wouldn't let myself get depressed though. It was time to move on.

Wendy and Julie came to take the remaining bits out of my head. I was pleased to see the back of the staples. More importantly, bearing in my mind my face had been peeled off down to my throat, I knew my body was rejecting them. With no infection caused, I no longer needed them. That was another bit of me mended. My face, shoulder and teeth had also improved.

The staples' removal was symbolic. All I could think now was home, home, home, despite how difficult it had been yesterday. When I was there I wanted to get back to hospital and now I had returned and they were putting me back together, I began to negotiate.

'I'll go home for good on Wednesday,' I told Wendy.

'No, you're not ready,' she told me straight, 'the following week maybe if you can get through a couple of days there this week.'

'I'll be gone permanently by then,' I replied. That was this hour's opinion, it literally changed that regularly.

Around 2 p.m. somebody I actually wanted to see came by. It was Chief Inspector Sav Patsalos and his wife Karen, also a cop. They came with no agenda and, even better, no grapes.

They just wanted to know how Kath and I were. It wasn't a police visit. These were just two very good friends and to see somebody offering genuine support and wanting nothing back meant the world.

Sav and I had had our funny moments over the years, in particular the memorable incident with the beard.

When he walked in the room, I thought of that instantly because I hadn't even recognised him once when I could see!

I had been out on traffic duty when Sav had got caught up in a domestic in the Kenton area of Newcastle. I arrived at the scene to find the usual garbage of effing and blinding in the street. I was always keen to be the ultimate police professional but I assumed that I was working with a new colleague because I didn't recognise the guy in the beard.

'Are you new?' I asked him when we were done.

'It's me, you idiot, it's Sav,' he replied.

I had never been very good with beards and for all I knew he might have one now. It didn't really matter anymore.

Sav was always my boss but he hadn't come in that capacity. He had come as a friend. At the moment I was shot, Sav was out having a typical Saturday night off in Newcastle. So great was his integrity that he got driven into the hospital in the early hours of Sunday morning and stayed for two whole days, still in the clothes he came in.

And he came as a friend then as well. That's why his visit today meant the world, because he didn't have to rush off and do something else, he wasn't killing time by my bedside.

Time stood still because it didn't matter. He knew I had hours, days, weeks, months and years ahead staring into the abyss even back then on that initial night, so it was the mark of the man that it really didn't matter if he stayed for two days or two years.

That is something I will never forget. Sav's first words were to ask how we were doing. I also appreciated that he'd brought his wife Karen. He simply brought his family to be with my family. There was no macabre voyeurism to stare at my injuries, to think 'it could have been them'. He didn't come as a boss, though I knew he had huge professional respect for me.

He came 100 per cent for Kath and me and when he left I wanted to tell him that I loved him. We had a friendship built out of adversity and emotion and I knew he would be there for the long haul.

I couldn't be sure about too many of the others when I was back home for good and people had forgotten my name and inevitably I would just be known as the 'Blind Policeman'.

And that day was coming.

I had been in and out of Sister Julie's ear all day about going home again. Thinking I was a comedian, the only way I could get to her was to call her 'Me Julie' like she was in *Ali G*.

She was a total professional but I was frightened of her. It was she who had told me that I was moving wards in what seems weeks ago now.

I couldn't argue with her medically but I was in such a state with sleep deprivation, the hallucinations, the staples, the darkness, that I genuinely feared her. Chipping away at her with 'Me Julie' was all I had to soften her up but it was working slowly.

'You can go home again tomorrow for a few hours,' she said, 'and if everything is fine then you can go home for good on Wednesday. Your room will be kept open and you will be on extended leave.'

Bloody hell.

Not just home, but a whiff of home for good.

It had been two and a half long weeks and the end was nigh.

My mind was racing again. Suddenly a huge door marked 'the rest of your life' was about to open. And I had no idea what really lay behind it.

TUESDAY 20 JULY 2010

'Welcome to my world,' I thought when Kath told me.
      Siobhan O'Dowd – her of the Facebook page – said
she now feared for her own life.

For goodness' sake. Why were there so many insignificant
people in this whole story who were given their moment of
fame when it had absolutely nothing to do with them whatso-
ever? You couldn't make it up – again.

Perhaps she would like to swap with me, spend an hour
with the consultant ophthalmologist.

Dr Shafique had returned.

Once again, he shone that torch into my eye and I wouldn't
have known he was doing it if he hadn't told me.

Then he uttered the words I knew were coming but I
dreaded hearing. I had known for longer than him, that he
would ultimately deliver the harshest of all cruel blows.

'I am very doubtful that anything can be done to save the
sight in your left eye,' he said.

I knew this, but I always held out hope.

Gutted doesn't even do it justice.

The what ifs began immediately.

It didn't really matter.

This was my lot.

'Just think outside the box and do something you wouldn't
normally do,' I pleaded.

'I am really sorry David, there's nothing we can do for you,'
he said. He had given his all.

They agreed to have one last look next Tuesday, but we all
knew it was futile.

I was clutching at straws and I didn't want to show weakness.

I needed divine intervention that would never come.

I might get justice eventually but where was my miracle?

The doctors told me not to get Kath to start pumping anything connected into Google. There was nothing they could do, and there was no precedent to help them do it.

I was sobbing inside but I had to be strong for Kath.

We didn't need to say anything to each other. The silence spoke volumes and we knew what this meant.

And, in the way that the NHS has to be clinical although it doesn't want to be, they were soon moving me on again.

'David, could you please sign here,' Mr Shafique asked.

It wasn't his fault. He was as gutted as we were but he had to show that level of detachment.

At least I got my Blue Badge. And to think that it used to part of my job taking these off people who had misused them. Now here I was signing for one.

There were 4,500 people registered as blind in Northumberland, he told me, but that was only 40 per cent of those who were visually impaired.

If I didn't sign, I wouldn't be able to access half the things I would need.

As if my world couldn't get any more surreal, I now pursued the usual chain of events, in that such a crushing blow would be followed by the next thing coming at me at speed, and it would normally have no relation to whatever it preceded. I was on BBC Radio 5 Live talking to Victoria Derbyshire, back in the media circus again. I felt I had justification for doing so. I wanted people to know I was still alive. Predictably, she had lots of questions. I knew the public also had a lot of gaps in their information. That's why I went live. I found myself saying that I bore no malice to Moat again. I don't know where that came from. It wasn't pre-determined. I meant it. It was the policeman speaking.

But I didn't really know what I was doing. I just enjoyed talking to Victoria. For me, it was a tonic and it gave me a big lift to have an opportunity to put my side across. I was talking in real time to a real person who was actually listening. You didn't get that in a newspaper interview.

Talking to Victoria was like talking to a counsellor. This was part therapy, part justice and whilst I was on the air, the feedback was coming in live and it was extraordinary. The real people were listening. I felt like the pride of Britain.

I lost some of my paranoia and found some peace with the media. For the first time I understood the size of all of this in the world beyond my ward. Being live and, of course, still being there for the reaction after, was the first time I connected with all the very kind people out there in a two-way relationship.

I was humbled.

'I'd like to give something back,' I said to Darren after the interview.

'We should look at setting up a charity,' he replied.

As Darren went off to investigate, the need for me to regain some power and control over my life became even more pressing.

Early in the afternoon, Gary Swinburne and Russ Watson came to see me. Watson was the Northumbria Police Federation chairman and Swinburne had been appointed my Federation rep.

These two were coming to help me, but it felt like they saw me as a small bit of paperwork that wouldn't bother them for long.

They asked me to sign things that in my state I couldn't understand and they didn't explain the content of. Beyond the fact that I was told it was an 'Industrial Injuries Benefit form', I couldn't know what I was putting my name to. I signed one form after another, with no idea what they were. Bureaucratic Britain ruled.

And when they left I told Kath exactly what I felt.

'What a pair of jokers,' I said. 'There go the fucking Chuckle Brothers.'

WEDNESDAY 21 JULY 2010

Home sweet home.

That's where I was heading, and this time I was ready.

But I wasn't.

I was just ready to leave.

Kath and I were excited but tense and our anxiety levels were off the end of the scale. We had been warned that there would be a lot of media interest but we really had no idea how much until a reporter was found skulking through the paediatric ward, opposite where I was preparing to leave for the final time.

Of course, he was doing his job and probably bloody well, but if I could just have my moment to leave with dignity, I would give that reporter everything. But now he had blown it.

I just wish they would let me leave peacefully.

Today there would also be a second post mortem.

As a FLO, I hated the post mortems.

What were they trying to prove by these post mortems? That the police had shot him, or he had been hit by a Taser or something?

The facts were clear. The outcome was the same. Moat was evil, and there was no justification for his actions or place for soul-searching on his behalf.

I didn't need to know any of this. I was going forward, getting ready to go home.

Lessons were coming thick and fast. This morning I was taught clock eating.

They gave me the breakfast and would say that my bacon was at two o'clock and my orange juice was at half past. I had never heard such nonsense in all my life. Maybe it wasn't nonsense but a spoon-fed David Rathband was not who I was.

Having said this, I did walk straight into the door of the toilet, head-butting it and giving myself a right clout but I wasn't about to tell the nurses that. I couldn't jeopardise what was coming. I knew this moment was in the balance and I had to take it.

'Are you sure about this,' Wendy and 'Me Julie' both said.

'You don't have to go now,' they said. 'You can wait.'

I was excited but Julie warned me that I would feel scared at home and it might all be too much. If I wanted to come back that was fine. There was always a bed for me.

I wasn't taking any of that seriously. I just knew that it was now or never.

Because of all the press interest we had employed a free-lance photographer who was taking everything so that we had control.

'I don't feel comfortable taking pictures of you in your bed,' he said.

'I'm asking you to take them,' I replied, 'because if *you* don't take them, someone I don't want to will.'

In a few short days, much as I despised the media attention, I had learnt how to play their game.

At that moment the boss of the hospital, whom I only seen on the day James Brokenshire had turned up, rushed in to kick our snapper out. They had tried to be loyal to the press and keep them all happy in their naivety but we had hired this guy to avoid a media scrum and frankly there was no difference in Kath taking a picture or our self-appointed paparazzo.

He was ejected, which annoyed me as he felt like an extension of our family. We trusted him. He was told to leave but he was also told where we were going. Nobody else knew. But I couldn't move at the speed they wanted me to. My confidence vanished. My whole body began to shake. At the moment of truth, I couldn't handle it.

I got to the door, but I was in bits. My legs went from under me. The only bit of my body that was still working as it did before I was shot couldn't sustain the rest of me. The weight of the emotion gave way.

Julie was right. This was harder than I ever could have known.

Everyone left the room except Kath and Wendy and we tried again.

They gave me about five minutes to compose myself.

'Now I'm ready,' I said putting my coat on again, less claustrophobic this time. Too many people to thank and too many goodbyes had made the moment harder. We had lingered and therefore it had become a big drama.

As I had thanked the staff the significance of the moment had dawned on me. If there hadn't been those goodbyes then it would have been much easier to walk through the door. Instead it had become a huge wall.

Darren went to the front of the hospital to act as a decoy.

Somehow, and heaven only knows how these things get out, the rumour was rife that my discharge was imminent. The press were at every single exit of the hospital.

I was helped out of the hospital with the same focus as I was brought into it the night I had arrived at the Resus Room.

Suddenly all I knew was a door had opened as I felt the rush of the fresh air. Wendy and Kath tipped me out of the wheelchair and dragged me the three or four feet to the car.

We had to get out of there quickly. I couldn't wait even for my photographer. There was no time for tears or long goodbyes now, as kind as everyone had been. We had to fly.

Reporters were chasing round to our exit, trying to snap me as I was bundled in to the back. I left almost as unceremoniously as I had arrived.

We fled at speed with Ash and the photographer right behind us in Ash's car. There was to be no big money shot.

But at the same time, if there was no picture at all, they would hound us until they got one.

Ash hatched a plan.

'I shouldn't really be doing this,' our photographer argued.

We pulled up at the Aldi car park in Cowgate just a couple of miles outside of Newcastle city centre.

There was no choice.

We had to stage the whole thing.

I couldn't get out of the car.

I was frightened.

They put my car up against the brick wall, and once the photographer had set up I forced myself out of the car and faked getting back in it. There were around nine pictures taken.

It was over in seconds.

But there was more to come.

Ash sped on ahead to make sure home was clear.

'There's two massive satellite trucks either side of the house,' he rang to say.

Kath was furious. All I could think was that I would never drive a car again. One by one all the things that I would never do again were being ticked off.

The reporters were on our drive as we pulled up just before half two. This was a scenario I had seen so many times over the years when innocent people get thrown, through no fault of their own, into the glare of the spotlight.

Now it was our turn.

One of the scrum was even taking an allocated parking space on our estate and ran across the drive as we pulled in. Our photographer was already in the house with Ash.

I tried to stumble out of the car and up the drive but I just looked like I was drunk. Ash opened the house door to drag me in.

'Get off my drive,' Kath shouted.

We knew exactly what they wanted. It was the full on frontal picture of my face.

'Just leave us alone,' Kath was screaming.

They just ignored her.

You know what I should have done? I should have rung the police.

Or better, I could have arrested the lot of them myself.

Kath's mum went round the house quickly and shut all the blinds so there could be no snaps through the window. This was the undignified way in which I was allowed to begin my new life. My family didn't deserve to be sitting in their own house as though they had just attended a wake.

'I feel like Elton John,' I laughed to Kath.

But it wasn't funny at all. It was distressing.

'Yeah well I am not happy being David Furnish,' Kath replied with the steam still coming off her at the blatant disregard for humanity that she had just witnessed.

And it didn't even stop in the house.

I turned on the news, and there I was. Rolling news meant that for today at least, I would never go away. I felt like I was hearing something happening to someone else.

Then the doorbell rang, and rang again and again and again.

Next the letterbox would rattle with press photographers' cards all landing on the mat.

All the time the home phone was ringing. Where did they get that number from? They could do anything and everything it seemed, and they wouldn't stop in pursuit of their story.

I was shattered and emotional, and it had rocked us all.

Nurse Julie had been right. Coming home was tougher than I could have ever known. When I was excited this morning, it was to reclaim my independence in my own home, amongst the things and the people I knew. Now I was here, it turned full circle and I resented the place.

I made an instant decision. We had to move.

All that remained in this house for me to care about were the people inside but the dynamic had changed forever.

Ash had become my protector, following me around the house, loyally watching out for me. Mia wouldn't leave me alone, snuggling up to me as I dozed the afternoon away. I felt that in the last three weeks, I had lost three years from her life. I hadn't seen her as much as Ash and Kath as we had kept her in school as much as possible to give her some sort of normality and routine.

My sweet little princess had aged so much in such a short time. She was becoming a woman in so many ways; Ash assumed the role of the man of the house; Kath was a doting mother and I was now the disabled child.

The blinds had come down and stayed down. Beyond them lay a new tomorrow.

THURSDAY 22 JULY 2010

That was the longest night.

We both broke down getting into bed. It was one of the few times where we had both got upset at the same time. Usually it would be one of Kath or I in tears. One of us would cry while the other reassured. Now it was both of us at once, fearing for the whole family's future.

Nor had I slept, twitching, sweating, and jumping all night. I was crying and screaming. Moat was coming to visit me more and more. There he was in the grey colour of death, as clear as day with his eye-less death face staring at me, his open flap of skin from above his left eyebrow opening up across to the right hand side of his face. His was the only face I could ever make out now.

And the bastard wouldn't leave me alone.

I was both a prisoner in my home and in my own mind and I felt only marginally better this morning.

I had tumbled down the stairs, leaving Kath screaming as I failed to negotiate the turn at the bottom on the last three steps.

The whole world now knew I was home and as one visitor left the house another would arrive. It was like a bus station, the back gate constantly banging with the sound of arrivals and departures.

There was, however, just one person I wanted to see.

'Hello,' Craig Jones said, shaking my hand and giving me a man-hug in my garden just as two other colleagues, Peter Lindsley and Jason Wright, were leaving.

It was early afternoon.

I knew Craig through his work in the Southern control room and we had socialised a handful of times. I couldn't say we were great friends. He had no reason to go out on a limb for me.

I sensed he was relieved to finally see me and couldn't get him over to the house quick enough.

Craig had texted me when I was in hospital saying he needed to talk to me and with that the seed was planted that all was not as I had been led to believe.

I knew he was going to tell me something about what had gone on in the control room on the night I was shot.

I had had an inkling for some time that I hadn't quite been told the whole story. Mike Costello from the homicide team had also visited me on the plastics ward although he had no reason to do so. I wasn't dead after all. He hadn't elaborated but he'd been the first to mention lawyers. He either had a profound sense of justice or he too knew something.

'What do you need to tell me Craig?' I asked him.

I put an end to the small talk and asked him straight.

I knew what was coming.

'I'm just really sorry,' he said. 'I tried to get them to warn everyone.'

'Gemma did everything she should have and held up a card saying it was Moat. I listened in straight away and knew it was him. I rang the supervisors and told them that they needed to get a warning out to the cops.'

He would have heard hundreds of crank calls over the years but he knew this was Moat.

Craig had a procedure to follow. The priority was to trace the call.

'I knew it was your shift,' he added.

As soon as the call finished, the control room tried to ring Moat back and reconnect the call to get him to hand himself in. He had already said that he was hunting cops and they had to come for him.

Predictably the phone was dead.

Craig rang the Northern comms supervisor in the Northern control room to ask if they were aware of the calls and to urge that a message be put out, only to be told not to worry, because it was with the CIM (Critical Incident Manager).

At the same time, the call was being listened back to and packaged up on an email to be sent to the Superintendent at Etal Lane.

'It was my worst experience in life ever,' he confessed to me.

At the moment that he heard me say I had been shot, he left the top desk in the control room and went outside.

He promptly threw up.

He told me how he had tried to get his superiors to warn the guys on the ground but he had been fobbed off.

'They did nothing,' I fumed.

I was angrier with them than I was with Moat himself.

Gemma, who took the call, was distraught because she felt she had screwed up but she had done her job by the book. No blame lay with her or Craig but he was beside himself apologising.

'Kath, you have to come and hear this,' I shouted to the kitchen.

The number of people in the last three weeks who told me that I wasn't targeted, that it was one of those things, that I had a job with risk in it and *now* I found out that my own force, risk-adverse by nature, hadn't bothered to put the threat out. This changed everything.

Nobody had made a decision. Moat had said he was hunting cops but we had no policy in place to deal with it. It just kept getting passed along a chain.

Craig relayed the calls to me word for word. There was no 'it didn't come from me' about him. He was happy to go on the record.

Of all the 4,000 or so people who I worked with, Craig was the only one who came forward with this intelligence. What more did anyone else know but was keeping to themselves?

'I'm really grateful for what you've told me,' I thanked him. Inside I was livid.

'I couldn't settle until I told you,' he replied.

And I knew the burden was being lifted from his shoulders.

I was furious but I also had a purpose which gave me a new lease of life. As unwell as I still was, I was hungry like a policeman once more, ready to start digging again.

This was the first time that I knew something had gone drastically wrong in the control room and that Moat hadn't purposely come after me, an idea that I had become obsessed by since he listed my collar number in his letter to the police.

I knew it wasn't my fault...

FRIDAY 23 JULY 2010

My sleeves were rolled up. I had work to do. My focus was back. My struggles with blindness took a back seat.

I lay awake all night. Moat dropped by again, of course. It didn't even fill me with fear anymore, I was so used to it. Plus I knew darker forces were at work.

The threat of the living was greater.

At the back of my mind, one thing consumed me.

I had to see the Chief.

What frightened me the most was that the information was being concealed. Tapes could be deleted, logs might go missing. I knew this could happen and I was paranoid it might. My police mind was absolutely certain that the quicker you got the evidence preserved, the better position you were in. And I don't think Sue Sim knew the whole story in the same way that she wasn't in the picture about armed guards not appearing outside my house while Moat was on the loose. I had to check she was as honest as I thought she was, and if Craig was telling me all this, what else weren't people telling me?

I was still furious this morning.

Kath was worse.

She wanted someone to pay as badly as I did as her life had changed almost as much as mine.

There couldn't have been a better time for the solicitor to turn up.

This was my old friend Paul Johnson's legacy. He had asked his solicitor Peter Southeran to come and see me.

Today was going to be legal day.

I told Peter everything about Craig's visit.

He was speechless, but now I was armed with real purpose. Peter was already ahead of the game and confident we had a case.

Kath was scared. The prospect of taking on Northumbria Police filled her with dread. I didn't think Kath had the stomach to still be fighting this in what – several years' time? I was adamant though.

It was nothing personal. To think that would be to misunderstand my motives. This was about someone putting their hand up and saying 'David, this could have been avoided and I take responsibility'.

That was my motivation.

That seemed the least anyone could do. But there was no chance of that happening. I knew that, because if Craig hadn't been so bloody honest, I would have gone to the grave ignorant of what really went on.

As Peter left, Sue arrived.

One in, one out.

The Chief had come to see me virtually every day, a rock by my side, professional politics not even on the agenda.

Now, I had to confront her. It became very obvious very quickly that I had information which I thought she knew but had actually been kept from her too. I didn't know whether to be angrier at this betrayal of her, or at the facts themselves, which clearly hung me out to dry.

It's not easy to deliver crushing blows like this to someone when they have stood by you at all costs and shown you the ultimate compassion and respect. But it wasn't personal and others had failed Sue. Why did I now know more than her?

'Do you know what went on in the control room when he rang in?' I said, no time again for small talk.

She told me she knew he had rung in and made the threats.

'Why weren't we told?' I asked her.

Every answer confirmed she knew only half the story.

'There wasn't enough time,' she replied.

'What do you mean there wasn't enough time?' I wasn't satisfied with that answer.

She thought they were just listening to the tape.

'They weren't just listening to the tape. The tape had been listened to on two previous occasions,' I told her exactly what Craig told me.

'No it hadn't,' she didn't know any better.

'Sue, I'm telling you,' I tried to help.

She had been informed that they were just listening to the tape and didn't have enough time. So I filled her in.

It had been listened to more than once.

Craig had rung several times to get a warning out.

The call was about to be sent over on an email.

They were the facts. Sue Sim wasn't in possession of them.

'No, that's not right,' she protested but only in good faith.

'I'm telling you that's right. That's exactly what happened. Then it was put on an email and sent to Superintendent Farrell.'

Somebody was covering up.

I was fuming again – for her, for finding out this way, as well as for myself.

I could feel her sitting there absolutely stunned.

She didn't move, twitch or flinch.

The realisation of cock-up and cover-up were dawning on her. I really didn't want to be the one to tell her this, but then I had only just found out myself.

'I'm asking you. Would you look into it for me?'

'Oh yes, I will,' she replied.

And she did.

Within seconds she was on the phone.

'I want the control room looked at. I want all the tapes retained and I want a report into what happened there,' I heard her say.

She promised me too that I would see the report as soon as she had it.

In my mind, I had thought that Moat was after me, that I was singled out for his venom because of our previous encounter. I had talked myself into believing that doing a recce at the Riverside Pub was a Moat trap to lure me there so he could recce *me* and in fact it had been one of his mates that had placed the call that Saturday teatime to track my movements.

I had convinced myself that he had rung the station to find out my shift pattern. I was wrong.

I told Sue that this was my fear.

'No,' she said. 'That's not true. Neither of the hostages knew you, and nor did he.'

It was obvious now from Craig's visit that Northumbria Police didn't have all the facts or indeed weren't sharing them evenly amongst themselves.

Then I realised that this would go on and on and on, and my testimony in time would be called upon at trial and that Raoul Moat had two accomplices with him who were passing themselves off as hostages.

My God, there was still so much that both of us didn't know.

Sue left, still on the phone and in a hurry.

And then I remembered her words as they echoed in my head.

'David, you must sue me.'

Four days later PC David Rathband returned to hospital to be told there was nothing more the hospital could do for his eyes. He would never see again.

He bought his first white cane himself.

At the beginning of August 2010, hundreds of people turned up for the funeral of Raoul Moat. Teresa Bystram from Weighbridge in Surrey travelled 300 miles with three of her eight children and told the world's media 'it was a better day out than Legoland' and that Moat was a 'good role model'.

Sue Sim provided PC Rathband with the report on events in the control room.

Chief Superintendent Jo Farrell gained a promotion.

Meanwhile PC Rathband launched his own charity so that no emergency serviceman would ever be short of funds in the future should a similar fate befall them. The Blue Lamp Foundation was born.

In November 2010, he was honoured at the annual Pride of Britain *awards.*

PART THREE – THE TRIAL

WEDNESDAY 2 FEBRUARY 2011

214 days have passed. In many ways, each of them has been the same. You can't know what I would give to have my sight back. Have I replayed every detail back a million times since? Of course, I have.

Have I had a good night's sleep since last July? Not really, no. Am I coping? I am learning to deal with it. Have I put my brilliant family through the mill and are they holding up? Yes, and yes again. God, I'd be dead inside without them. I owe Kath so much and we remain without boundaries. Have I learned a lot more since the night in question about the night in question? Oh yes…

But today is the day I have been waiting for.

Today is the trial.

The papers are calling it the 'Raoul Moat trial', which disgusts me. He was a coward, not man enough to face democracy and the judicial process. And then there's the forgotten man in all this – not me – but the innocent guy who hardly gets a mention. Chris Brown, who just walked into somebody else's story and paid the ultimate price for no logical reason other than that that little Stobbart girl put the lie out that he was a copper. What a terrible price to pay.

The trial is about the other two – hardly spoken of until this point. The public won't even know their names.

Karl Ness and Qhuram Awan.

I lump them together. Spineless, cowardly shits, and Moat's accomplices. May justice take its natural course.

I'm buzzing, to be honest, dead excited and looking forward to going through the front door and having my moment in court. I pray that a jury of their peers sees through them.

Only ever losing two cases in court, I have a sense of right and wrong, and I lived for my job. Those days are now sadly behind me.

Today is the first day I am both a victim and a witness, a member of society and a serving officer, all in the same trial, all in the same courtroom. This is new territory. This is my trial, as it is Chris Brown's family's. This is not Raoul Moat's trial.

There's no doubt that Ness and Awan are guilty of something but the only way Chris's family and mine can get any justice at all is to nail these bastards. It really is *our* trial. Two men, hardly mentioned at the time, are in the dock but as the process takes its course, the innocent will get their say and the public will see that Moat was never working alone.

We are led by the barrister Robert Smith who prosecuted in the Sharon Beshenivsky trial in 2009. I'm upbeat about that because he's one of the best, and that was a trial we all followed. Paul Sloan defends for Ness and Jeremy Carter-Manning for Awan. Good luck to them. They are going to need it – and I think they know it.

Northumbria Police want me to enter discreetly through a side door but I'm having none of that. I shall be marching through the front entrance in my uniform.

I want my day in court.

I feel nothing for Sam Stobbart, the other principal witness. Kath and I both think she is afforded some protection because she is so young but in our eyes, even if she didn't realise how things would turn out, she knew what she was doing was gambling with Chris's safety.

I am in an odd situation. It is *my* trial, *our* trial, but I find it difficult to be involved in it. It's like looking into a bubble where everything's going on and being outside of it feeling like it doesn't affect me even though it does. As the day has got nearer, I have homed in on that thought.

This is my trial.

Things stepped up a gear a couple of weeks back when I went for a pre-trial visit. Although I have been into the courts many times, I wanted to go now I was blind so I would know where everything was. I couldn't allow myself to be trumped psychologically on the day because I had been deprived of my sight.

That was a fiasco though – they showed me a court that was the opposite way round to the one the trial would be held in. It was no use to me. Then they took me to another room. That was no good either. It was a lot smaller than Court Number One which we would be in and to which I had been many times previously.

I stood in the witness box so I could get my bearings and was hit by emotion, even though it was practically empty. I couldn't let that happen on the day. I needed to make sure that my testimony was going to be *evidentially* rather than emotionally about what happened to me. That's the subtle point – removing myself from the situation.

I had always got nervous giving evidence in the box but it was different this time. I wanted to be able to turn up and act as a cop but I was turning up as a victim too. And that didn't sit well with me.

Out of my comfort zone, I am not confident that I will be able to handle it. If I go as a cop, it's dead professional. You read your statement, give your evidence and it's all very matter of fact. As a victim, it's much more emotional and, of course, Kath and the family will be there. It won't be the 'Moat trial' by the time I take the stand. I know already that the headlines will read that PC David Rathband broke down in court and the trial hasn't even begun yet.

To go in there – albeit with my uniform on – as a victim of crime was going to be tough.

Could I, the victim, deal with nutter relatives shouting rubbish from the gallery? Only time would tell. I deliberately haven't been part of the police investigation so I only know as much as I need to know in relation to what happened to me. It is important that my opinions of what took place are not tainted by rumour.

I know a small bit of what happened to Chris Brown but it is not my intention to sit in court to listen to the key witnesses lying. Most of the people I have dealt with in court over the years do just that. To take the oath is a bloody joke. In its simplest terms, it's archaic. Most of them would burn the Bible. I know that once again I am about to sit through a pack of lies.

My plan is to give my evidence and go. I shall return for the summing up and that's it. Judge Justice McCombe will look at it evidentially and he'll give an indication to the jury. He's impartial of course, so that's the time to go back to court to get an overview of what he thinks.

I am in no doubt. These two are guilty. Even with the best barrister in the world for them, against the worst for us – which isn't the case by the way – I'd put my house on these two going down for a very long time.

My passing out parade after joining Northumbria Police in 2000: I took great pride and satisfaction in sending bad people down. I'm proud of the fact that in five years I had one of the best records as a traffic cop in the entire Northumbria police force.

My patrol car after the shooting: this was the lowest moment of my life. I had been shot twice but was still trying my best to think like a cop and follow any kind of procedure I might have been taught to deal with circumstances like this. I had given my all.

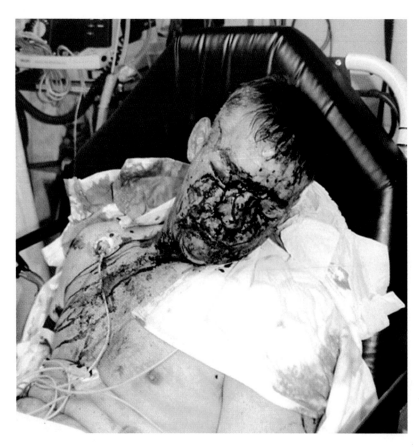

Although the doctors were very non-committal, Kath is adamant that at no point did she think I was going to die. Knowing how poorly I was, I find that warming. It wasn't based on any medical assessment or on having read my medical notes, because she hadn't. She just knew me better than anyone. There was no way I was dying here. That's why I had fought so hard in the car.

The Rathband family, then and now: Kath is my life and her love for me has no boundaries. I have two amazing kids and I live for them now.

Rathband the golfer: still winning trophies even after the events of July 2010.

TOP LEFT Me with Chief Constable Sue Sim of Northumbria Police.
TOP RIGHT I completed the London Marathon in April 2011.
BOTTOM LEFT Just over twenty-four hours before my twin, Darren, had been in his house, just outside Adelaide, when he got the call. He flew to the UK straight away.
BOTTOM RIGHT Kath and me.

The Rathbands with Nick Clegg, Adrian Chiles and Christine Bleakley at the *Pride of Britain* awards.

Kath and me on our first date after the shooting.

Raoul Moat: deceased

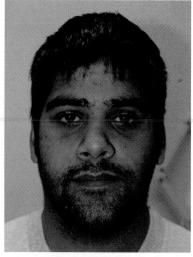

Karl Ness and Qhuram Awan: sentenced to life imprisonment.
Ness will serve a minimum of forty years and Awan twenty.

THURSDAY 3 FEBRUARY 2011

I shall be called next week to give evidence. People who don't know what closure means keep telling me *this* will be closure. There is no such thing. I know from working as a FLO. What you may understand as closure, I recognise as the look in their eyes becoming less haunted. You can't close when every day sees a reminder. All you can do is to park it. I can tell you now – it's there until the day you die.

However, I do need to get through this next week and see what is on the other side. So much of my driving ambition in life has been towards locking up bad guys. I can at least begin that process and tick that box, which is a great comfort. It will be one of the last moments in my career, though, where I am able, as a serving officer, to influence the course of justice.

How I will feel as a victim, I can only guess. Kath is concerned and upset by the advantage that Ness and Awan hold in having sight. I am going to have to deal with that as I do every day now. That's why I went for the pre-trial visit. I do possess the psychological edge though, in that I'll be dealing in cold hard facts.

They're denying the charges, of course – conspiracy to murder, attempted murder, possession of a firearm with intent to endanger life and the big one, robbing a chip shop!

From yesterday's very early scene-setting exchanges, I know the public will be stunned by two things.

Moat didn't just shoot Chris Brown. He took him out in a full-on execution, having hatched his plan during his eighteen weeks in Durham Prison. He didn't just fire a gun at him, he terminated him. Moat had boasted to his barber that he had some things to sort out and would 'probably be back inside by Friday'.

Karl Ness is implicated as he was receiving texts from Moat as he lay in waiting underneath the open window where his ex Sam Stobbart was sitting. Ness was in a stolen Transit van around the corner.

'We'll miss you mate if it all goes down,' Ness texted Moat on the night of the Birtley shootings. If that doesn't position Ness as being Moat's right-hand man, then I don't know what does. Indeed, as Moat fled the scene, Ness drove to Albion Road in Byker where he dumped the van and summoned his mate, Qhuram Awan, for a pick-up.

The second outrageous claim, that gives everybody a picture of what we're dealing with, is that Moat claimed to have shot Stobbart deliberately, so she could walk away with some compensation.

What an incredible guy! And believe me this was just the beginning.

FRIDAY 4 FEBRUARY 2011

Delays today. Frustrating delays.

Kath has been back and forth to court while one of the barristers sorts out another case of his which is nearing a conclusion, plus one of the jury is heavily pregnant and has complications. Another's child has chickenpox.

Since that awful day, *we* have had no contact with either of the other two families caught up in the triangular drama that is Moat's sick world but today that changed. Chris Brown's mum, Sally, asked to meet Kath at court.

Little has been said of Chris and his family. Like Ness and Awan, most people probably couldn't name him, or recognise his picture.

For the first time I was able to draw a line between him and Sam Stobbart who I think is calculating.

Kath says Chris's mum was lovely and their meeting highly emotional. In many ways, it settled them both. Painfully, Chris had only known Stobbart a month.

Apart from this, we've achieved little today but at least Ness has now admitted being in the car that Moat was using when he shot me. This was now undeniable fact and would surely cast aspersions on everything else. And after Moat calmly wandered back to that car, what was he doing...?

Just laughing.

That's all.

I'll be generous and dismiss it as distasteful and un-gentle-manly. Nothing surprises me about this man any more. I knew he was volatile and anti-establishment. Normally, my perception of people is correct. I take only small comfort from getting him spot on.

While the shotgun was still smouldering and I was fighting for my life, Moat was having the best craic he'd had in years.

Ness claims to have been shocked, pretending it was the first time he had ever seen a gun. He is also trying to wriggle his way out by claiming to be a hostage.

We know this because my colleagues carried out a search at Holme House Prison in Stockton where Ness was banged up and they found a letter which could have only been intended for his girlfriend, Tara Collins, in which he was actually coaching her to help *his* defence!

'Raoul turned up at yours going crazy and telling in detail what he had done. I got there and Raoul was pointing a gun at you, he told me everything he had done, we were shocked. I will never forgive Raoul Moat for what he has put us through... that should help a lot.'

This small-time gangster was clearly oblivious to the fact that a text can trap you these days and that the police knew he had been communicating with Moat at 1.07 a.m. on the night of Chris Brown's shooting. Yes, Ness, it did help a lot.

Thanks very much!

Ness clearly doesn't understand that lies come back to haunt you. Heaven knows how his barrister keeps up with his story.

I've only just learned myself about this texting in the past week though I *did* know about the images of Moat and Ness shopping in B&Q and the CCTV will be played during the trial.

You may remember these because they were the first images released after Moat came out of Durham Prison and show a slimmer man than we had all been looking for, calling for many people to ask why photographs weren't automatically taken when any prisoner leaves jail. This footage is one of many nails in Ness's coffin. Clearly, they are shopping casually and Moat hasn't got him round the neck in some sort of hostage position.

Ness won't know either about what we refer to in the force as fishing trips. To him, that is something you go on with Gazza. Not us, we had been there for some time with one big almighty trawler.

In preparing the prosecution, Northumbria Police applied to listen to all of Moat's calls from June and July, whilst he was still inside. Back in June, the indication was that he was planning to purchase a gun. The word 'gun' was never spoken itself. It was always language like 'have you got that item?' My understanding is that £500 gets you a gun, and it's as easy to do so as getting any drugs you want in any city centre, as long as you know where to go.

In all, around twenty-six people have been arrested in connection with this case. My colleagues went fishing – you cast a huge net out to catch the big one. Bring in hundreds of minnows and you'll close the case. Anyone who went to see him or spoke on the phone, we've been talking to them and our tapes are secure. It's all nailed down in evidence.

This is how you unravel Ness's story piece by piece. None of these so-called 'friends' of Moat will now be able to come to court this week and say 'Oh no, I was with him' because we pulled them all in. The chance of them cross-referencing with each other are now minimal.

My boss describes it as being like a corridor.

Bang.

He walks down the corridor shutting each and every door.

Bang.

All of these Moat accomplices are all doors.

Bang.

One by one, you slam them shut.

Bang. Bang. Bang.

Your lies catch up with you in the end.

I only have the truth to tell.

Whilst the investigating team went fishing, of course other stuff came to light. Northumbria Police found a sawn-off shotgun near the patio of a guy – 'Mr R' – who was then arrested. The weapon was sent off for testing *but* the firearm was different to the type that Moat had shot me with. The firearm particles *didn't* match Moat's and there was no DNA association either. They could link the weapon to 'Mr R' forensically, though they can't to Moat. He has been charged with possession of a section one firearm, which would give a minimum sentence of five years, and denies all knowledge of the gun, despite the ties seeming to link him to it. He *is* an associate of Moat's but they can't link the gun to Moat so we remain none the wiser as to who the armourer was.

All of Moat's other 'mates' have disassociated themselves with him and want nothing to do with the case. Who the defence will call as witnesses is anybody's guess.

It doesn't look good for Ness and Awan.

Apart from staring at the barrel on the night, I haven't seen the gun. Once the case is finished, it is my intention to do so. My blindness is an irrelevance in that process. I have to do it as a policeman and as the victim. I want to feel it to see if it is the same sized gun, adamant that it was longer than the gun Moat was ultimately found with, because on 4 July he seemed too far away from the car to have a sawn-off shotgun. I had always felt that. That would mean only one thing.

The gun that was used to shoot me is still out there.

MONDAY 7 FEBRUARY 2011

K ath went to watch Sam Stobbart in court today. Again, it settled her. She wanted to feel hatred for her.

Why, after all, would you make up that lie about Chris Brown being a policeman? It all starts there.

I know Kath is curious to get underneath Stobbart's skin. Violent psychotic men we can understand in a strange kind of way, but woman to woman is a different dynamic. She wanted to know one thing. Knowing Moat better than anyone, how could Stobbart have been so calculating to put Chris Brown at risk?

She knows pretty much the same information that I do in terms of evidence, but this is the one witness she would have bought a ticket to see.

You can feel nothing but contempt for Ness and Awan – they chose to make those decisions – and much as I have little time for Stobbart, she had many decisions thrust upon her.

Kath now says she can't hate her. She understands now why she said those things. From a woman's point of view, no woman wants to hear about another being dragged down the stairs by her hair. She was in a violent abusive relationship and she and Moat had a child together.

It wasn't easy; she was caught in Moat's world and told that lie to protect herself. He was a ticking time bomb and I firmly believe that the only reason he hadn't killed a probation officer or a social worker previously was because he couldn't get to them. Police officers, on the other hand, are a ten-a-penny.

It wouldn't have mattered if I were a female, or a horse-mounted officer, Moat had built up such a head of steam in prison that he hated any figure of authority and vulnerability counted for nothing. He felt society had failed him but I believe he was inherently evil. That's the question you always ask – nature or nurture?

He was evil by nature for me.

Sam Stobbart was the catalyst; her reaction to him just lit the blue touch paper.

Kath studied her performance with new-found sympathy but at no stage in court am I aware that Stobbart said she missed Chris. She concentrated on positioning herself as a domestic violence victim and that sits uncomfortably with me.

I can't really know if her tears in front of the jury were regret for herself or for Chris. For goodness' sake, Moat and her had been arguing over custody of their puppies that night!

It is my turn on Wednesday and I'm well aware that my waterworks may flow too. The difference is that I'll let my drama take its natural course.

WEDNESDAY 9 FEBRUARY 2011

'Let's go and get this done,' I say to Kath as I wake this morning.

Today is the day.

Of course, I didn't sleep well – two hours at most. I rarely do now.

'You're really quiet. What's the matter?' Kath keeps saying.

Sitting alone at the breakfast bar in our house, I can just about manage my porridge, trying to get into some sort of zone where I can believe that this is just another day at work. I've done this dozens of times before.

'Are you nervous?' Kath asks.

'It's just a normal day at work,' I reply.

Maybe I am answering on auto-pilot. Perhaps Kath detects that. It's the only way I can really prepare myself. This day has been on my mind for some considerable time. All I ask is that the press afford me the dignity of walking in as a policeman.

I know I am the star witness and that the defence don't want me there.

They can't argue with the facts though. They already speak volumes and we have barely got underway. My expectations are that Ness has no chance and I'm not hopeful for Awan's fate either. My fear is of some sort of red herring like a psychiatric report to say that either of them was incapable of thinking for themselves or some other nonsense the barristers come up with.

I hope the jury don't fall for that. There's certainly persuasive CCTV evidence for Ness. Not just the B&Q moment but also several shots of him leaving Moat's house, ironically, one of the most filmed buildings in the North East because Moat was so paranoid. He rigged up a whole movie set there himself. His own evidence will ultimately feature in the prosecution of his mates! That will be a sweet moment.

Those tapes show how they had been very busy on the Friday, as Moat got dropped off by Ness and his girlfriend. The jury will also be told that Ness was carrying a bag. He claims it contained an air rifle. The prosecution alleges it had a shotgun in it. One witness claims it was steroids.

All I can say is they must have been using *some* steroids if they think a bag carrying a shotgun weighs the same as one carrying steroids!

My head is clear, though.

I am ready.

We arrive before 9.30 a.m. and I make my way to sit in the police room with Alison Brown, my FLO. Kath and Ashley head into court; Mia is at school. Outside court the press are considerate. Quite how Kath and I will look later when the TV news shows the cartoon courtroom sketches is another matter.

Ali begins reading my twelve-page statement aloud to prepare me.

'Just stop, I've had enough. I don't need to know any more,' I shout.

The noise in the corridor outside has been driving me nuts and she has reached the point in my statement where I have been shot for a second time. It's about ten pages in. I've heard more than enough and I know how this one ends.

At around 11 a.m., I am called.

I feel empty. I know exactly what is coming.

Some officers exaggerate, others understate; occasionally some big up their part. I only deal in the truth.

I want what I know about the case to be evidence-based so everything I am learning with the jury is new to me too. I have met the investigating team twice but not to find out any of the evidence and I have asked Detective Superintendent Stephen

Binks, the head of the inquiry, if I can sit down with him for a couple of days *after* the trial.

Today I can only answer the questions that I am asked.

I am confident the defence will want me away as quickly as possible. You never know how a defence barrister will act but I'm sure that, given the deliberate public profile that I have had in the last six months, I just don't see it being any benefit in them turning on me. The jury would see they were clutching at straws and they won't see any weakness in me to exploit. There will be no chink in my armour and I know I hold the moral high ground.

Why Ness and Awan are not pleading guilty is beyond me. They say that they were held hostage. I don't see that as a defence to murder. The only defence to murder is self-defence.

At the end of the trial, if they are convicted, I want them to lose some of the things that I have lost: I can't ever see my family again but I will always have them. They may be able to see out of a window, but they won't see their family apart from on visits. Only then will I find my satisfaction.

They won't rot in jail, because in time they will be released. Moat fired the gun but these two aren't gentlemanly enough to stand up and admit their role in proceedings, hiding instead behind their pack of lies. That is what really rankles. Still they squirm, when they should know that they are beaten. They are among the world's most horrible people, who don't have the morals and principles to say 'sorry, we were wrong'. They have previous convictions too, though unlike Moat, not with me.

My only concern as I approach the box is not to trip. The saddest thing for me is having to be guided into the box, unable to enter it alone. My stick feels like a sword, and I feel hollow and lonely as I hand it back to the FLO, Chris Clarke. I don't want it to fall over and distract me while I am giving evidence.

For months I have choreographed this moment with military precision, visualising how I would stand, talking through in my head how to come across naturally.

As I take to the stand, I'm struck by how quiet the room is.

It's the most silent I have ever heard a courtroom. You could hear the proverbial pin drop. Speaking into a microphone, the sound is crystal clear. The only jarring to the clarity is one of the reporters scribbling away, either with a really rough pencil or a very cheap pen. It's slightly irritating but all the same, I sense the jury hanging on my every word.

I don't know if this is out of awe or respect. It seems strange and unusual that the trial is in Newcastle. There can't be a person in that jury who hasn't seen me on TV or is unaware of the case. Perhaps it sends a chill down their spine to see me there in the flesh. Obviously, I can't see *them* but that does not stop me, as a blind person, sensing their deep intake of breath and knowing inside that they aren't at just any other trial.

All I want is to retain my dignity and professionalism and for one of my superiors to come up to me afterwards and say that mine was the best evidence they have ever heard in court. I want to do my job today. Putting my uniform on this morning rather than a suit helped, giving me back my shield. In the moment itself, I don't feel a victim. It's great to be a policeman again.

I am aggrieved *not* to see Ness and Awan however.

They can see me.

The jury box is directly opposite the witness stand, twenty feet from me. I am standing behind an open lectern on a raised stage. To my right is the Judge.

Directly in front of Justice McCombe are the barristers' desks and about nine feet behind them is a big glass screen with two six-inch gaps – one at the top and one at the bottom – almost in a private annexe to the court. Ness and Awan are in there. All the sound in the court is played into there, so they can't miss anything. I may have known this court from previous experience but I didn't know this feeling.

I'm determined to eyeball them, as ridiculous as that sounds. When the Judge speaks, I turn to him. I know *they* are looking at me. When their barrister talks, I face both Ness and Awan.

A stumbling blind man, unconfident of his bearings, will help nobody. I am not that man.

I asked Kath yesterday what she would do when she first laid eyes on them, knowing I would attack them if I could. She wasn't sure, shaking her head repulsed. She just knows that they are lowlife scumbags.

And then it was time.

I have told this story so many times but this is the only occasion that really matters. I know the detail word for word.

I've learnt my lines.

My pre-trial visit may have helped me geographically but it didn't tell me how I was going to feel. You can't know at that stage the difference between an empty courtroom and a full one and knowing that the world is watching, I succumb to my vulnerability.

I falter a couple of times as I realise this testimony is my toughest, my well-told story finding an audience as though for the first time.

Of course, I am right back in that car, and I can see him coming round the corner. That's why I have to pause regularly, as my words race ahead of the moment of impact which returns again and again. I'm trying to tell my story as evidence and without emotion. I hope the jury are sympathetic that in my world it isn't Wednesday 9 February 2011. Suddenly, I'm back there in the early hours of Sunday 4 July 2010. And tears are rolling down my cheeks. I hope I am telling this story for the last time.

'Did you enjoy your job?' QC Smith asks me gently.

'Yes, I did,' I reply. 'And I still do.'

Composing myself, I know those words make a statement.

The judicial system is on my mind. I know the games barristers play. These guys are guilty. I know their defence has nowhere to go but I also recognise a man on damage-limitation. To my surprise, I am cross-examined.

To not be questioned would of course radiate the message that the trial was a write-off. If you have nothing to ask me, then you know to tell your clients that this is only going one way. Of course, he *had* to cross-examine me, even though I wasn't expecting it.

And as he begins, his game dawns on me.

'I am not being critical of your evidence, but let me take you back to March,' is the defence's mild opening.

I know instantly from experience and instinct that he knows he is beaten but is now positioning his clients. Why talk about a mild scrap metal offence rather than the main event? He's establishing characters and patterns, attributing blame to Moat.

I can see where he is taking the jury. He's homing in on *my* original fear of Moat from that previous meeting, so the jury can see from my honest evidence how Moat is intimidating and therefore could have placed Ness and Awan under duress, indeed taken them hostage. This, frankly, is his only card, and I think he knows it.

I am wise to it, making the point that back then he wasn't angry at me in particular. That meeting just shows he was anti-establishment, angry and bitter at anybody in authority.

I've knocked him back for sure. He has no further questions.

It was done.

I have been in there an hour. Or maybe less.

The defence must have mustered no more than four questions, a token two to three minutes with me. Reading between the lines, that is damning. I hope the jury get that point too and I feel pretty confident that we are sending them down.

I had done my job. I had done what I had come to do. I simply told my story calmly as I have done on numerous occasions since, briefly faltering for a moment as I slipped back to victim. For the most part, the policeman just told his story.

My day wasn't quite over, though.

This morning I had overheard a conversation between Steve Binks and Alison Brown.

'All her applications for criminal compensation have been rejected. She's got a bill of £3,000 to pay for Chris's funeral,' Steve had said.

I don't know if he had told Ali this for my benefit, or if it was just casual conversation. It left me preoccupied.

Kath's meeting with Sally Brown had left her very emotional. I knew now for the first time that I had to meet her too. Over the weekend Kath told me that the courtroom experience felt like we were in a movie, one of those chilling Lynda La Plante split-screen dramas, watching our lives running parallel with Moat and his cronies. She had felt sick thinking about it. The prosecution had put up a timeline of events for Saturday 3 July starting with that innocuous game of golf. That was the thing that really got to Kath.

She has found a way of dealing with the big stuff but this small detail was a painful reminder of the everyday routine of our old lives. This has now gone forever and that detail brought it home. Something so harmless and irrelevant in this complicated story became a tipping point. She felt it was like watching our lives on two separate train tracks getting ready to go bang. Sally Brown had said exactly the same thing.

Here we are now, thrown together, through no fault of our own but with one common thread – Moat.

I remembered one thing of Sally from when I was in hospital. She said she would never speak to the press. I found that quite honourable and it was that which made me decide that I had to be the spokesperson against Moat. The only other option was to let Sam Stobbart have her moment and I didn't think that was right.

When my witness statement was being read this morning I sent Ash home to let the dogs out and told him to return with my cheque book. Kath and I were united in what was the right thing to do.

I wanted to pay for Chris Brown's funeral.

So after my testimony I asked Kath if I could be left alone and if somebody would get Sally. She walked in and we both started crying.

'I appreciate everything you *haven't* done with the press, and I understand why,' I begin, choking.

'That's the reason why I have done as much as I have. I want you to realise this has never been about me, it's about what happened to Chris *and* me.'

Sally can't hold back her anger and emotion.

'Have you had any help with the costs of anything?' I ask, already knowing the answer.

'No,' she replies, 'everything has been refused. I can't even get criminal compensation for him.'

Sadly, I am not surprised by this. My understanding is that Chris had walked out of the house carrying an iron bar and in the eyes of the Criminal Injuries Compensation Authority that isn't grounds to pay out.

If you are armed yourself, add to your own downfall or are the instigator, *or* have lots of previous criminal convictions, they are unlikely to pay out. By carrying that bar, he had nullified his claim.

'I am going to give you something now from Kath and I. I don't want you to be offended, please accept it in the spirit in which it is intended. Don't open it now.'

Sally doesn't work and I just don't think it's appropriate that she should be paying off her son's funeral for the rest of her life. As anniversaries come and go and suddenly it has been five, maybe ten years since Chris was shot that payment will still be going out to pay for her son's funeral. To those who cite closure, that's the reality of life after Moat.

After twenty-five minutes, it's time to part. I don't regret not seeing Sally sooner, but I am glad we have met now. The moment hadn't been right until today and I knew the moment would come. Today, it feels right.

Money means nothing to me but since my niece Naomi's death and the fact that my sister Debbie has always felt that she wasn't dealt with properly by the police at the time, I have always wanted to do the best by people as a FLO.

As we part, the irony is not lost on me. I came to court this morning as a policeman. I stood in the witness box as a copper and as a victim. I leave this evening, back where this whole story began when I came home on the Friday night – as a FLO, comforting Sally Brown.

THURSDAY 10 FEBRUARY 2011

I went for a run last night to clear my head. I jogged the furthest I have ever run without stopping and then slept for England for the first time since it all happened, nearly seven months ago. Any runner who is not a serious *serious* runner will tell you that always happens when you pound the streets, whether that's your intention or you've just gone for a mild workout, listening to your favourite music. Running is a therapeutic emotional sieve.

Of course, I couldn't get the trial out of my head at first. I replayed every line time and time again. Most importantly, I felt proud. I am confident that I did a good job.

Yes, there were moments. On the way out of the courtroom I broke down but nobody saw me crying. My legs – the same legs to which I had somehow transferred power on 4 July to walk to the stretcher when my colleagues couldn't get me out of the patrol car – well, they went. I had been standing upright for an hour. They just gave way through emotion.

I had been cool and collected inside the court but Kath could see me going on the way out.

'Don't cry now, the press are behind you,' she said.

My right leg kept giving way.

Raw emotion took over.

I am happy with that though. The court is my office and in it, I behaved like a professional. On its steps I was a victim, and I don't think anybody would be surprised that I caved in there. I did my job – that's the main thing.

Kath told me that Ness and Awan never moved. Dodgy defendants are normally fidgety. Not these two lowlifes, devoid of emotion. Their suits were ill-fitting too. It was probably the first time that they'd worn them and by all accounts they didn't look the part. She also backed up what I sensed. Some of the jury *were* sat open-mouthed at what they were hearing. They, too, were now sucked into my world through the lottery of jury service. They, too, would now be faced with sleepless nights, aghast at the mindlessness of what they had heard. They too would have Moat with them for the rest of their lives.

And do *I* feel closure today?

No. It's just another nail in their coffin. That's all I feel.

I've been *taught* closure as a FLO. I've been on courses to help me understand it and help victims embrace it. And now I see how stupid and unnatural that is. You can't get emotion from a textbook.

As odd as it is, the best analogy is to think of this week in terms of Christmas. Tuesday was like Christmas Eve, full of anticipation and excitement that the big day was just around the corner. Yesterday was split into two. The morning was Christmas Day morning – feeling good. The afternoon was that predictable sensation after you've opened your presents and had your Christmas dinner and when it's all over, you reflect on the banality of it all. The extremes of excess that got your juices flowing a day before leave you empty 24 hours later.

That leaves today. Boxing Day. When you wake up and you're not really sure what all that was about, and when you have done it all there's nothing left.

Today I am flat. I no longer buy this notion of closure. I officially think it is rubbish. You don't close anything.

One thing has changed though. I had been planning just to go to court for my evidence and the summing up but now I've gained the same sort of resolve which made me find the strength to get on the radio when I was waiting for the dog handler to shut up.

I want to go every day now, determined to play my part.

They won't take seriously the defence's request today to 'give Awan more calories', nor his visit to hospital yesterday as the defence try to portray him as not physically strong. I hope they see through the games but register the irony that he went to the RVI Hospital – the very one which housed me in my darkest hour.

I feel more contempt this morning for these two than Moat himself. What happened to me was because I was caught up in Moat's game. The problem with these two isn't what they did but what they didn't do. If they hadn't enabled his actions as they did he wouldn't have got anywhere near me.

Without them, there would have been no car, no weapon, and no chain of events, pulling so many innocent people into Moat's path of destruction.

Professionals like Craig, who vomited on the night outside the control room, wouldn't have got dragged in to this trial and my action against my own employer. Yesterday he had to go through it all again as Moat's chilling, but ignored, five-minute call, from just moments before he shot me, was replayed to the court:

Raoul Moat (RM): 'Hello there, this is the gunman from Birtley last night. What I'm phoning about is, is to tell you exactly why I have done what I have done, right? Now, my girl-friend has been having an affair behind my back with one of your officers. This gentleman that I shot last night, the karate instructor, right, now I… Yous bastards have been on to me, right, for years. Yous have hassled us, harassed us, yous just won't leave us alone. I went straight six years ago when I met her and I have tried my best to have a normal life and you just won't let up. Yous won't leave us alone for five minutes. I can't drive down the street without the blue lights flashing. Yous have stitched us up for years; you have been in court, stitching us up, so the fact of the matter is, right… She has had an affair with one of your officers. If he had not been a police officer I would not have shot him.'

Call handler (CH): 'Okay.'

RM: 'It's as simple as that, right? But the thing is, you know, it's been going on for a while. I went to jail, right, I was stitched up by yous for hitting my kids which I did not do.'

CH: 'Right, right.'

RM: 'I went to jail for something I didn't do; I could have taken a community order, right, but what happened is my Sam had a discussion with my barrister… if I went to jail for three to four weeks… my barrister promised us and they let us down. She said she would have us on a retrial and get the not guilty so that after me and Sam could live together.'

CH: 'Uh-huh.'

RM: 'Now I have went to jail, right, longer than I should have.'

CH: 'Hang on, hang on a minute, you're losing me, yeah.'

RM: 'I went to jail longer than I should have for something I didn't do, right? Which justified that in your own head, right? Meanwhile, while I'm in there doing that for my missus, right, she's having an affair with one of your officers, right. She's winding us up, saying that yous are going to stitch us up using him.'

CH: 'Yeah.'

RM: 'Right. And I know that he is this and that is going to cos he's a multiple black belt, that he is going to kick me arse all over the place.'

CH: 'Right, okay, sorry.'

RM: 'And I have had nothing but grief… but I have had a genuine relationship with her for six years, which is why we have stayed together, and I have gone straight. I have had a totally legit life with her, I have opened a business, and I have been shafted. You police have took too much off me over the years.'

CH: 'Okay.'

RM: 'Yous won't leave us alone. And now yous think you can take me missus. Now, I didn't mean to shoot her like that, right, that was…'

CH: 'Okay, okay.'

RM: 'Right. He deserved it, right, but she, right… you can run ballistics – I was altering those cartridges, right. That one was half the powder, that… it was meant to get her compensation because obviously, I'm not going to be around in a few days, right, it was meant to just give her a little injury so she can get lots of compensation.'

CH: 'Okay.'

RM: 'Like, for the bairn. Now that I have found out that she's critical I'm not happy about it. I did not mean that, you know what I mean?'

CH: 'Right, right.'

RM: 'I can't, I can't. To be honest, I'm quite surprised she's critical, you know, but I didn't mean that. But the fact of the matter is I'm not coming in alive. Yous have hassled me for so many years. If you come anywhere near me I'll kill yous. I have got two hostages at the moment, right – come anywhere near me and I'll kill them as well. I'm coming to get yous. I'm not on the run – I'm coming to get you. You have made me unwell. Yous have made me do this cos yous just won't leave me out. You know, yous just won't leave us alone, right?'

CH: 'Can you confirm you have got two hostages?'

RM: 'I confirm I have got two hostages.'

CH: 'Right, and where are you?'

RM: 'I am not gonna tell you where I am.'

CH: 'Okay, fair enough.'

RM: 'I'll call again (inaudible) don't worry (inaudible) I have (inaudible) with yous.'

CH: 'Right, can you just confirm who you are? Can you give me your date of birth please?'

RM: 'Yes, it's June 17 1973.'

CH: 'Right, okay then, thank you very much.'

RM: 'Right. I'm very sorry for what's happened to Sam, that is not what I meant.'

CH: 'Right.'

RM: 'Okay. But I tell you something else, that this other idiot in the paper that's saying I pointed a gun at him – you know that he's had to, like, you know, his dad's had to console him and all the rest of it?'

CH: 'Yeah.'

RM: 'He was accused, right. I heard rumours in jail that he was sleeping with my Sam. Now… I have spoke, I was talking to Sam's dad yesterday and he said he heard the same rumours as well but he didn't believe it was true. But he was definitely trying to get into her. So listen to me when I tell yous he was the first one – he ran and hid upstairs leaving his wife and leaving everybody else, you know what I mean? He did not stand there and let a gun point at me because, had I pointed it at him I would have shot him, because I believe he was getting into her. There's a lot of nonsense going on behind my back while I have been in jail. She has changed, she's not half changed. And every, every time I spoke to her and tried to be reasonable she wouldn't let us anywhere near the bairn.'

CH: 'Right, right.'

RM: 'She wouldn't let us go up to her house, she wouldn't discuss anything and she was taunting us with one of your officers. Right. Now I have had enough. I have had enough of yous. That jail made us unwell. I came out a different kid, you know what I mean? I lost everything through yous, right? Yous just won't leave us alone, right? So at the end of the day, yous killed me and him before that trigger was ever pulled.'

CH: 'Right.'

RM: 'You know what I mean?'

CH: 'Okay.'

RM: 'Yous are…'

CH: 'We are trying to help you.'

RM: 'You're not trying to help us, you're not trying. Yous wanted me to do myself in and I was going to do it till I found out about him properly and what was going on – and as soon as I found out he was one of your officers I thought, nah, yous have had too much from me. You will get your chance to kill us, right, you will get your chance to kill us.'

CH: 'Right, we don't want to do that, we don't want to do that.'

RM: 'Aye, yous wanted me to kill myself but I'm gonna give yous a chance cos I'm hunting for officers now, right?'

CH: 'No. Please don't do that. We don't want any more killing, all right?'

FRIDAY 11 FEBRUARY 2011

I shuddered hearing that transcript back yesterday. It's also bloody hard work to listen to.

Deluded, misinformed, hell-bent on causing destruction and without a care for the consequences. His constant use of the word 'yous' almost makes such a serious and damning, chilling piece of evidence comical. Nobody is laughing though.

This is the call which my mate Craig listened to and urged his superiors to act on. It is probably the most important piece of dialogue in my life. The clues are all there but it wasn't acted on in time. Reading that back now, can there be a person alive who can give good justification as to why that threat wasn't passed on to the team out there on the night? Hindsight is a wonderful thing but I'd be a bad cop if the warning it provided hadn't put me on the move. Failure to pass that message on put us all on the back foot and placed Moat in control. You can argue that many moments were the key ones – from Northumbria Police receiving a telephone warning that Moat was a threat on his release, to my decision to sit at the A1/A69 junction.

This is the defining one for me.

The test of course comes if this ever happens again. Heaven forbid the senior officers in the control room would do the same again. Hopefully in future, they would alert the troops and then work on the data, not the other way round.

The jury also heard evidence from Sam Stobbart's mum, Lesley, and Lemur Singh, another who'd been caught in the crossfire.

Mr Singh is the fish and chip shop owner in Seaton Delaval, who Moat held up on the day after I was shot. At the time, nobody was saying publicly that this was Moat's handiwork, and – forgive the pun – a raid for £100 in cash seems small fry compared to what he was up to his neck in. I don't know if he needed the cash or if by this stage he was on some sort of adrenalin-kick, pleased with himself at leading the police a merry dance, but it seems odd. Moat was still brandishing a shotgun during the raid. Witnesses place Ness and Awan in the black Lexus outside.

To absorb all this yesterday was exhausting. It wasn't some Crimewatch reconstruction. My stance remains the same, that to retain a high profile reminds all concerned to keep focused but already I need a break. I've a sense too that the key players have already been called. Today Karl Ness's mother is due. I doubt we'll learn much.

So, despite my intentions to attend every day, I am not going to court this morning.

It's a welcome relief therefore that Kath is keeping me busy, driving me to Stoke for a white collar boxing event for the Blue Lamp Foundation.

It's a great way to end the week, channelling my energies into helping future David Rathbands. But it's not closure. There's a still a hell of a long way to go.

MONDAY 14 FEBRUARY 2011

The boxing on Friday night went down a storm. I'm grateful too that the Chief came along. That doesn't surprise me. Sue has never wavered in her support for me. I have never become an embarrassing piece of paperwork that won't go away once the dust has settled. I am still one of her boys.

I have to keep busy, or I'll be trapped in this darkness for the next forty years or however long I have and the boxing was a welcome break from the trial.

On Friday, Maureen Ness – the defendant's mother – took to the stand, telling the court that she thought Moat was 'a bit of a loner' and that she had always warned her son off him but she was concerned that *he* had always admired and feared Moat.

She also went on to clarify another letter which Ness had delivered to her daughter-in-law Kelly on July 3 which said 'Don't be alarmed but I'm being held hostage by Raoul. I'm being treated like a gent. Raoul is a nice bloke but he has problems, don't we all? He's a mate of mine and I will do as much as I can to help him. Tell my mother and tell her not to go to the police as I will not be back if she does'.

Well, what can you say other than this is the most unusual hostage scenario any of us have ever heard of? I didn't realise Ness was smart enough to attempt to put his alibi in place as events were unfolding, though on a second glance, it's really not the brightest piece of prose, is it?

The jury also saw the moment Ness and Awan were arrested, walking along the B6344 in Rothbury after a dog-walker had become suspicious. This, of course, confirms they were in

Rothbury. Significantly, the arrest took place on Tuesday 6 July, early in the week. Clearly when you're just wandering freely around in the woods with no sign of Moat, you're not in a hostage scenario.

This must have given Detective Chief Superintendent Neil Adamson the confidence to say at the time that the net was closing, even though it was another three to four days before the manhunt reached its conclusion.

I've had the weekend to reflect. Buoyed up by the boxing, I remain determined to be in court as much as I possibly can. I'm concerned that the 'star witnesses' have had their moment and that the jury remain focused while some of the less juicy stuff plays out.

I'm waiting on a letter too, which should have arrived by Friday. The police had until then to respond to my litigation against them.

Their previous lengthy correspondence denied liability for what happened to me, despite Sue Sim telling me that I had to sue and her passing me the file of a secret investigation into what went on in the control room that night. What was the story behind those harrowing tapes?

The force's solicitors had asked what the police could have done better on the night, which was surprising, given that they repeatedly failed to pass instruction of the threat to the ground units. Of course, this left me confused so I asked Sue to come and see me, given that I was suing on her instigation.

The Chief had originally been informed that the call from Moat had lasted six minutes and had only been heard once in the control room but I was the one to break it to her that it had actually been played back twice and had been about to get a third analysis. She had commissioned this report when I told her that she was about to find out that *this* was the truth and not what she had been led to believe.

I am hugely grateful to the many people who have shared hidden or private information with me since my shooting.

You can see how hard it could potentially be to piece all the elements together given that I was near death for a considerable period.

Imagine though if I had found out via some TV investigation in ten years' time everything that some of my honourable colleagues have told me in the last six months. That is not the correct way for the force to operate and I attribute much of that disclosure to Sue. Under the previous Chief, I believe these people may well have been hounded out.

I've been told that my case could take a considerable amount of time to resolve.

So, you see, there is no closure. It just goes on and on and on.

With all this going on, the boxing could not have come at a better time. We nearly doubled the total funds for the Blue Lamp Foundation in one evening on Friday. I am thankful and humbled as we head towards nearly £100,000 raised so far. The fact that we've raised this much money in this difficult economic time, and when there is still some sort of negativity in fund-raising towards the police, has given me renewed energy and vigour.

When I woke this morning, *this* gave me something to aim for, and going forward, I have to have reasons to get up in the morning.

Every year at the *Pride of Britain* awards, there is a category for individuals raising money for charity. It's now in my sights. I want to be the first person ever to win two *Pride of Britain* awards.

TUESDAY 15 FEBRUARY 2011

On Sunday I had a tip-off that one of the witnesses had been in to change their statement and had been asked if anyone had got to them. The answer was yes. This doesn't surprise me. It's the kind of rubbish I expect given the characters involved in this trial.

It just makes it all the more strange as to why the trial is in Newcastle. It is not normal for such a high profile case to be tried on the doorstep of where it happened, especially given the huge number of accomplices caught in the net of Moat's world.

And I felt totally at home today. In fact, evidentially it was a fantastic day, and I was surprised by what I heard.

I sat bolt upright and did a double-take when I learned that I had been shot with an unmodified shotgun cartridge.

'Fuck, Moat screwed up. I'd be dead if he hadn't,' I thought.

Chris Brown was shot three times in all – in the knee, left throat area and the back of the head. The two shots in the leg and the neck were single shot shotgun cartridges which had been modified. The execution shot in the back of the head was unmodified.

Moat had a sawn-off shotgun which means in theory that the shots from the cartridge can spread out quicker than from a full-length shotgun. When the shot spreads out, you have less chance of hitting something. Moat was tampering with the guns so in effect what he aimed at Sam Stobbart was more like a bullet, which he had concocted himself using fishing weights.

I have no idea how he found out that you could do this and everybody today whom I asked was clueless to explain where he had got the knowledge from. Prison, I assume. It seems to be the work of both an idiot and a genius but *I* remain convinced that he picked the wrong 'bullets' for Stobbart and myself. You remember in the call to the control room he didn't realise he had injured her so badly. He was intent on killing Chris Brown, but took a risk with her.

Karl Ness, the accomplice, worked at the Get Carter Cars garage, ironically just near the police station. The prosecution today linked that garage to one of the cartridges. Furthermore, one of the cartridges that hit both Chris Brown and me had been removed from the gun afterwards and had been found in the Lexus, driven by Ness and Awan. As well as the B&Q footage, there is also a till receipt from Bagnall and Kirkwood in Grey Street in Newcastle.

This is a fishing shop!

Piece by piece the prosecution were linking Ness and Awan to Moat, to the weapons to the car, and at the very end they introduced a blue bag with excellent DNA evidence from both Ness and Moat, both on the chord and neck of the bag. Two cartridges had been found inside the bag as well, both forensically linked to them and found within the police cordon at Birtley right after those shootings. This was the bag that a witness later claimed was carrying steroids!

Lana Potts, the 22-year-old daughter of Ness's girlfriend, Tara Collins, had told court yesterday that she had found a blue string bag on the top of the fridge at the beginning of July and had climbed up to see what it was. She discovered a 'bullet' and believed there to be more in there. Subsequently she had been shown a text by detectives sent from her mum's phone to Ness which read:

'Lana not happy cos she didn't know you left that thing in the kitchen til Raoul asked.'

I think that tells you everything, though hers had been a curious, mumbly performance – the only time I can ever recall an interpreter being used in court for a British person – so incoherent and inaudible had she been.

I had always been under the impression that I had been shot with a modified shotgun. I was stunned with my own conclusion that Moat had made a mistake. That bullet should have gone straight through me and blown me to pieces. It would have done if he hadn't messed up. The bullets meant for his next victim after Chris *were* meant for a police officer, but he messed up and fired those at Sam Stobbart instead.

Of course, most of the really bad stuff links Ness to the case more than Awan at this point but it's still early days.

From what I heard today I am convinced that the prosecution has been very clever and is setting the scene, producing a mobile which had been dumped up the A69 with Ness and Moat's DNA on the front. This was the same phone that was used to call the control room, warning that Moat was about to shoot a policeman. In effect, they are showing that Moat and Ness are inextricably linked and are about to position Awan as the facilitator who drove them and fetched them after Birtley.

I could see where it was going.

Strangely, some of the evidence made me laugh. The police had recovered a second gun from Kingston Park, just a few miles outside of Newcastle. The gun was made in 1890! Where were these players in contemporary warfare getting their ammunition from, and if you take the eight out that's my collar number too.

Tango 190.

The trigger was broken on one barrel but the firing pin was still active. That's how antiquated the gear was. Significantly, a cartridge from Birtley matched one found at this same address. I wasn't shot with this gun, however. A Lincoln did for me.

All in all, this has been a key day, forensically linking Moat and Ness to the bullets. It also shows some of the brilliant work which the public rarely see. The DNA stuff was fascinating.

The forensic specialist, when asked to handle the bag in the witness box, refused to do so without rubber gloves. That bag has been up and down the country for tests from London to Wetherby and back again, but I thought that her refusal was brilliant because it showed to the jury how careful the forensics guys were and that they don't make mistakes. Even at this stage she wouldn't contaminate any evidence and the jury would conclude that this had been the way all through the process.

The defence had little to offer in return. I don't recall them even cross-examining the two forensic witnesses. I sensed Ness and Awan's teams were going through the motions. If they had been my defence team, I would want them scrabbling for everything but they only seem to have a mild 'under duress' card to play for Ness and Awan.

Moat's accomplices will probably be called towards the back end of this week, and they'll either fade away and their lies will unravel themselves, or their barrister will play a blinder for them. Either way, there is every indication that the jury will be sent away on Monday of next week to consider their verdict. That's bloody quick, about twice as fast as I expected. I can only assume that the writing is on the wall.

The financial cost of all this has emerged today as well.

Cheap at half the price, the bill for Operation Bulwark so far is up to £1.4 million. Much of that has been spent on overtime which is ironic considering that I know about fifteen officers who worked for nothing and that I have to yet to clock off that shift! I must be owed millions by now.

At least the force isn't wasting any more taxpayers' money having separate trials for these two – and it's better off spending that much money getting a murderer off the streets than it is on a stupid statue outside the new police HQ in Wallsend which was revealed last week.

We've only gone and blown £50,000 on a large O with a ball bearing in it.

And we were getting slagged off left, right and centre for wasting so much money on a load of scrap metal, which, of course, is where all this began back in March 2009.

And worse, this wasn't just the 'Raoul Moat trial' any more. The *Daily Mail* now labelled us the 'Raoul Moat Police Force'.

WEDNESDAY 16 FEBRUARY 2011

Court was boring today.

I left for different reasons from yesterday, not for effect this time but because the whole day didn't have the same impact on me. It was dull! And not gritty enough compared to Tuesday! My thirst for drama had waned.

To be honest, I struggled to follow some of it.

Today was about phone technology – Northumbria Police had instructed a 'cell analyst' called Duncan Brown to look at a number of significant locations across the North East, but his evidence was so full of pie charts and graphs that I wondered if the jury could really be following it too. I hope we didn't baffle them with science.

I did learn that all of Moat's calls had been recorded in real time, dating back as far as 9 June – so nearly four weeks before he went nuts. Well, really nuts anyway.

He never referred to a gun in those calls. It was always 'Have you got me that item?' That, of course, leaves questions, outside of the trial, for future operations. The clues were all there.

Curiously, Moat's phone was registered to an address in Kenton, just outside Newcastle, and under the name of a Mr Trimit.

'Trimit – what an odd name,' I asked myself. 'Can that mean anything? Is it an anagram of something? Nah, he wasn't that clever.'

Trimit doesn't exist, of course. Moat had been using a phone owned by one of his friends to ring when he was in prison.

He made one emergency call on 30 June from inside because he was out of credit. Durham Prison obliged!

Unbelievable, I know, that you even have these rights. That 'emergency call' was to the world-famous Mr Trimit and that phone was being picked up by his mates.

The calls were becoming more and more frequent, getting very busy up to the period just before he came out. He had been trying to get 'Mr R' (the guy alleged to have the gun under the patio and the ties in the garage) to come to the prison as soon as he could, and for him to speak to somebody by the name of 'Stevie Walton' to get all the information from him. Clearly Moat spent his eighteen weeks in prison brewing and plotting.

When this 'emergency call' finished the analyst was able to show that 'Mr R' immediately rang the address in Kenton where Walton answered. They weren't even subtle about it, or were just incredibly naive about how the police work.

The prosecution was cleverly establishing the scene, and walking down that corridor again slamming those doors shut.

This phone registered to 'Trimit' was the mobile Moat then used himself when he left prison. I'm not sure at this point if it is the one found on the A69.

That's how this morning began in the court, with the prosecution establishing this timeline.

I also sat through the Home Office pathologist's evidence which clinically took us through the injuries sustained by Chris Brown. These turned out to be different to what I had understood them to be up to now.

Chris was shot from just a metre away in the right-hand side, down an imaginary line from underneath his arm to the fleshy part of his chest just below the rib cage. The single bullet from the shotgun cartridge travelled through his chest wall, through his liver and embedded itself in his heart. That alone was a fatal injury.

The second shot was further away, penetrating the left side of his neck and coming out the right without piercing his voicebox or veins. This wouldn't have been life-threatening.

At this point he was probably staggering just before collapsing on the ground. The third shot – the execution blow – blew his brains out as he lay on the ground, almost dead anyway.

All this puts yesterday in perspective because I can see how bloody lucky I was compared to Chris. I would be dead if Moat had shot me with the same bullets he shot Chris with, smashing straight through my skull. I remain convinced Moat got the ammunition mixed up.

Yet none of this was reported yesterday, which baffles me. It's not that I'm just approaching this from a police point of view with an eye on the end game. I'm just not sure that the journalists understand that the DNA and the linking of all the cartridges, the phone calls and the fishing weights to it, is ultimately going to be the key in the prosecution's argument.

Sky News are hardly running any of this despite their intense focus on Rothbury at the time; the newspapers are concentrating on the Chief having to defend police cuts, which the media, of course, then put back into the context of Rothbury, questioning how they will cope with reduced numbers and budgets should it happen again; the Metro Radio website just says 'Ness's girlfriend was worried about him after the Birtley shootings' which I think misses the point. Especially if you knew that on the Saturday she went to the funfair in South Shields. Yeah – extreme concern, I would say.

It's still looking like Monday or Tuesday for sending the jury out. That was the inkling I was getting today from Detective Chief Superintendent Neil Adamson who kindly came to sit next to me in court.

'We've worked really hard on this. I hope we've done you proud. I hope we get the conviction. I want it really shoved up them,' he said.

I still couldn't understand though why the defence were so passive. This was making me a little edgy.

'Why don't they try and undermine or belittle something?' I said to Detective Chief Inspector Steve Binks.

'Because they can't. They can't argue with any of it. All they can do is to wait for it all to come out and try to go for duress,' Steve replied.

I want it over now, because it seems to be plain sailing and I have a nasty feeling that there's a low-baller coming around the corner.

The defence don't have to tell the prosecution who their witnesses are. I've been told that there are four to six witnesses for Ness and Awan and it concerns me that we might have missed something and somebody will come out of the wood-work to contradict something that we've overlooked or, more likely, to tell a pack of lies.

Otherwise why would the defence just let it run like this?

With no evidence to contest, it just doesn't seem right unless that's why Ness sacked his barrister a week before the trial, normally a sign that any suspect has been told 'Look, you're in the shit, you're going down'. The new defence barrister either knows that he has inherited a load of nonsense, or that a low-baller is coming.

Interestingly, they have intimated that they will seek extra time for consultation from the Judge. Normally, after the prosecution have summed up, there will only be a slight adjournment but the feeling is that the defence will ask for a delay.

If Ness and Awan don't have something up their sleeve, then they're in the shit, but I'm in the police and I'm a cynic. It makes me nervous.

THURSDAY 17 FEBRUARY 2011

I dropped off twice in court today. I had been listening so intently to every detail all week that I was exhausted. Plus the seating does your head in. It's like being at some old picture house with really uncomfortable seats and you're packed in like sardines too. On top of that, I had to endure Sam Stobbart whispering away just four feet behind me, commenting on every little detail.

Becky, Chris Brown's sister, wasn't there today. She had been up for the week and sat through Monday, Tuesday and Wednesday but had to go to hospital with the stress of it all and was being flown home this morning. Heaven only knows what she must be going through, getting dragged into all this and hearing the graphic detail of where the bullets went into Chris.

There was more telecoms analysis too which didn't help, baffling me with all the graphs. The work that they've done on the phones has been extraordinary but it was so complicated that I struggled to follow it. I can only hope, for the second day running, that they didn't lose the jury too. It's a necessary evil to be so meticulous in establishing these timelines but you've got to be switched on to keep up with it. I hope it didn't do any damage, the important thing was to link the evidence to the phone patterns. They look like good, respectable people, I am told. Heaven forbid one of Moat's cronies had penetrated the twelve.

The call data showed them working independently but all meeting up at different points. Half the houses in the North East seemed to have been mentioned but we found out about a new unit at Blaydon which was linked to Awan, who wanted to start a pizza delivery business from it. With great skill, the barrister linked all of the phones but was at pains not to include this unit until the very end of the telecoms analysis.

This is where one of the guns was hidden.

In Awan's lock-up.

Leaving it to the end was a decisive blow.

The general feeling from Northumbria Police was that it had been a very good day.

In the afternoon, the court heard highlights from Ness's nine interviews following his arrest. Tellingly, in Awan's testimony he had said that he didn't know why Ness had gone to this unit and that there wasn't a gun there but when pressed on this he had changed his mind!

This gun in the pizza parlour was never found. The only two which the police had recovered were the Lincoln which shot me and the weapon under 'Mr R's patio.

Nobody knows where the third gun is but presumably if there was a third gun, as yet unused, then you have to assume that Moat's network was even broader than we knew. Some of those people are still out there. And so is the gun.

'It was like something out of a film,' Ness had said in his statement.

Good God, what kind of movies does he watch?

FRIDAY 18 FEBRUARY 2011

Reporters on my doorstep; Mia bullied at school about me today; an uncomfortable stand-off in which I feel hugely mis-portrayed. Those are the headlines.

It has hit the media that I am to sue Northumbria Police. Under no circumstances had I wanted this to come out during the trial. I don't want the jury getting distracted.

They've heard the truth, the whole truth and nothing but the truth. I don't think you can argue with the facts. The timing of the story shouldn't and mustn't put them off the scent.

A reporter at the *Evening Chronicle* in Newcastle has annoyed me. He's been ringing all week. I've given him stuff in the past, but he is going to learn the hard way now, after writing that I would probably have to pay back all the benefits that I have received so far if I am successful in my claim.

This is low-rent journalism.

The only benefit I have had is a payout from my *personal* insurance plan. For God's sake, I even had to buy my first white cane myself.

My friend, and PR man, Robin Palmer rang him to have it out. The journo was passing the buck saying his editor said the story was running and that it had been in the *Sunday Post* at the weekend. Yes, it had. For about three lines.

I'm unhappy, too, that he thinks that this means that my relationship with Sue Sim is now strained, pointing out that any legal letters would be addressed to her, although I had spoken highly of the support she had given me.

Yes, any legal letters do have to be addressed to her and I did speak highly of her. I still do.

Worryingly, though, dark forces are at work. The Chief told me that nobody from the press office had spoken to any media, though Northumbria Police of course did acknowledge that they had received the paperwork. The reporter told Robin that the press office *had* commented. Clearly, somebody was lying. And not for the first time.

Everybody at home is upset and irritated. Furthermore, we're not sure when we will be back in court. As we expected, the defence have asked for a break. They need to consult with their clients – or get that low-baller out – and after what I heard today they are going to have to work quickly.

At least that means on Monday I won't have to sit there as I did today with one of Ness's friends, who had also been arrested, sitting behind me.

I know, it's crazy.

Evidentially though it was another great day.

Ten out of ten.

Again, I struggled to concentrate. Directly behind me and three seats to my left, Ness's mate sniffed his way through proceedings, rolling phlegm in his mouth and eating in court even though he had already been told off on a previous after-noon after standing before the Judge had left. To be in the same room as him is bad enough. I don't even consider him worthy of a seat.

The stenographer was winding me up as well, though for a different reason. They just do their job but as I now only deal in sound, the beep of the recording machine was driving me potty in an otherwise still courtroom.

On the day that Ness and Awan were arrested, it was hardly front page news. At that point, the media attention was all about Moat. Even so, my force had really got cracking straight away.

Ness and Awan had been assigned 'urgent interview' status which means that Northumbria Police had been able to proceed without them having a solicitor present. This will normally happen in cases where the threat to the public's lives is still out there.

Only in his tenth interview was Awan challenged.

It's a pretty standard operational procedure to let someone like that dig a hole for themselves, and then produce something which unravels the train of deceit behind them. Keep them rambling on and on. Crooks can't help themselves.

The police had a letter.

Awan had sent a note which included the phrase 'I'm safe, safe, safer than safe' but brilliantly the paper had 'Burn It' at the top. There are very few really smart criminals, as you can see.

Seeing the writing on the wall, he then admitted in interview that he knew about the gun at the pizza place.

But that wasn't even the best bit. Our barrister brought in an air rifle today which the firearms experts showed did not fire properly.

This was clever.

The rifle was introduced with one thing in mind. Next week, we suspect that the general defence will be based on the fact that the air rifle was the gun which had been carried in the blue bag but the rifle is three times longer than the sawn-off shotgun and doesn't fit in the bag. They've introduced it tactically now to undermine in advance anything which the defence might try to use next week.

This made me very proud and confident and happy that at least I am not stewing over the weekend like Ness and Awan must be.

What can their barrister say to them on Monday? You're in the shit, or we're going to fight this tooth and nail?

There doesn't seem any hunger for the latter. The 'Burn It' letter has Awan nailed.

In his previous interview he had told police that he had been a hostage, that he wanted to help the police and that he was going to come clean. Then came the letter and he had no answer for why he had failed to mention this minor detail!

'I am scared of life. I've nothing further to say,' Awan had replied when challenged last July.

'What do you mean?' came the reply.

'I'm scared of life,' he reiterated. 'I've nothing further to say.'

Clearly he would never have mentioned the letter if my colleagues hadn't shoved it under his twitching little nose.

You'll note that he didn't say that he – the hostage – was scared of being shot by Moat.

In fact, the testimony which resonated the loudest was the fact that, after Moat had shot me, Ness and Awan went back to their tent and wanted a chill-out day. Yes, a chill-out day. A 'day off'.

All this killing business had left them knackered! Put your feet up for twenty-four hours and we'll pick up where we left off on Monday. Can you believe it?

They were talking it up under interview as though it was a day's work. I go to the station to lock people up. They go around shooting people and it leaves them tired. God bless them, eh. And Awan had also claimed that he had only met Moat once before!

This trial was proving to be a pendulum of emotions and a circle of deceit. Disgusting attitudes like that repulsed me, but I could also laugh at them for their idea of an honest living.

On the downside, I heard transcripts of the exact dialogue between Moat and the two of them when he returned to his car after shooting me.

Moat told them that he'd shot me in the head, which had left me slumped onto the radio. Then he said that he had put another one into the back of my head.

I loved that.

Genuinely, I found that very uplifting and it made me laugh. Humouring the monster was a victory I could still have. He had got it all completely wrong. You recall that after the shot between the eyes, I had lifted up my left shoulder. He hadn't slotted me in the back of my head at all. Clearly though, he had walked off confident that there was no way back for me.

It also emerged today that Awan had driven into Newcastle city centre on the Friday or Saturday to go shopping. All these incidental details, which embed them in a greater evil, namely 'planning' and 'conspiring', are damning evidence.

He had gone clothes shopping for the three of them! At Oxfam and the Cancer Research shop.

A man with style!

Awan claimed to have been concerned that the police might have spotted him in town but seemingly was not bothered enough to avoid parking on Grey Street, one of the busiest focal points for shopping in the North East!

I was busy congratulating myself on what great work Northumbria Police had done when I realised I was ahead of myself. Awan had told them all this himself.

Interestingly, too, in the most telling piece of body language that I been aware of in a courtroom in all my years, Awan and Ness no longer sat too close together but were some four seats apart. Their barristers had also clearly told them to smarten up. Today they were almost sharply-dressed.

I'm told they're playing games with their facial hair too, varying its lengths. Ness seems to be trying to distance himself from all the images of him which the jury have seen in photographic evidence and CCTV. As an officer with sight, I would have spotted the look. A couple of days later, the penny would have dropped. Without it, I've proved to myself today that I still have a lot to offer. I can dissect information more clinically than ever without external influence or distraction. Isolating the words and the tone of what criminals say is now my best skill. I can only concentrate on their pauses, their innuendo and their contradictions from now on and I won't miss any of it because it is all I have.

We'll see how good their games are next week, when they are called, and I can't wait. We're going to pull them apart, and they've nothing left.

All they have is the 'under duress' card, which clearly is bullshit. What decent person is left at a campsite alone, goes shopping for clothes, meets a friend and *doesn't* say anything? Awan had met a mate of his but didn't say much more than being slightly miffed! Just about the most unreal kind of hostage scenario ever.

He had also added that it didn't matter if Moat took his car. He'd just claim it on the insurance.

Yesterday Ness told how he had gone round to his girlfriend Tara's house with Awan and decided to go in for a couple of minutes, only to find Moat holding her at gunpoint.

'You're coming with me. I'm taxing your car,' Moat had said, indicating that he would pinch it.

Moat had planted that insurance seed.

I don't believe any of this actually happened, though I do believe Moat *was* in the house. I am sure he just told his accomplices that they were off. The Senior Investigating Officer indicated to me today that Ness's girlfriend has some strange affiliation to him and loves him so much that she would never shop him. Otherwise, if Ness's girlfriend *were* being held at gunpoint, why didn't she ring the police after they all left the house?!

All eyes are now on next week. Chris Brown's mum is due back after the weekend too. They are going to take her to Rothbury as she has never been. Painfully, she *has* already visited Birtley and yes, she has cashed the cheque, which I am pleased about.

The prosecuting barrister is anticipating Tuesday and Wednesday for defence.

We'll have to wait until then before we find out what that could be.

MONDAY 21 FEBRUARY 2011

'Raoul Moat was my gay lover.'

Obviously Moat wasn't *my* gay lover. That would be one hell of an ending to this story. Not sure the current Mrs Rathband would be too keen either.

No, don't be ridiculous. *The Sun* is carrying an exclusive with a guy called Carl Redford who is claiming a four-year affair with Moat from 2002, whilst living near Moat and Marissa Reid, the mother of two of his children.

One thing led to another apparently, when Moat visited him and found him in the bath. How do you get into someone's house when they are in the bath?

Redford is quoted as saying 'we satisfied each other' but Moat was desperate to keep it secret because of his hardman image as a bouncer.

You couldn't make it up. Gazza, Ray Mears, a funeral 'better than a day at Legoland' and now, Moat's gay lover.

I have to tell you, I pissed myself laughing. I think I'm allowed that privilege. Of course, I am not homophobic so I would never laugh for that reason but to think that Moat, the self-proclaimed epitome of Geordie masculinity was in denial about his true feelings makes me smile all day long.

I don't even know if the story is true, but it doesn't matter. I will take any chance to have the last laugh.

'At first I was sad. Then I thought – good riddance,' Redford said when he found out Moat was dead.

Too right.

My only concern is why this should be coming out now, in the middle of the trial, when so much better, brilliant evidence is coming to the fore?

Apart from that, it has been another day from hell. I have been depressed all day, waking with my face killing me this morning, annoyed that the defence have asked for an adjournment, and still really hacked off at Friday's press.

It's as though somebody has it in for me. My dental work has cost £3,500, and two lessons a week to walk with a cane have been paid for but as for the scandalous comment about me losing all my benefits, the force have done bugger all to help me.

There will be a press statement later in the week to redress the balance, but all that takes time, costs money, and zaps energy which I don't have. By 3 p.m. most afternoons I am knackered, and today has been one of the worst.

A pellet from one of the gunshots had popped in my head. A bubble of fluid has burst, leaving me sore and with a quarter of an inch depressed hole in my skull.

While all this was going on, I was being assessed for hours on end by an Injuries Management Consultancy firm. The nurse kept referring to my 'accident' which really pissed me off but I just sat there and bit my tongue for four hours.

'You're categorically not ready to go back to work,' she said.

Not what I wanted to hear.

I've been telling everyone I'll be back in April but nobody at the station is talking about it. In fact there are so many changes coming up at Northumbria Police that it seems impossible to make decisions. We don't know if we will have a new Chief, and what effect that will have. Nor do I know where I will be working. I'll need mobility training too and somebody with me at all times. The day when I walk back into Etal Lane looks as far away as it did when I was lying on that stretcher seven months ago but I've got to believe it's coming to achieve some level of normality.

Unbelievably, this is the first time that I have been assessed at home and it's left me feeling really disabled. It was draining and humiliating and did nothing but have me identifying gaps in my new life.

The garden needs sorting but I can't do it alone. Kath can't do it because it will hurt her back and I wouldn't dream of asking Ash to go round the house with a petrol strimmer. My aim was to get the garage cleared out so I could use the running machine but it's full of so much crap that I tripped on a sheet of glass the other night and nearly sent everything flying. My boxes from when we moved remain unpacked. Mia is still down from the bullying at school, and that wasn't even the first time. Plus Kath has to go to London in the morning on important business and I hadn't even remembered. I am at the beck of the call of everybody else, and it's pissing me off, and sooner or later, it's going to annoy everybody else too.

I think I need to get back to court.

TUESDAY 22 FEBRUARY 2011

I have never laughed so much in all my years. What a complete contrast to yesterday and Friday. There has been real tension in the Rathband household, particularly since Friday. Some days, the consequences of that night just never seem to end. It goes on and on. Today though, has been a good day – the more lies and deceit, the better the day. The extra day off had fired me up.

Karl Ness has been in the box.

At times I had to stop shaking my head in disbelief so the jury *wouldn't* see me on this occasion. This is different to when I wanted them to catch me arriving and leaving at key moments in the last few weeks. Some of it was so hysterical that I just didn't want them to think I was unprofessional.

'I thought he was going to kill himself,' Ness testified, recalling Moat on the night in Birtley.

Chris Clarke and I nudged each other.

'Didn't he say earlier he was going to wait for him?' Chris and I whispered to each other.

Moat and Ness were in the van near Sam Stobbart's house.

'Hang on,' Moat had said. 'And if you hear one shot just go.'

Then Moat had sent a text to Ness saying that he was being slagged off and he was just going to 'do it'.

Ness claimed he took this to mean Moat was going to take his own life, even though he'd never mentioned it before. What's more, why would you hang around if that were the case? None of it was logical.

Remember too, that Moat had changed his Facebook status to 'Watch this space, something is going to happen...' Ness denied knowing about this.

So Ness had accompanied this supposedly suicidal man to B&Q and shopped with him as Moat systematically altered the weights for the gun, but now suddenly thought he was on suicide watch? If you were going to blow your own brains out, you would be so careful in your preparation of a weapon, wouldn't you?

It got better, believe me.

'I couldn't resist it. The tent was a bargain,' Ness justified.

Well, I could have been on the floor at this point.

This was possibly the single most surreal line I have ever heard used in defence in a courtroom. He wasn't taking the stand, he was taking the piss.

Well-known camping expert Karl Ness couldn't resist buying a four-man tent with his mate Raoul Moat, within hours of him coming out of prison… *because it was a bargain.*

I nearly wet myself.

Was that all their barristers could come up with it? All that money spent on defence and that was their best shot. Presumably this was Legal Aid money too, which would make it all highly ironic. *My* taxes were funding the defence of these two clowns. I was paying to send these two down, but you know what, it would be worth every penny.

I lived for keeping scum off the streets.

This cheered me right away. When I arrived this morning, I was still expecting that low-baller, especially after the day's adjournment yesterday. But it never came.

All I know is that there were some issues raised with the Judge out of court this morning. My understanding is that the two opposing barristers are at odds over the timeline of events. Namely, at what point does conspiracy to murder *become* conspiracy to murder? This seems a technicality to me.

Nobody has denied any of the evidence against these two, but I sensed a wriggling coming in the next twenty-four hours which the defence might be about to introduce. At what point did these two become conspirators according to the legal definition of the word? That is for the prosecution to prove.

After that, it was a full day in the box for Ness.

'Our barrister can't wait, he's rubbing his hands,' Detective Chief Inspector Steve Binks told me. 'Let's see if Ness can answer any tough questions!'

We're now looking at Monday or Tuesday next week for the verdict. There is no sitting on Thursday afternoon which suits me fine as I'm back in the hospital. I'm guessing the Judge has golf inked in the diary.

To date, Ness has only squirmed his way up to arriving at Rothbury in his fine work of fiction. Awan has yet to step up to the dock. Comparing both their efforts is going to be hysterical.

There had been one gunshot at Rothbury, Ness had said. This was the world's most unconvincing hostages' first opportunity to flee Moat.

Except this was total bullshit.

There were no gun flashes, no reports from firearms officers at the scene, no members of the public dialling 999, nothing from the helicopter above.

A total fabrication.

The defence hadn't even been convincing in their opening gambits trying to establish the character of the witness.

Offering Ness the opportunity to show how he had gone slightly off the rails at the age of fourteen, committing a series of minor offences following his father's death, he could only say that it had brought his family closer together.

There was no emotive language. No 'massive impact' line or 'I was devastated' reflection. He was a poor actor, a shifty character and now, given the chance to speak up on his own pitiful life, he had little to offer. I hope the jury got exactly these messages. They had no witnesses to call because there were no witnesses.

So that meant there were no surprises today. Except, how stupid Ness was.

Take this, for example.

After his mate Moat had supposedly taken his own life in Birtley, Ness told the court how he drove off back to the Get Carter Garage and rang Awan. Earlier Awan had been at the garage to 'tinker' with a Corsa!

So, your best pal has just blown his brains out and what do you do next? You go back to work in the early hours of a Saturday morning while your mate 'tinkers' with a Corsa.

Not even last-minute emergency repairs for a top client who needed the car first thing in the morning, just a bit of tinkering. If one word could condemn a man, I hope it is the verb tinker.

A text message from his girlfriend Tara put an end to the tinkering though. There would be other nights to tinker, for sure. When your missus texts to come home, then all tinkering must end. You are duly summoned. Amazingly, when they got to Tara's, there was Raoul Moat, back from the dead, wielding a shotgun around her house.

Tara Collins was so bothered, of course, that when Moat left the house, she did what everybody would do in that situation. She dialled 999.

Except she didn't.

Maybe she had some tinkering to do too.

'He (Moat) threatened to do me Mam in,' Ness had answered somewhat tinkeringly in court when asked why Tara Collins hadn't called the police.

'Why did you write the letter?' QC Smith was now tinkering with him.

'Her head was that much in bits that I wanted to refresh her memory,' he replied.

Clearly, this is a fair response.

Yes, her head was that much in bits that she went off to the funfair on the Saturday.

I assume Tinkerbell must have been there.

They have had seven months to concoct this bullshit and it was like something out of a film.

'There is nothing there to cause me concern,' Chris Clarke said as he drove me home. His car got home tinker free.

This was my happiest day in ages, and to top it all, when I got back two pellets of shrapnel from Moat's gun that were still embedded in my hands and skull came out of my flesh.

Every little moment like this when another piece of the Moat circus falls apart is as close as I get to a good day. That just left about 200 pieces still inside me all carrying his DNA.

Clearly, Moat was very much still with me. At least today went some way to closing the door on two nasty little bits he had left behind.

WEDNESDAY 23 FEBRUARY 2011

'Enjoy it, you bastard,' I whispered as Karl Ness took the witness stand for a second morning running. I was looking forward to this. Robert Smith QC had warmed him up yesterday but with time in short supply, he was saving his main artillery for this morning.

Ness stared ahead at the court, a rabbit in the headlights.

Both he and Awan were still suited, the latter ill-fittingly dressed like a bad funeral director who had to borrow a jacket at the last minute. There is no emotion or relationship any more between the two. They barely fidget like most guilty suspects too and they both knew QC Smith was about to shine those headlights their way once again, and this time there would really no hiding from the glare.

Robert was brilliant, quick and so far ahead of these two lowlifes, mocking them with the irony of Angus Deayton in his heyday.

Systematically, he pulled apart the timeline of events, showing Ness on the CCTV at Moat's house on the Saturday at 1.08 p.m. Ness, who had said that he *hadn't* supplied Moat with any firearm other than the shotgun, had the blue draw-string bag on the footage!

'Are you sure about that? Are you absolutely sure?' QC Smith asked.

'No I haven't [supplied it]. I'm absolutely sure. No,' Ness replied.

'Well, we'll have a look at the video shall we? What's that in the bag?' Smith continued.

Pause.

'It's an air rifle,' Ness responded.

You recall that this was cunningly introduced last week to plant the seed.

Ness was lying. Any such air rifle would have been around 60 centimetres; the sawn-off shotgun just over 25cm.

Robert let Ness talk him through the footage, saying that it was an air rifle, and that he had taken it in the house.

'Let's have a look at some pictures then, shall we?' He was almost telling a story, calmly narrating.

'So, can you confirm that that's the blue bag?' Robert mocked.

'Yes,' Ness replied.

'And that's the air rifle. Now Mr Ness, that rifle won't fit into that bag will it now?'

He was going in for the kill.

'Well, it's how about you arrange it,' was the best Ness could do.

'You'll see there, we've tried to arrange it, and it doesn't go in Mr Ness. Let's have a look at this video again shall we? Is that you, Mr Ness?'

Robert was loving this.

'Yes,' the defendant squirmed.

'Is that the blue bag?' came the quickfire accusation.

'Yes,' Ness mumbled.

'What bit did you put in the bag Mr Ness?'

There was a rhythm rising now.

'I put the butt end in,' Ness protested.

'What's the butt end?' Robert asked.

'It's the bit on the handle.'

Ness knew more about guns that he would like to admit.

'Well, look at the picture, Mr Ness. That's a completely different shape to the air rifle. Shall we have a police officer produce the gun?' He motioned to one of my colleagues.

'That's funny, it's exactly the same shape. I put it to you, Mr Ness, that you supplied Mr Moat with that shotgun. You took it to the house on Saturday, the day after he was released, an hour and a half after he came home,' Robert twisted the knife.

All Ness could offer back was no better than 'I can't recall' or 'No'. His story had run out of steam. Any conversations he might have had in the car with Moat? No, he couldn't recall them.

'Mr Ness, can you recall him saying that he was going to shoot Sam Stobbart?' he went for the jugular.

'Nah, I can't recall that,' Ness denied.

'But you said you were with him all the time?' Robert inquired politely.

'Well, he might have gone out. It was noisy,' was all Ness could muster.

He just lied to everything and you could hear it in his voice. When he was fibbing, his vowels shut off really quickly, whereas in normal conversation they are prolonged. A linguist would tell you that minimalistic language meant you were hiding something. In fact, scrap that. Any old fool could spot it.

I was loving it.

Every single second.

I was only sad that I no longer had the eyesight to watch him squirm. That upset me, that he still had that advantage of vision over me.

There wasn't even any of that 'Rot in hell you bastards' shouting you always get from the gallery at some point in a trial. The court was quiet and the prosecution's words were the only tune anyone was dancing to.

There were no chavs making scenes of themselves. Instead, sitting dignified, a couple of seats away from me was Chris Brown's mum, Sally.

'I heard a scream and one bang,' Ness recalled the night in Birtley.

'No you didn't,' said Robert. 'You heard four shots didn't you? And that's why you revved the engine, started the van and waited for him. You didn't drive off because you thought he had killed himself. You knew he hadn't killed himself. Why would you have stayed?'

This was tough on Sally. I wanted to be there for her. She has gone through much of this on her own as she barely knew a soul in the North East. Just when she thought that most of the graphic detail about Chris was over, we were back there once more and I could feel her shaking again.

'Stick in there,' I said to Sally after Ness had said that Moat had only told him the following day that he had killed Chris. Clearly this was bullshit.

Of course moments later, it was my turn.

Ness described how they had pulled up, driven past me on the roundabout and headed up to Heddon-on-the-Wall where they dismantled a phone to avoid being tracked and placed it in a green plastic bag behind a street sign so that they could find it again. This was the phone they had rung 999 with to warn that they were going to shoot a policeman. Ness had actually taken detectives afterwards to the lamppost to show them where they had hidden it.

It all seemed very planned out.

They then came back, went round the roundabout and headed southbound on the A1 but did a U-turn on Scotswood Road, the main approach to Newcastle city centre from the West. They had gone past me.

Back they came northbound on the A1. Moat told Awan to park the car and turn the lights off, running up to the corner and pulling the trigger.

'I heard one bang, then two seconds later heard another one,' Ness said.

He claimed he couldn't see me or my car.

'Are you OK David?' Sally asked.

It was my turn to sit there with my head in my hands, tears rolling down my cheeks.

Amidst all this deceit and personal torture, I hadn't foreseen that I would share this moment with Sally.

I'm glad I did. It felt appropriate that we were both able to help each other. Finally, we were united in grief.

'Moat got in the car with a nervous giggle. I could smell the gun burning,' Ness told the court. 'I just froze and thought he was a sick man.'

Though, of course, he had also told the court he was his best mate.

For the record, I don't believe they *couldn't* see my police car. My lights were well above the concrete wall. Plus, they had driven past me twice.

'I've done the copper,' Moat had said. 'I don't think he's dead.'

As Ness was relaying this conversation I remembered that Awan's statement had said that 'he knew I was dead' so which was it to be?

Ness went on to say that Moat reloaded the gun and they carried on, actually getting stuck in the police blockade on the West Road, and driving up through Denton before hitting the A1 for Rothbury.

Steve Winn, who found me, has told me since that he had been shitting himself on the night, fearing that Moat would return to the scene and might have shot him or someone else. And that's exactly what he did.

One of the things that police always look for is 'visits to the scene'. That would have been on everyone's mind in the aftermath. Cold, calculated killers like to collect trophies. That's a common pattern.

Moat did head back but couldn't penetrate the police cordon. The inner cordon was set up to preserve the crime scene which was around 50 metres over the roundabout where I was shot. The outer cordon was another 250 metres or so further back. This was the key area for forensics and a fingerprint search.

Instead they had to use Slatyford Lane which was the diversion. One policeman recalls waving a black Leuxs through between 4 and 6 a.m. but that can't have been correct. Someone *would* have seen them though.

Ness claimed that they stopped Moat from shooting another victim whom he also thought was a policeman but turned out to be a council worker in a bright vest, walking his dog early in the morning.

'I'll get him,' Moat had said, but they persuaded him out of it, driving on to Rothbury, where, unbelievably, at 7 a.m. they tried to get into a shop which hadn't yet opened, only to be turned away.

Nobody rang the police.

At one point, Moat got out of the car and threw a dead badger – killed at the roadside – onto the windscreen of the vehicle. Ness told the court it made him feel sick but Moat wanted to take it back to eat.

And to make a hat.

That's right. Our killer on the loose had time for a barbecue and some needlework to make that great disguise which was sure to throw my colleagues off the scent – a hat made out of dead badger.

Moat even sent his two accomplices for a needle and thread.

It's difficult to know at this point if Ness made this up. Given what an idiot Moat was, maybe it *was* true. You couldn't make it up, could you?! The jury were certainly laughing, which shows that by now, they felt the same as I did. On the night of my shooting, when I looked him up on the police computer to find out what had happened with the scrap metal, had I missed the bit where it said 'Birthplace: Yellowstone Park'?

'Had you thought to stop any of the eight cars which had driven past you before the police came, and ask a passer-by to help you?' Ness was asked.

'We didn't no,' he replied.

QC Robert Smith had nailed Ness.

No doubt, in my mind. A great questioning turn of phrase ('Why did you do that, Mr Ness?') together with a ton of evidence, had shown the lies about the air rifle, and when exactly he had seen the gun – Ness finally conceding that he had seen it on the driver's seat, whereas initially he had said it was under the chair and he was oblivious to it.

Ness's claim that he heard one shot where there were four, and then drove off feeling sick were a sham. After all, Moat had sent him a text saying 'If this goes down, I'll get to the car'.

This was what I was waiting for. He is the facilitator. It was poetry in motion watching the prosecution wrap up for the day, reeling off three consecutive lies that Ness had told and was then forced to admit were rubbish. After he had said in interview last July that he wanted to help, he still failed to tell the police that he got the Transit van they used cleaned up. Robert Smith sent the jury home with these lies ringing in their ears.

'This is it,' I thought, rubbing my hands that justice was to be done for both Chris Brown and myself.

You couldn't *not* be moved by Sally's raw emotion sitting next to me. She was hearing so much of this for the first time.

'Please don't hold me responsible when they are convicted,' I said to Chris Clarke, 'I *will* shout something like enjoy it you bastards.'

'David, you can't,' Chris said. 'You've been really professional, and you'll go down in people's estimations. Don't do it.'

'You're right,' I conceded.

I'd give anything to see my family for twenty minutes, to take in my new house for five. I wish I could do my job for another hour, but I'd give all that to be able to see them squirm in that box. How I wish my eyesight could come back just for an instant to see how uncomfortable they are.

So, if Sally stands up and lets rip when the verdict is delivered, I won't be holding her back.

THURSDAY 24 FEBRUARY 2011

I had to fast last night in preparation for today. It wasn't that my stomach was churning with the graphic detail of yesterday and the shared emotion with Sally. One minute I was consoling her, the next vice versa. No not at all, I was getting a real high all week with what was going down in court – hopefully those two. Today I had to return to hospital and that's why I couldn't eat last night.

By 8 a.m., Kath and I were at the RVI. It had become a second home since last July. Of course, on the drive in, all I could think was for Kath to keep driving. Take me to the law courts. That's where I wanted to be.

I'd never been met at the door of a hospital before, now everyone is so kind to me, treating me like a private patient in a public hospital, chaperoned away into my private cubicle. It's a far cry from when I used to come here before the shooting.

It had always seemed so busy but now the all-modern Leazes Wing felt like a spacious department store. I had been a regular visitor before last July, most notably when my little finger needed treatment after chasing a car thief named Lee McDonald up onto Osborne Road in Jesmond. McDonald had run off and I had followed him out of the car, placing my arms on his shoulder. The little bugger turned round and snapped my finger off.

Back then, I was stitched up and promptly sent on my way. Today I was getting the five-star service with gold knobs on. But now there was a smell that got me. Hospitals always used to smell chemically clean. Now, I couldn't get one particular smell out of my head every time I went back. It's a sickly odour of fresh meat and I can't get rid of it. Regardless of how swish the modern wing was, it still smelt to me as though I was out the back of the butcher's, blood dripping from fresh meat. I hated it.

This is a result of my blindness. Having no sight means I am relying on other senses. My hearing is 40 per cent sharper and I miss nothing. This is both an advantage and a problem. I can hear everything, even stuff I wasn't meant to. But, it is also an inconvenience because my hearing isn't yet tuned. Just as when you tune a radio dial and narrowly miss the station you can sense there is talking but can't quite make out the words. I have yet to learn the skill of tuning out all the dead noise to listen past the crowd. It's mighty uncomfortable.

On 4 November last year, I was at the Police Review Awards on a table of ten with the Home Secretary, Theresa May. I could hear her but I know she didn't think I could.

'Isn't he fantastic? He's an absolute credit,' I could make out, but I couldn't decipher everything amongst the general cackle of the night. I had to live off snippets.

It has been the same at the Metro Centre, when I walk past people. I catch the 'ice' at the end of the word police and then I might hear 'man' directly after. I don't hear enough to know what they are saying but it is clear when people are stopping and staring.

'There's that blinded policeman,' I assume they're saying.

On the upside, it gives me a head start.

'You're only little, about 5'4', I said to the nurse as the porter took me down to theatre this morning.

'How do you know that?' she asked.

'I can tell by your gait,' I replied, 'You're taking little short steps.'

'And *you're* about 5'10', I said to the porter.

'Blimey, I am, how did you know that,' he confirmed, surprised.

'I can tell by the way you walk and I can feel you behind me.'

My head was on the pillow and I sensed him lurking.

'That's an amazing ability,' the porter added.

'It's all I've got,' I replied.

Despite missing the trial, I was excited. It has become part of the healing process now that every time I removed a pellet from under my skin, I destroy a little bit more Moat.

'I'd have my head cut out, tipped upside down and jet-washed and then put back on again if I could,' I said to Kath.

Today we would identify a few more pellets with the senior registrar.

At my pre-ops, I signed my consent forms but had no idea what I was putting my name to. I think I am long past asking medical questions. Everything I signed now was guesswork.

In theatre, the drugs kicked in straight away.

'Let me know if you can tolerate this,' the anaesthetist asked, mindful of the motion sickness which had made me violently ill on my second day in hospital last July.

He knew there would be no protests coming from me. I was out for the count as his sentence tailed off. Normally I like to say goodnight before sleep, medically-induced or otherwise, at conventional bedtime or mid-morning. I didn't even utter the 'g'. I was gone.

Mr Chalmers and the surgeons got to work immediately, cutting under my right armpit, then at my right forearm and onto my left index finger. The pellets which had come away in court needed attention. The dead skin and scarring was cut away and re-stitched. There was a further pellet in the pad of my thumb on the pressure point. That had to go too, entering from behind the knuckle to avoid damage.

There was still debris in the left side of my mouth plus a pellet in my right eyebrow and three more in my right cheek, which had become lumped together in the jaw bone. Another came from my left temple and my left eyebrow. On it went, and remember that these little fellas have been living in me for seven months now. You can see why, psychologically, I needed to get them all out, however long that took.

In reality, whilst every removed bit of ammunition is a victory, I will go to my grave with Moat still inside me.

My head was infected where the pellets hadn't healed, so they took swabs from it. I'll have to return to have it cut open at some point. I wanted them to do it today but I have to wait, possibly for up to three months because of the infection. My guess is that there are close on 200 pellets still in there. At my last dental visit alone, there were twenty-seven pieces above my teeth.

On a daily basis, the pain is relentless. On a scale of one to ten, the agony is about two, but the discomfort is a nine, just droning on every single day.

It would be like this forever now. If it wasn't one job, it would be another. The next step is to get my eyes re-fitted when the scar calms down in my right eye although I can't say when that will be.

Before all of that, I have to go back to the GP to get my medication reviewed. The sleeping tablets no longer work. Originally I had begun with one Amitriptyline per night. Then it had become two, and gradually four, and just about six weeks ago I began piling in half a dozen a night. They are a non-addictive anti-depressant but can be prescribed as a mild sleeping tablet. I didn't want to become addicted to anything so I took these. You can see that I was taking more and more, with less and less effect as we approached the trial.

The doctors thought I was clear of danger, bar the risk of infection or someone knocking my face if we happened to be out. I would pick at the pellets constantly, and every one that came out was cause for celebration.

I could no longer have an MRI scan because of the magnetism. The scan would send the lead pellets spinning and God only knows what that would do to my insides.

I was now one of those people for whom every day would have a medical challenge.

Going through Heathrow had been bad enough in the last few months. Four times I had been searched, even though they knew who I was and clearly wasn't likely to be a shoe-bomber or have a dangerous rucksack. Those scanners at the airport picked up everything.

Kath said I had been talking shit all morning.

'I need to finalise my garden tidiness,' I slurred as the drugs kicked in.

I had been gone three and a half hours by the time I woke and was back home for half twelve. I was only expecting to be operated on for about fifty minutes or so. Still, every pellet out meant the world to me so I was happy for them to continue for as long as it took. I knew avoiding thumb damage would be tricky but they had spent three times as long as I had anticipated.

By coincidence, it had been the right day to go to hospital rather than court.

I scoured the local news in the evening to see what had happened, knowing that it would have followed the same format as yesterday, but I could barely find any reporting. Maybe they all had golf?!

I was most curious as to whether QC Robert Smith has finished with Ness, or if he will be back on in the morning. I rang to get word.

The court had found out that after the robbery at the chip shop in Seaton Delaval the night after I was shot, Moat had thrown the money into the car, shouting 'Wonga'.

Did he think he was in the *Italian Job* or something?

From there they had gone to McDonald's in Ashington and were passed by a solitary officer in his patrol car.

'Raoul said "Will I get him?"' Ness told the court.

'What's the point, you're eating,' Awan had replied on the night.

'Yeah, I know, I'm having my McFlurry,' Moat responded.

I know now who that officer was and believe he has been told that he could have been next if Moat hadn't been busy stuffing his face. To think, that the price of life came down to an ice cream. Every one of my colleagues would do well to remember that.

Who can't picture Moat right now, that big orange face and those cold killer eyes, sitting in a drive-thru car park hoofing down his food and devouring his ice cream, while on a break between killings? Why interrupt a McFlurry for some copper who happened to be driving past?

Given that this was the most wanted man in Britain at this point, it is worth noting that they didn't even attempt to hide at the sight of the patrol car. Their casual actions suggest they were all pretty chilled about what they were doing. Besides, another cop would surely come along soon.

It was just unbelievable.

Having heard all this I am not seriously expecting Qhuram Awan – or Shaun as his mates called him – to be called to give evidence. If his own team don't put him on the stand, and there is no obligation to do so, then our barrister can't cross-examine.

That will be their fear, that after Ness's evidence, Awan is knackered.

At best, he can say that Ness is the one who is lying and can hope for the lesser sentence of assisting an offender but if the original offence is murder and attempted murder, then the sentence would still be life. Ness will always be known as a liar in the criminal fraternity now. Awan should reflect overnight.

He is going down too but has the chance to do so with some honour. If you ever found yourself in this situation would you lie and wriggle your way through with all the evidence stacked against you or would you stop making up stuff, admit you did it, and go down with a little dignity intact, saying you did it to stand by your mates? I suspect Awan is just a silly boy who got caught up in all this. He has one chance to put more distance between himself and Ness. Robert Smith will be on to him the moment Awan takes the stand.

FRIDAY 25 FEBRUARY 2011

'Enjoy it Ness,' I whispered again.

The defendant brushed past me after another morning on the stand.

I loved that. It could have been much worse.

'You're a liar', QC Smith had repeatedly accused.

'No, I'm not', Ness would reply.

'You lying bastard', I stopped myself from shouting.

Ness was recounting how at the moment Moat shot me, he was 'scared' for me. That's really big of him. When asked what he did about it, 'nothing' was all he could reply.

You can see why I wanted my moment.

His style though, cut me apart. He had no remorse, as if what happened to me was of no significance to him. He stood there as though he couldn't give a shit, and when he needed to clarify his story, he failed to do better than 'can't remember'.

I had to step outside to cool myself. I was seething inside, angry and on the brink.

It had been a long sleepless week listening to lies and bullshit. When I got into the lift a traveller attending some big gypsy trial tapped me on the shoulder to say good luck and that I was a hero. With that warm gesture I started welling up.

Detective Superintendent Jim Napier had already told me that prison had been breaking Awan, a massive morale boost. He hadn't taken well to his new home and intelligence had been intercepted that he had been trying to contact his sister to get her to remove a further phone. The sister had refused to, which is just as well since my colleagues had got there first.

The phone evidence had already been damning – Awan was covering his tracks and could see what was coming.

Then he entered the dock, playing the sob story from the off, selling himself as a weak and feeble man, prone to black-outs and breathlessness. He didn't seem to have them when he was wheel-spinning away from me as I lay there dying in my car. He was now poorly *again* with his Warfarin; his pulmo-nary arteries were playing up. I'm not surprised. Both he and his defence didn't get the fact that this lost them any moral high ground.

When my name was mentioned for the first time during his evidence, I am told he turned to acknowledge me.

All this seemed like a game. Was he pitching himself as reasonable and courteous? Was he trying to appear just an average guy pretending to show respect to his victim. He wanted the jury to note it.

His snivelling was relentless – at one point trying to get emotional, saying how he had just gone along with everything because he feared his family would be killed.

But it was early days and I was confident he couldn't keep it up. It didn't seem to add up that you would pitch yourself as a suffering, unwell man, and then raise your game to start talking street.

He didn't hesitate to drop Ness in the shit.

'Moat has gone acka,' he said, recalling the call from Ness after the shooting.

Ness had always maintained that he had driven off from Birtley on the Friday night after hearing one shot. Awan told the court that wasn't true, that in fact Ness had rung to say that Moat had gone fucking mental, shooting Sam and her boyfriend and that he had killed Chris.

In one sentence Awan made a mockery of all the lies that his mate had told in the previous few days.

Whilst I think Awan was closer to the truth than Ness, it was merely damage limitation. Awan could see, or had been told, that they were both doomed. He knew they weren't getting off and not sitting together last week was bearing fruit now. He was guilty, but he wasn't *as* guilty. That was all he could hope for.

But there was nothing really new coming out of his mouth. Just the word acka. We had all learned that.

'We'll just go over that last bit again,' Awan's defence barrister began, straight after the break for lunch. 'What did you mean by acka?'

'Well, you know. It means mad or pissed off,' he replied.

'What exactly did he say to you?' QC Carter-Manning asked of Ness's phone call.

'He'd shot Sam, shot the boyfriend and killed himself,' Awan clarified.

As for Rothbury, Awan was sticking with the bullshit hostage line.

Surely, the jury weren't going to be swayed by any of this. None of it fits. For a start, they were still trying to ring Moat! Once he picked up, twice he ignored them.

'Make for the river,' Moat had texted them, 'there's cops everywhere.'

And then Moat cut and ran.

Ness and Awan were on their own and walking straight into the arms of the law. Moat had abandoned them. It was game over but they were still trying to help him because they were part of it. They were Moat's scouts in the woodlands of Rothbury.

'It was a spaghetti junction of feelings,' Awan waxed lyrical, showing the frustrated playwright within.

Or perhaps, it was a McFlurry of emotions when he had realised he had better come up with something quickly.

'He made my stomach churn,' Awan called for the violins to strike up, plucking at the heartstrings of twelve reasonable men and women.

'I was a rabbit in the headlights,' he whined.

No, that was a badger and you were going to make it into a hat.

He claimed he was fearful, but he had then had gone shopping for sweets.

'You never hear of people going after the police,' Awan told the court after relating how Moat had said 'Let's go and shoot some police'.

He must have been playing the wrong video game if he thought it didn't happen. Instead he stuck to his line that he believed Moat was just going to give the cops a message by shooting out the tyres or the bonnet of their car or something.

'He was a sick, sick man,' Awan concluded.

Finally after seven months of bullshit, he had got something right.

Awan had got caught up in the moment and his fate was facing him. He had a small amount of previous – a shoplifting caution from the age of eleven and a fixed penalty notice – but now realised where he was heading. He was just twenty-three, and his free life was over. And he knew it.

He had put distance between himself and Ness but realised that he should have done so a long, long time ago. Ness was Moat's number two, calculating and complicit. Awan wanted to be seen as the poor old soul who had to go along with it. He was way past the moment where he could put his hand up and apologise. Instead he had to stick with the cobbled-together bullshit that they had concocted.

As a policeman, have I ever seen a more clear-cut case in thirteen years of coming to court?

No.

Most days I would tell myself that life wasn't fair. Heaven forbid that these guys wriggle their way to a lesser sentence or, years from now, walk free on parole. They wanted to help Moat and between the two or the three of them, they've invented all this bullshit. Moat himself was seemingly smarter – he'd sorted his exit strategy.

From the moment he shot Chris Brown, he was always going to be shot or shoot himself. Those were his words. Set on living rough, they would camp in the day and drive into Newcastle by night. The fact that Moat set up camp in Rothbury with these two on the Saturday says to me it was all pre-determined and he had hatched this plan whilst inside. You don't just rock up in Rothbury. Moat lived in Fenham, twenty-five miles away.

I afford Awan a small amount of sympathy, just for having been so stupid, but Ness knew exactly what was going to happen before Moat got out of prison. The phone analysis proves that.

'I'd love to see Raoul Moat stand there and face this jury,' Jim Napier said today.

It would have been therapeutic to have seen all three of them there. I've often visualised it but the nicest thing for me is that those two can see I'm not dead. That's why I've been all over the media for the last six months. That was their daily reminder that I didn't give up and had lived to fight another day, and every time *they* saw the news, an anniversary, a London marathon, a Blue Lamp walk, anything… then they knew roles were reversed and they were no longer the hunter. They were the hunted.

I survived. Moat lost and suffered, and his death was painful. I know that because it bloody hurt me. I may have lost my sight forever but I win. He won't be walking down the street coming looking for us. He's gone.

Ness and Awan may walk free in time but they are unemployable, and that's a comfort. The dark world from which they have come is the only place they can go back to, and they will be on licence forever. One crime at any point in their life and they will be straight back inside.

Meanwhile, Sam Stobbart walks away. She too, has turned up at court with a different look – her hair now a different tint, again trying to differentiate between the Sam Stobbart of then and the Sam Stobbart of now.

'I want to talk to her,' Sally Brown said to me today.

I didn't.

I couldn't bear to be in the same room as her.

'I really want to ask her why she left court crying on Wednesday,' Sally was angry.

Ness's mum had also been at court; Awan's father came and left because there wasn't enough space.

Not one of them had the decency, conviction or the balls to come up to me and apologise for their sons. Their lack of moral conviction disgusts me.

I've been brought up differently. It makes me laugh when I think how, when Ashley once kicked over a neighbour's flowerpot, I took him round to apologise and paid £40 to replace some cheap £3 pot plant just to keep him clean and out of trouble. That's what I subscribed to as a human being, and that's the young man who has stood by me like a rock since that fateful day.

Plus, as we were now finding out, you don't want to mess with landscape gardeners.

Shit, it's just dawned on me.

That is why Moat's phone was registered to a non-existent Mr Trimit.

He too was a wordsmith.

MONDAY 28 FEBRUARY 2011

'It was like a cross between Grand Theft Auto and Jason Bourne,' Awan opened in style.

'I told you it was a film or a video game,' I said to Robin Palmer, my PR man.

He was that stupid he thought he was in a movie.

What a way to start the week. And he had had all weekend to think about it.

QC Robert Smith wasn't taking any chances, calmly recapping on Awan's lies from Friday, just for the avoidance of doubt.

'I never said that,' he would occasionally interrupt, constantly gulping through litre after litre of water.

Awan was keen to re-clarify that Ness had rung to say that Moat shot himself, then went on to say he was confused by all the legal visits he had had.

'Mr Awan,' Robert interrupted. 'You need to be very careful because the line you are about to step over is very dangerous and I suggest you think very carefully before you cross it. I do not want to draw you over that line.'

I couldn't believe it.

It was as though he had been about to shop his own barrister, as if there had been discussions that Awan had got his lines wrong and had since been corrected.

I have never heard a moment like this in court.

But his lies ran so deep now, that he is trying to convince himself. He has been living a geeky fantasy and all he could fabricate was from that world where most of his friends also seemed to be. It was simply garbage, bearing no reflection on reality.

'I didn't want to piss him off because of the underworld, and you know what the underworld is like in Newcastle,' he deluded himself.

Nobody had ever heard of Raoul Moat in the underworld! At best, they knew him as a woman-beater, a child-beater and a steroid-user. Oh yes I forget, more recently, the gay cavalier.

'Oh you know it's not Brooklyn, like New York, where they are shot every day,' he responded when asked why he hadn't taken seriously the shooting of a cop. 'Last time I heard of a cop getting shot must have been at least last year down south.'

Ladies and gentleman, Newcastle is now The Bronx.

'Oh really,' Robert Smith replied, saying less rather than more for dramatic effect.

He knew the jury would be smiling inside about that, if not outwardly guffawing. This is the QC of course who in this same law court two years ago to the day, pulled Yusuf Jama and his accomplices to shreds for the murder of Sharon Beshenivsky from West Yorkshire Police. Sentences ranging from life down to eleven years were handed out. Awan would have done well to Google the case before going off into fantasy land.

'If Raoul Moat had said he was going to kill my family, that meant he could have got it done. He could have just rung somebody,' the fantasist continued.

'Did he know you?' Robert goaded.

'No,' said Awan.

'Did he know your family?'

'No.' Awan was boxed in.

'Did he know where you lived?' The prosecution was almost mocking.

'No.'

Every no represented the slamming of a door in Awan's personal corridor.

Bang.

'So you took him round to your sister's house to drop a letter off? Why did you do that?'

Awan could only half-splutter a response, saying he was frightened. He had been caught out.

Of course, whenever someone threatens to shoot my family, I always take them round to my house to show them where they live too!

Becky, Chris Brown's sister, had just managed to stop herself shouting 'Just tell the truth, you lying bastard,' before having to leave the room.

She too had had enough of sitting through lie after lie.

If I hadn't been involved, I would have been laughing. It was just embarrassing.

At one point Awan had said that he didn't understand a question about one of the nights at the camp in Rothbury only to then repeat back everything he had been asked in the original question.

'Mr Awan,' the prosecution paused, 'Don't try and be clever.'

Repeating back the question was only done for one reason. So, he had a few more seconds to invent a few more lies. Instead, he had been found out and buried his raspy voice in more and more water. Give a guilty man a prop, and he will work it to death.

This was box office drama.

'I was shitting my pants,' Awan raised the tone.

'What do you mean?' Robert asked.

'I was really frightened. I was scared beyond belief,' the liar continued.

'What about?'

'My family… myself… getting shot in the head,' he was still shitting himself.

And of course, that's when the CCTV came into play.

A fragile, timid, weak Awan, so unsure of himself and in such great fear for his life was right up there on the video, buying a chicken wrap!

'Were you shitting yourself when you selected the chicken wrap?' continued Robert.

'Yeah, I was,' Awan recalled.

'So the minute you selected the chicken wrap, you were shitting yourself? What else was on your mind?'

Three jurors were starting to laugh.

'I was hungry,' he reasoned.

'So you've just found out that your friend and the bloke you are with has murdered at least one person, and shot his girlfriend – if you shoot someone in the stomach, you'd expect them to die, wouldn't you – and there you are, buying a chicken wrap. That's not the action of somebody filling their pants,' Robert nailed him.

He'd be shitting it now though.

Then came the bombshell that had one juror crossing their arms as if to say they weren't listening to any more of this bullshit, and another with their hands on their chin like they were mouthing blah blah blah.

'I need to confess,' Awan meekly offered.

Finally, at last, someone had some spine.

This, I had to hear.

'I'm a comfort eater,' he delivered the best punchline yet.

I hope you can see how I have managed to retain my dark sense of humour during the darkest of all days. McFlurrys, badgers and chicken wraps. Gazza and Ray Mears.

Where would it end?

Some moments after the jury had picked themselves up from the floor, I would suggest.

Ali was relaying the body language to me. Four of the jury, she said, had already passed sentence.

You can see now why I said I didn't think Awan would be called by his own team. In his stupidity, he obviously felt that he could work an audience in a primetime show, and would walk away with rave reviews.

'So you went to Sainsbury's? Tell us about that then. Were you filling your pants then?' Robert had the metaphor of the hour working overtime.

'Yes, I was,' the comfort eater didn't know when he was beaten.

'So who told you to go and buy all the stuff?'

Our prosecution was just warming up.

'Raoul did,' Awan apportioned blame. 'He said to go and get some clothes and something for the barbecue.'

'Is that all he said?'

'Yes,' Awan replied.

'So who told you to buy a duvet?'

'Raoul did.'

'But you didn't say that,' Robert motioned to the CCTV.

'Why did you buy some shorts? Did Raoul tell you to buy some shorts?'

'No… he didn't,' Awan was falling into the classic trap of being able to lie about the big stuff convincingly but failing miserably on the incidental detail which most crooks neglect.

It's this stuff which always establishes the pattern of deceit. Never mind where the gun came from. Do the details of this man's own story unravel before his very eyes?

He had also bought some trainers – because he wanted to. His were knackered. Yes, this followed the traits of a textbook hostage. Take a break for some shoe shopping.

On the way back to the camp in Rothbury, Awan had avoided a passer-by who later testified that he looked quite happy and at ease with himself.

'That must have been how I appeared,' he squirmed. 'But I wasn't.'

This had already been submitted as uncontested evidence.

Awan had also bought a radio so Moat could hear the news. The ego at large wanted to know how he was being reported. There were also sausages, mobile phones, t-shirts, boxer shorts, and of course, as we know that Moat's gang had a very unique diet, Reggae Reggae sauce.

The good lads also bought some soap so they could wash themselves down after their long weekend. Decently too, they had picked up some toilet roll.

On it went, getting more and more comical.

And then I would get angry again.

Every time he used my name I wanted to rip his throat out, throwing in a casual 'PC Rathband' like there was no harm in doing so. If he was trying to show respect, he was way off the mark.

'I'm so confused,' Awan said. 'The police bullied me.'

'Pardon, you were in a police station and they were asking you questions about someone who had shot and murdered somebody? Were you offered a break in the interview at any point?'

Even Robert didn't see this coming.

'No... I just wanted to get it over and done with,' he replied.

'So you weren't bullied?' Robert asked.

'No, I was just in a police station for the first time and I felt intimidated,' the garbage continued.

Any sympathy I felt on Friday, thinking he might be an innocent bystander, was gone. His own evidence had convicted him. Where Ness would say 'I can't recall', Awan would make an excuse and dig a hole fit for... well, a badger really.

Every time he was asked a question, he repeated it back. The more he talked, the more rubbish came out of his mouth. He had even written a journal entitled *Diary of a Hostage* though he claimed Moat had penned some entries for him! Laughter is a great medicine and frankly I had just taken an overdose. Can you imagine if Terry Waite had done the same? He'd still be chained to that radiator in Beirut now.

QC Smith asked Awan what Ness had said when he came to his garage for an hour that night.

'Nothing,' he replied.

'He was in there an hour, and he said nothing?' badgered Robert.

'He wasn't with me for a considerable amount of time.'

How long was that considerable amount of time? Awan confirmed it was mighty considerable.

'About five minutes,' the silly sausage replied.

They both left the garage at 4.16 a.m. to drive to Lemington where Moat had been dropped from Birtley by a taxi driver after Ness had dumped the getaway Transit van. How lucky was that driver then as he recalled to police that Moat had something in a bag, and had headed off to an address in Shipley Street. The prosecution allege that this was a pre-arranged meeting and that Awan's car drove him and Ness there.

Stupidly, thinking they would get off on the hostage ticket, they neglected to remove any of the receipts from the tent in Rothbury. Why they were keeping them, I have no idea. Perhaps Awan was going to put them through the books of the non-existent pizza parlour in the name of a pre-launch team building weekend. Most people don't keep receipts for long unless they are self-employed. They probably weren't hanging on to a proof of purchase to return any of the items, like perhaps the bog roll, because as we know it would be pretty much unused.

Awan hadn't filled his pants at all.

But the receipts are damning because they create the timeline which matches up to the CCTV. They don't know how easy they made it for Northumbria Police and how hard for themselves.

Awan made a massive play for a good ten minutes or so about how he wanted to do his father extremely proud and that was the reason for the pizza parlour which never got off the ground and was obviously now going up in smoke. They had yet to make any dough, in every sense of the word.

In fact, they had only got round to storing his mate's beds and furniture in the unit. Oh yes, and a gun of course. They had got no further than installing a practice pizza oven. He explained how his dad couldn't spend any money he made from alcohol in his own convenience store. And he swore all this on the Koran.

Then he went on to describe the cider he bought for himself on one of his shopping trips! I'm sure his dad has never known greater pride.

He was knackered, and looked it, asking to sit down, still sniffing and gulping water, playing the medical card but every time he did so the jury would remember an earlier exchange about Awan's medication.

QC Smith had asked him about his work as a doorman and if he had ever used any violence in that job. He admitted that he had but said they normally handled problems in pairs – there were the talkers and the toughs. Awan said he was more of a talker. He hadn't needed his Warfarin then.

He had driven the Lexus for six days, ferrying Moat around after the shootings. He never offered the keys to anybody and when he told Moat he took medication for blackouts, Moat just told him to 'fuck off'.

'He wasn't bothered, so I just left it at that,' Awan had told the jury.

'So you did without your Warfarin then?' QC Smith had asked.

'Yeah, yeah,' he had replied.

'I feel really sorry for him,' Alison said.

I had a little too on Friday but my perceptions had changed. At that moment at the back end of last week, if he had stood up and apologised, admitting that he had talked nothing but shit and was just a stupid little boy who went along with his Hollywood fantasy led by two wicked monsters, I would have asked Northumbria Police not to press charges, but he was a spineless little rat who didn't have that in him.

Now, however, he had dropped himself in it. Watching the QC playing with him was payback; Awan, overusing the word 'honestly' every time the next whopper was coming out of his mouth.

At the moment of his arrest in Rothbury, he had spotted the police about fifteen metres away but went back to phone Moat to warn him. With the police helicopter overhead Ness told Awan to keep walking towards the police.

'Why didn't you stop?' he was asked.

'I just wanted to get away,' he answered. 'I just wondered if he would get involved in an exchange.'

Where had that word 'exchange' come from? That's military language. You might hear a cop say that, but not a member of the public. That's the calculated dialogue of someone lost in a drama, living out his own computer game. They weren't the words of a hostage.

He would certainly recognise the next two words as he had seen them on his screen many times.

Game Over.

TUESDAY 1 MARCH 2011

'Raoul did,' Awan said again when Robert Smith asked who told him where to go. When asked who told him to get stuff for the barbecue, the answer was that Raoul did. The questions changed, but the answer was still the same.

Blame Moat.

God, wouldn't this trial have been so much better if Moat had stuck around for the final part of this story. I wonder if the answer would still be the same then. Probably not, because Moat – remember – was such a legendary underground figure in Newcastle that Awan would have filled his pants again.

'Drive straight on, turn left, come back round,' had been the instructions.

So, on the night they came into Newcastle to shoot me, Awan had always said that Moat had rung the police after they had passed me on the way up the A69 from Hexham.

The phone analysis had revealed the time that Moat made that call of course, and I had actually caught them on film on my ANPR camera inside my car. They passed me as Moat was on the phone saying he was going to hunt a cop.

'Where was Moat?'

'He was in the back of the car.'

'Have you heard the transcript of the call, Mr Awan? There's nothing on the call about directions.'

He hadn't heard the call, and was lying again, going on to insist that Moat was in fact pointing the directions.

'Pointing from the back of the car, Mr Awan?'

Moat then told him to turn the lights off, though he accidentally whacked the hazards on instead.

'He ran up to the police car, and then I heard a bang, and another bang,' he continued.

'And what did you do think he had done?'

'I thought he'd just shot the car.'

Smith then pointed out that Awan had labelled Moat a maniac and a dangerous man.

'And you only thought he was going to shoot the car. Oh right, Mr Awan.'

When Moat returned to the car Awan said he was frozen.

'So you didn't drive off at speed then?' QC Smith enquired.

'Oh yeah, I did, cos Raoul told me to,' he replied. 'I just put the pedal to the metal.'

Well, this was a whole new ball game – it left me a bit acka to be honest.

'Did you think then what he'd done to the policeman?' QC Smith asked.

'No, I didn't think he'd shot him. I just thought he'd shot the car.'

Awan said Moat was laughing when he told him that he'd shot me on the way back up the A1 to Morpeth.

'How did that make you feel?'

'Frightened. I was filling my pants,' he replied.

Robert Smith would always quote from the original police interviews after the arrest to show that Awan was lying. It wasn't a case of putting words into a shaky witness's mouth. This was the original text. And of course, Awan finally had the starring role in that movie he always craved.

'Have a look at the CCTV,' Robert said. 'What's that in your right hand?'

'Oh I don't know, I can't see.' Awan replied.

My God, he must be thick.

'Have a closer look,' Smith continued.

'Oh, it's a wrap.'

For effect, the prosecution pretended not to hear.

'A what?'

'A wrap,' confirmed Awan.

'You weren't filling your pants then, were you, Mr Awan?'

The footage had nailed him. He hadn't been filling his pants at all. He had been filling his wrap.

The police statements showed again he was a liar, repeatedly telling the police he was now telling the truth only to later confirm that he had misled them over a series of ten conversations with the detectives. QC Smith pulled lies from pages 46, 43, 52, 57, all over the damn shop.

Awan said how he prayed for me, which is touching given his cider-swigging in Rothbury.

'I thought the police officer was in good hands, I was not quite as worried, knowing he was in the hands of the NHS,' his heart clearly had gone out to me.

Yeah, if he'd only pulled down the window and said not to worry because I was in good hands just before he put the pedal to the metal and went all acka as he 'tooled it' up the A1, I'd have probably been a lot more chilled, lying there, bleeding to death, blinded.

I couldn't take anything seriously since the Grand Theft Auto/Jason Bourne moment and this just made it worse. Everything he says makes me think I'm in his film, touring Newcastle in some gangster movie. He even called the campsite 'the fort' and 'the safe house'. I assume he has nine passports and a secret identity and some phone with a bloody tape recorder on. When I think how I have told Ash and Mia never to lie, that's all he does.

'I am really starting to feel for him. He has a really hard life, and I understand what he has been through with the police victimising him.' These were exclusive extracts from the bestseller *Diary of a Hostage*.

'Why did you write that?' asked QC Smith.

'Well, it was flattering him,' he wriggled.

The problem was that the new Dan Brown didn't have a proofreader on the camping weekend. If he had, then it would have been pointed to him that at times he was writing 'we' but as a hostage, of course, he wasn't part of any 'we'. He was an 'I' in the narrative. Equally the police, to whom a hostage would turn, should not really be labelled as 'them'. At one point, glorifying what they had done so far in their great adventure, he rounded off a sentence with a barrage of exclamation marks!!!!! He couldn't stay in the role. Schoolboy error that. When you're sitting on such a hot manuscript as his, you should always hire a proofreader.

Of course the budding movie maker would be aware that every great motion picture needs a big finish, and he got his moment alright, literally caught on film with the police helicopter overhead.

'I panicked,' he told the court.

Supposedly sent for some papers, he had run into the police, so turned back and rang Moat for fourteen seconds.

'You panicked. You're a hostage. Why didn't you just walk up to the police and say he's down there why don't you help me?' Smith reasoned. 'Panic? Why would you ring the person that is holding you hostage?'

You can almost see Awan's final credits rolling, high fives all round, and the director dreaming of his Oscar next year and calling time on that day's filming.

'That's a wrap,' he would probably say. And Awan wouldn't know if it was time for chicken again or if he was still in a movie.

The best was yet to come.

Awan's witness statements continued with him saying how much he wanted to help the police. Though, of course, he didn't tell them about the letter.

Well, not until the sixth or seventh interview, anyway.

By the next interview there was another letter and later a third. This is the *'Burn It' Trilogy*.

'It slipped my mind,' he said when asked why he hadn't mentioned them before this point.

QC Smith pointed out that on page 54 of his witness state-ments he was now telling the truth.

'This is where things may differ,' he said.

'Please don't show this to my mum or dad because they will spill the beans,' the letter had said.

'What do you mean spill the beans?' he was asked but had no answer.

'Why did you write burn it?' QC Smith persisted.

'I just wanted my sister to have it,' he continued.

'Yes, Mr Awan, but why did you write this letter?'

Pausing to take a big gulp of air, he practically sentenced himself.

'Well, it's incriminating, isn't it?' he said.

I couldn't believe it. I knew he was stupid, but that was just the icing on the cake.

'That's 2-0,' I turned to Robin, chuckling, the chicken wrap having been the first own goal.

Three female jury members were rocking with laughter; two of the men were shaking their heads; many of the others sat there with mouths open. Robin said it was a picture.

'What do you mean incriminating?' Robert Smith couldn't believe his luck.

'Well, it's incriminating,' he repeated.

This was a Smith trick. Even I could see this now. Latch on to a key word, and ping it around the courtroom for all to hear. I thought this was genius.

'Well, it's incriminating because I've told her to destroy it and you've found it,' he had said it three times.

I could leave now.

Except there was more.

Around lunch time I got a tip-off that the prosecution had served notice that they had additional evidence to submit.

'Mr Awan, I know the other day you said you wouldn't go anywhere unless you had a supply of Warfarin. Is that correct?' Smith led him up another blind alley.

'Yes, that's correct,' Awan replied, confirming that he hadn't taken it with him.

'What I am going to do now is show you some photo-graphs,' Robert had his slide show ready to go.

There were three photos prepared in a booklet.

'That's the inside of my car that, it's the centre console,' Awan confirmed.

'Can you see the tissue? What's underneath that?'

He must have thought it was concealed.

'I don't know, you can't make it out,' he said, not knowing where this was going.

He was told to turn the picture. In the bottom left hand side was a receipt.

'Is that the receipt for your four sweet chilli dips from McDonald's?'

He confirmed it was.

'What's that underneath it?' Smith went on, again knowing the answer in advance.

'Oh I don't know. You can't make that out,' he lied again.

It was his Warfarin, sitting there in the Lexus.

He took that trademark gulp of air again.

'Yes, that's my Warfarin, but it's empty. There's nothing in it.'

But there was.

The jury was shown the exhibit with a tablet still in it.

'That's the wrong stuff,' he protested. 'That's brown Warfarin and it's only one milligram, and I'm on ten milligrams a day. When I went to prison I was given a blood test, and my results were only 1.3. I had three days of the correct dosage so that shows I hadn't taken the correct amount.'

'Yes, but that's your Warfarin Mr Awan,' the prosecution delivered calmly.

I knew *this* was my moment to leave today, ensuring I tapped the door as I departed. Oscars all round.

Awan had just given it to us on a plate. He had told the jury he was in prison. They wouldn't have known that. There is a massive pre-determination of attitude if you're already inside, rather than loitering on bail. You never tell the jury you are already inside.

No wonder he had to have two extra breaks today and asked to sit down because he was weak. The burden of his deceit was weighing him down. He wasn't the only one to feel faint though. I passed out when I got home, unable to eat. Alison had to tell me to take my watch off – my hand was like an iron. There was a red line of blood racing through my flesh, as the pellets tore me apart again. It had been a brilliant day but alone at home, the reminders were still there. If I hadn't taken a shed load of antibiotics in the early evening I would probably have been heading back to hospital. In bed by 7 p.m., I knew one thing. If I could survive two strikes from a shotgun, I wasn't having blood poisoning on my death certificate.

The sooner I could hear the words which the armed guards had said to me when Moat shot himself repeated, the better.

WEDNESDAY 2 MARCH 2011

'**B**ang, bang,' she roared.

I stopped dead in my tracks.

There were about twenty of them and I had heard them coming as I left the underground car park.

I froze.

'I hope you don't think that's funny,' Ali turned round to say.

She motioned as if to fire, Ali told me afterwards.

These scumbags had nothing to do with the trial of Ness and Awan. Normally in the police you expect to be called some pretty choice names, but I was devastated that after all the months of goodwill that the vast majority of the public have shown to me, just as the trial was nearing to a close, somebody thought it funny to have a pop.

And for what purpose?

Despite what people may have read or seen in the media, it takes me all my courage and energy to overcome my vulnerability each and every day. My house is my fortress and despite having moved there *after* the shooting, I know it inside out. For the last four weeks or so, I have put myself open to the public, which is something I have to do to make sure justice takes its course. But it's not something I enjoy.

Entering the court today, I couldn't have felt more upset or intimidated.

Thankfully, Northumbria Police will press charges against this idiot, clearly showing off amongst her friends. What a trophy to win, that she got a laugh for frightening a blind policeman.

A detective came down from the fourth floor of the courts where they had found her. She has been arrested on a public order offence and for intimidating a witness.

This was a very dark moment that took me right back to the car. It's not how I wanted to enter court today. Once I had settled, I hoped that the jury would hear of it, even though they aren't supposed to watch the news. I knew that would work in our favour.

We were coming to the end of the trial. There would be no more comedy but there would be no more lies either. We would hear the highlights again in the summing up but essentially we were done. The jury would be sent away in the next few days and finally I could start to think about the future. At last, we were in the home straight.

It didn't mean there wasn't any legal bullshit left to endure – far from it. In fact, whilst I found the barristers' discussion fascinating this morning, it hit home that they could still be arguing the toss in five, seven, who knows how many years' time.

There is resistance, you see, to the word 'duress'.

Essentially, only Awan has ever put up much of a fight to the evidence, though it was a pretty lame effort. Nobody has ever denied that Ness and Awan were with Moat, nor drove him around in their cars, performed countless favours and errands for him, had dialogue with him in and out of prison etc etc… On it goes.

But, from the off there has been this lingering rubbish that Ness and Awan were hostages. That was the plan to get their sentences reduced. Robert Smith had been brilliant in court for the prosecution – his opening speech alone had lasted four and a half hours. The defence had been going through the motions, dealt a helpless hand. Robert saw it coming – their one shot at getting anything out of this trial was to play with the law.

That is what this morning was all about.

All the law books had been out, throwing up legal rulings from 1925 in the search for stated cases on which to draw precedents in the case of Ness and Awan.

There was, simply, no historical example that 'duress' was an escape clause on the charge of conspiracy to murder. In murder or attempted murder you can't play the duress card. That's there in black in white in the statute book but there is no ruling on the charge of conspiracy to murder, which they are also facing.

The Judge began comparing this case to the Nazi concentration camps. Did the people who built the death camps conspire to commit murder? In which case they would be held responsible and there would be no duress. Most of them, I felt, probably didn't know what they were building, but what if they had a rifle in the back under orders, was that conspiracy to murder under duress?

Should the Judge decide that you can't have duress, then Ness and Awan are knackered on all of the charges. He would have to direct the jury accordingly and tell them if they find them guilty on the evidence that they have heard, then they must be found guilty and duress is neither here nor there.

If the defence then appealed on the conspiracy charge in relation to duress, we could be off to the High Court, the Supreme Court, and even Europe. Then it will never end, though Ness and Awan will have begun time for the other charges. To the layman, it's a needless delaying tactic which might soften the likely heavy sentences coming. To the legal profession, they could be about to create the next stated case – a precedent – and this case, if a McFlurry, an ex-footballer, and a TV survival expert hadn't already put it on the map alongside the monstrous crimes, would forever be quoted and referred to, long after all of us are dead.

So you see that this will never be truly over.

This is the game now, and it's no surprise to the prosecution. That's why so much was made of the medication found on Awan's dashboard. The receipts and incidental detail like the cider show a pattern. The casual conversations and wandering off shopping may have come across to the jury as banal but they weren't.

But this was as close to the low-baller that the defence could get, and Robert Smith had smelt it early. By never under-playing any of the seemingly irrelevant detail that established the pattern of behaviour and mapped out their deceit, he had, from the outset, been at pains to show that actually there was no stress, and therefore duress, at any single moment. He had batted the low-baller back before it even came flying in our direction.

You would hope, therefore, that in the next few days no legal precedents would be set, and that the jury too could see through the games. Society never moves on if brave pioneers do not force changes in law but this was not a case in which anyone should be seeking a starring role in tomorrow's law degree. The duress card was a wriggle. This wasn't a moment to be a legal hero.

Conspiracy to murder under duress has never been tested. The Judge now has to take a moral position. We'll know more only in the next few days.

There is no sitting tomorrow and we return on Friday, though that too was up for debate, given that there might be an unfair advantage having the last word into the weekend. Finally, some two weeks on from when I thought it might all be over, we look like we are heading for the end.

Lawyers get heavily criticised but I left today convinced that Robert Smith earned every penny. He knows his stuff, and whilst dryly ruthless in the courtroom, was the warmest, dearest man out of it.

He was fuming about the 'Bang Bang' woman. Like me, he had seen enough scum over the years. But he was buoyant overall and confident on duress. He said I had been fantas-tic giving my evidence, that I was humble and dignified. As

I thanked him for everything he had done, especially nailing Awan yesterday, he warmly implied that it had been more than a job to him. He had a sense of right and wrong, but the disparity between the deceit of these three and the impact on the lives of those who were now suffering seemed to drive him on with legal brilliance and a compassionate heart.

'I hope you don't mind the times I leave. I've been trying to leave at the most opportune moments,' I apologised for playing the game.

'I know exactly what you have been doing and it's fantastic,' he replied.

That meant a lot.

It was good to retire early and to have a day off tomorrow. I haven't felt right for two or three days.

I am literally limping wearily to the finish.

I just about had the energy to set up the sweepstake on how long it would take the jury. Giving nothing away here but look out for the guy in a police uniform with a white cane walking off with a wad of cash if it comes in at two hours and forty.

THURSDAY 3 MARCH 2011

For once, I slept soundly last night.

Knowing that there was no court today must have helped. My hunger for the trial was gone; my belly full from a feast of lies and deceit. I just wanted it over.

I awoke today to find that they had thrown the book at Bang Bang woman. I still don't know her name. My colleagues had done a job on her.

She was still being held at teatime yesterday and is now out on bail. In her police interview she had turned on the waterworks, probably barely able to fathom how one mindless gesture could get her in such shit.

And now her house had been raided too. That was the price she was paying, and I was pleased. Northumbria Police were sending out a message: Don't fuck with us. Justice will be done.

Bang Bang had claimed she was indicating to her sister that she wanted her phone back. I told the DS that I had heard her walk past me and say 'That's that policeman' – the phrase I had heard more than any other since I was shot.

'Oh that's interesting,' he said, 'she never told us that. Well, it doesn't matter anyway because there was a witness standing in the window above who saw her in a rifle pose and she's come forward.'

There were still some decent people out there then.

'We've raided her house and raided her previous house and seized her computers,' the DS continued.

We were pursuing her over-vigorously. The Chief was mortified by what had happened and had sent someone down to see me straight away yesterday to check I was fine. We all know Bang Bang will probably walk away with nothing more than a £100 fine, but my colleagues want to make a stand.

Remember, she *didn't* know who I was but *did* admit in interview to having gone on one of those Raoul Moat websites. It had gone right to the top of the Crown Prosecution Service. I bet that's a mad moment of her life she wishes she could have back. She will be charged and her name will end up in the paper. That's a heavy price. I'm just waiting to find out if she likes chicken wraps and McFlurry, and if she knew Gazza and Ray Mears.

I had the day to reflect and Moat was bugging me once more.

The court had heard all of Moat's previous – multiple – arrests and then some. That night when I hunted him on the police computer I was only looking for the time I had pulled him over. Some of the detail of what went before though was shocking. On a conspiracy to murder charge, he had walked free after threatening to shoot the ex of his then girlfriend, who was just sixteen at the time.

Another girlfriend had had a similar problem but retracted her evidence saying that she and Moat were now reconciled. Violence was always his answer; he looked a predator too. Amazingly he had never done time until the eighteen weeks in late spring last year which led to all this.

I'm sure, like me, you have one question.

Why?

FRIDAY 4 MARCH 2011

Dr Crippen removed my stitches this morning. You may know her better as Katherine Rathband. And if you don't know Hawley Harvey Crippen... well the good doctor only murdered his wife in one of America's most famous cases of the twentieth century! That's all he did, and they didn't even have chicken wraps then.

I had stitches that needed to come out. I'd also had every pain going and every needle and tube inserted in me in the last half a year or so, that frankly, if my wife wanted to be brutally ruthless with me, then so be it!

It was back to the RVI this morning to see Mr Neo. Three weeks ago he had cut my bottom eyelid and re-stitched it. My right eye had gone saggy as I had no eyeball. In the next couple of weeks I will be back again to have my eyes remoulded. It was only a ten-minute consultation but then they needed to see my hands and take swabs. I remain badly infected.

It is water off a duck's back now. I've spent a lifetime trying to avoid hospitals, and here I am virtually with a mortgage on the place now. No pain can ever match what I felt after being shot, so really nurses and consultants can prod, poke and prick and I barely notice. One thing never changes though, from the moment we were in the Special Care Baby Unit with Ash to the Seven Nights in Rothbury.

Time always stands still in a hospital.

The importance of what goes on inside overrides every meaningless bit of nonsense going on out of it. Who hasn't come out of a hospital and turned on their mobile straight away only to be underwhelmed by all the garbage that was sent to you while you or the people you love were at death's door.

Put that into the context of the little old lady who came over to acknowledge me.

'Hello, I know who you are, I've just been watching you, and you're a marvellous couple,' and then she toddled off.

Hospital was always a reality check.

I would inevitably be back here soon, and then soon again after that.

Next week, I have a trainer coming to the house, which is something. This is for my mobility training so I can be guided round buildings when I return to work. At least my employers are taking that seriously, especially as word came out yesterday about some departments being re-aligned in the cuts. Some of my colleagues who are superbly trained in searches on anything from royalty to drugs are being disbanded. That is what we are facing in the recession. There is no word on Sue's job for a few weeks or so, but I'm not hopeful. At this point, I am sure I am on my way out but I am not declaring that publicly of course. Why should I?

The job I love has had its heart ripped out. I still have the same instincts and some sharper ones too through my sense of hearing. I'm not about to chuck it all in. I will stand firm until they kick me out. They will have to pay me to go. They have a duty of care to me, which they neglected in the control room that night, so I will stubbornly remain an officer. The irony will not be lost on you that in these times of austerity and people being made redundant, Northumbria Police need at least two (because of holidays, sickness, and shift patterns) trained extra people to accommodate David Rathband. Even I can see that is a waste of time, but why should I do anything other than hang in for the long haul?

I think Alison gets that. She has about five years left herself.

There are only so many times you can dedicate your life to fighting evil, and it gets to you.

On the way out of court this afternoon, there were about half a dozen alcoholics, thieves and smackheads loitering. The court had seized £1,200 from them as the cash had been the proceeds of crime. All we could hear was 'fucking bastards' and 'cunts' on the landing. Seven months ago, I would have locked them up. We both got in the lift disillusioned and thinking the same thing. How long can you put up with the scum for?

For the first time, it is sinking in. I don't want to face the lowlifes any longer. I will always enjoy the knowledge that my colleagues will still be locking up the devil's children, but in reality, I am done. Deep down, as much as the police are trying to create a role for me such as visiting schools to give road safety talks or giving talks to FLOs, I know I will never arrest another Ness or Awan again.

Yesterday, with no court, I was sitting in the house and I picked up the wailing police siren of a traffic cop, about three miles away.

'I used to do that,' I said to myself in the past tense.

Given the world today, I am more likely to be a token novelty interest on *Dancing on Ice* than I am to drive a police car with all lights flashing, nailing the next Raoul Moat.

‡

The current Moat, of course, was dead. His accomplices remained. Now it was time for closing speeches. Strangely, I almost have a season ticket now at the law courts. You will remember that I was only going to give my evidence and return for the summing up and verdict, while Kath had been there on day one. That had been too much for her, whilst I became addicted, overwhelmed with the notion that I had to supervise the detail. It gave me great pleasure seeing the brilliant job Robert Smith was performing. Trial by irony and mockery was more cathartic than the facts themselves. I loved his tone.

Oddly though, today he seemed unable to pronounce my name. On at least three occasions he stumbled on Rathband, adding the 'H' after the Rat. I don't know if it was his accent, or if he was thinking ahead, it was just bizarre.

I didn't hear anything this afternoon I didn't know already. Nor did anyone of course, but it was worth witnessing to know what focus the jury would take away.

'Their story is riddled with incredibility,' Robert said. 'It's one thing to assist an offender to escape but what they did is far more serious than that. They were each parties in law to the offences which followed and were in agreement with Moat they should be committed.'

He pitched Ness as Moat's 'loyal servant' and Awan brilliantly as 'not the amiable buffoon he has tried to portray himself as'. He reminded the court that Awan was the driver carrying Moat in his hunt for police officers.

Awan's whole demeanour was labelled 'an extraordinary performance in the witness box'.

I know too the QC hates them and it's more than a court case to him. He hates lying bastards. I know that from the way he talks to me. His drive to convict people who shoot police officers knows no boundaries and he was the first choice for the CPS to front our case. Ironically I heard that Sloan, defence for Ness, was the second choice, and people will struggle to get their head around that, in law, you suspend your personal feeling, and that the guy who was our second choice to prosecute ends up defending that lowlife's right to a fair trial.

A payday is a payday.

Every time Robert Smith talks to me his smile is as long as a Cheshire Cat. I waited for him again today to thank him for everything and he was beaming, and he had just been narrating this work of fiction for three hours off the cuff. He is very confident and very humble and the verdict means everything to him. Whilst law is a game, this one has touched a nerve for so many people.

On Monday, the defence will respond. They may string it out all day, but in reality, they should only waste five minutes of everyone's time.

Much of what happens now is down to the Judge's direction. Should the jury find them under 'duress' for conspiracy to murder, then so be it, but it seems an irrelevance given the chicken wrap, McFlurry, B&Q and countless other nonsensical details.

The Judge seems to have implied that we may be on new legal ground and that it could be acceptable to allow duress on a conspiracy to murder charge for the first time in British law, but this is a smokescreen. The twelve upstanding members of the community need to be clear that this case of duress is bullshit, so chilled were Ness and Awan.

Now is not the time to seize legal glory and search for a precedent because someone has put the statute book on the table as the last chance saloon. The fact remains that the law may be a grey area, but the chicken wrap, like most things in Newcastle, is in black and white.

They had a million opportunities to break free, and human nature dictates that if police officers think these guys are guilty then they will find evidence to show that and when the police put a file into court the best thing to do is not put anything in to undermine it. The only wonky area in all this is that there are thirty minutes missing footage in Rothbury before the moment of arrest but that proves nothing. They *had* been walking away and had ample opportunity to flag cars down but didn't.

Your only concern now has to be if the jury are nuts too. I am not insecure about this but I have always felt the justice system to be an ass. Twelve members of the public with what-ever is going on in their life or three judges with an encyclo-paedic knowledge of the law – who would *you* trust more?

The latest sweepstake betting is now two hours forty-five minutes from me. That's as long as it will take to read every-thing out and nod. Ali is more cautious at three hours fifteen but then she did miss about a week of the trial or so. Even so, the times are small. If there were any element of doubt we would be into days, not hours.

They have to be seen to consider the evidence, so once that door is shut and four or five of them shout guilty as I expect, you just know that someone will suggest caution.

'Hang on a minute,' the foreman will say. 'Let's have a cup of coffee and go through it again.'

Juries can be known to stretch it out and whatever is said in that room remains private – not even the Judge will know. No member of the public is allowed to question a juror and they can't tell you their decision process. I am now getting into my worst fears scenario. I know they are guilty, but it's not my decision.

We're nearly there though, and then once it's over, I face the future. I await the resolution of my action against the police; perhaps foolishly the London Marathon is on the horizon and I must face the first anniversary this July.

My face isn't ready to go to back to work yet and there are already signs that I am becoming just another statistic. The Department of Work and Pensions rang after court to tell me they are coming to see me in the next couple of weeks for a medical to see if I am worthy of benefit.

While some have never done a decent shift in their life and claim benefits left, right and centre, this esteemed member of the medical profession will judge if I am fit for £60 benefit a week – and it will cost a hell of a lot more to send him or her round to see me for that medical.

It's an absolute piss-take.

Kath read the letter to me yesterday, and I only had one reaction remembering the last communiqué I had had, which made no reference to me being blind. All I had was a facial injury and a frozen shoulder!

MONDAY 7 MARCH 2011

I'm sending twenty-three bags of rubbish to the tip. I've spent two hours pulling at a thirty-foot rose bush in the garden. Life must go on, and blind or not, the garden isn't going to do itself. Anything would be better than sitting through any more of this trial.

I left at lunchtime, fed up of listening to all their shit, just getting angrier and angrier at the way Ness and Awan's defence were defending them. QC Sloan had said how compelling my evidence had been – in fact he remarked how you couldn't *not* be compelled. He reflected that I had been a total professional and how tragic it all was, and then I read his tone to be 'Now, disbelieve everything else you've heard'.

I couldn't believe it.

It was as though he knew that he couldn't take the moral high ground from me. He was obviously aware of the huge public outpouring in my favour, and that it would be a big error to play me off. He would lose the jury who surely had some sort of memory of the events of last July anyway, and if they didn't then they would have noted my timed exits from court, and would never forget my testimony.

That's why you don't shout anything out when court makes you angry. Always remember the end game, and let the jury picture you once again back on the stand in uniform giving evidence as a trusted policeman rather than an emotional victim, even though I was, of course, both.

He was right about my evidence, and he couldn't question an ounce of it, but to then glide on as though the rest of the evidence was nonsense left me fuming. I did nearly shout out, but remembered myself. Instead I withdrew for a fag and a cup of tea before returning for more of the same.

The argument was based solely on Ness and Awan being under duress, that Ness didn't know anything about going to shoot Chris Brown and had driven off thinking Moat had shot himself. On that basis, he couldn't conspire or be a murderer. Ness must be innocent as he hadn't texted Moat back.

This, of course, ignored all the other phone analysis from inside and outside Durham Prison and the fact that, whilst Ness may not have texted back for twenty minutes as Moat sat underneath the window in Birtley, he had said that he would 'miss you mate if it goes down' and had a Transit van parked up around the corner.

This was the trick.

Nothing that was damning was referred to; anything where there may be reasonable doubt was suddenly the lynchpin of the argument and that was making me nervous. The game was simple: compel the jury to consider 'reasonable doubt' and if they did with substance, these two bastards would be out and roaming around within a few miles of my house again. All the jury had to do was favour one barrister over QC Smith, or ask themselves could anyone be so stupid as to behave the way Ness and Awan did and conclude 'surely not' and suddenly there was doubt. What if the jury had felt these two were innocent all along? I do remember the laughter in the courtroom at some of Awan's answers, but it seems a distant memory now. My mind was rocked with paranoia that all this had been for nothing. Never had I experienced any end-of-trial nerves previously in my career.

It had all been so clear cut.

They *were* in the car after all, and repeatedly lied in witness statements and in the box, and looked anything other than hostages in all the CCTV footage and photographic evidence. And then there were the 'Burn It' letters too. The jury had to go back in their memory banks and remember the previous five weeks or so, and not be dazzled by the bright lights of the closing speeches. This was just spin; fact had come before. It was time for strong minds.

Heaven forbid that all twelve couldn't find them guilty, or indeed ten of them. Imagine if the jury were split and there was a retrial. I can't do this again and be putting my life off again until the start of 2012.

If it came to that, Northumbria Police's resolve would be even stronger and the Crown Prosecution Service would find yet more evidence but could they justify it? As it is, such is the pressure now to bring a trial within six months of the offences that we have all been running from day one. QC Smith and my colleagues have done brilliantly, but with more time, we could have nailed them further. The phrase reasonable doubt would then only apply to any sweepstakes on the length of the sentence.

But now, since I have come home this afternoon, I am convinced they will get off. I've always looked at this case objectively through the eyes of a policeman giving evidence rather than as a victim craving justice, but I have been heading towards an about-turn for several days now. So confident was I that Ness was the right-hand man, and that Awan had self-destructed in the courtroom, coupled with all the hard evidence which nailed them that these doubts had only manifested themselves after all the witnesses had been called.

Once we deviated from everything the prosecution had thrown at the pair, and it came down to the legal game, that's where my heart started missing a beat.

It began with the technicality of whether you could be guilty of conspiracy to murder under duress late last week and ended when Sloan effectively told the jury that if they had any doubt, and they would have some doubt, then these guys must walk free.

I'm on an emotional roundabout, concerned that the jury have had two days' leisure time to see the light and with it the 'reasonable doubt'. That is because today is Monday and I've just sat through the mind games. On Friday, when they left for the weekend, I was convinced that in their minds, Ness and Awan had already been convicted.

I can now only see the wrong end to this trial; the human frailties of twelve swayable members of the public are in my mind night and day. I need to hear those words that it's over, yet every second we get closer to the verdict, I convince myself that we get closer to acquittal. It's painful watching the defence twist every detail to sow the seed of doubt.

In a nutshell, they have now only one question to answer. Were Ness and Awan hostages? If they start there, and remember the chicken wrap, they can get to the correct verdict.

It wasn't just the fear that twelve decent members of the public could have doubt that was distressing me. It was also my disgust at the game.

I felt that the defence sounded like a waffling wordsmith who avoided the uncomfortable moments, yet had the skill of language to make a jury think again, stating that Ness hadn't been Moat's henchman at all. To my disbelief, their pitch was that he was Sam Stobbart's right-hand man, 'in consort' with her *and* betraying Moat himself by not spying on her to see if she had a new boyfriend while Moat was in jail.

Unbelievable.

Ness didn't think he was carrying a gun in the bag. He knew it was steroids, as Moat had told Stobbart that he had ordered a load of growth-enhancing 'gear' for when he came out of Durham Prison.

I was watching a jigsaw at play. You could throw all the pieces up in the air and it would fit, and you could do the same again and it would fit another way. The defence did everything to make it fit, and of course, some pieces would conveniently go missing when they tried to complete the puzzle.

I had seen all these tricks before. Wasn't it much smarter to realise that only somebody with something to hide would need to resort to such devious methods? If you were confident in your innocence, then your innocence would speak for itself.

'Don't get hung up on the verdict,' Ali said to me earlier.

Even though that was the right thing to say and I had handed the same advice out many times over the years, it meant nothing.

You can't lean in any direction as a FLO.

However certain a verdict seems, nothing can be. To give a family false optimism can only come back to haunt you.

What struck me today as the only source of hope, given my increasing pessimism, was that Sloan's closing statements for Ness only lasted a couple of hours, which seems a minuscule amount of time given the length of this case. Carter-Manning, defending for Awan, was already on before lunch and is only expected to need another twenty minutes tomorrow before the Judge sums up. This reminds me positively that much of the evidence stands uncontested, and since duress can't be used in a charge of murder or attempted murder, the jury have to find them guilty. Let us not forget, these bastards drove the cars for Moat.

Awan, Carter-Manning claimed, was a victim of 'terrification', an entirely new word in the judicial system. This was such an extraordinary case with so much bullshit that the defence's latest attempt to get these two acquitted was to invent previously unheard of nouns.

'If I had to fit a case where duress fits the reality of the situation, then this is your case,' he said playing on duress again.

Awan wasn't physically fit to rough it camping, he added. Too many chicken wraps perhaps? I've been on camping trips myself and I've certainly never shopped that much! He reminded the jury too of his character and how he apologised for any errors in court.

Yes, I remember how apologetic he was too. I think he said sorry nine times after admitting the evidence was incriminating, frequently ending sentences with the word 'honest' like most who doth protest too much.

I'd rather think of it as Awan's 3Ss – shopping, shitting and shooting. That seemed to sum it up for me.

But I am nervous, fearful of the consequences. Newcastle is a small place and I live halfway between both Ness and Awan. They'll come again, we always say, and unless we move abroad, I'll bump into them, because you always do in the North East.

Goodness only knows what becomes of them if they get out. They can't go legitimate because their lives are ruined, but they may also become extremely dangerous villains because they got off with it, seeing themselves as untouchable because they know they assisted someone to murder but walked away scot-free.

It doesn't bear thinking about.

But it was the only thing on my mind.

TUESDAY 8 MARCH 2011

'I can't believe anyone would do something as sick as that. She deserves everything she gets,' Colin Swaine told *The Sun* yesterday.

Mr Swaine is the grandfather of 22-year-old Kelsey Donkin. Donkin is Bang Bang woman.

Her family have now disowned her.

I would have done the same. Her grandad told the reporter that she was in court to support a friend on another case and that it was a prank to look good in front of her mates. Heaven only knows what her pal was up on, but attempting to trump it in a game of one-upmanship was all part of the 'my ASBO is a badge of honour' mentality that I loathed.

I'm glad a police source leaked her name for all to see.

Forgive me – what I meant to say is that I am glad the reporter dug so thoroughly to ascertain all the facts. How strange too that the reporter Robin Perrie was the same one whom I had given an interview to in December. However do these things happen?

I am acutely aware that it will be my turn to face the media soon. I had initially promised that I would give one interview to Ben Chapman at Tyne Tees Television on the delivery of the verdict, but now I'm having second thoughts. I even snapped at my PR man Robin about it on the way in this morning. Tyne Tees sensed I was backing off and wanted to know why. I just feel it is time to get some sort of sense of perspective and whilst my door is always open to the media, I lose the moral high ground if I stand on the steps of the courtroom asking for privacy but then later on that night I am giving a full-on interview to the TV in a half-hour special which they have pre-planned.

I have to go back on my agreement. It *is* the time to be with my family.

Celebrate won't be the word, but whatever emotion we will all feel at the verdict must be a private one.

So drained and angry am I by what I have witnessed in that courtroom that I am now veering towards giving the traditional statement on the steps of the law court, dressed in my police uniform. I know that the sight of myself fitted out for work will resonate to the watching world that I remain a professional who continues to fight against the lowlifes of society. It will also get me into some sort of zone where I will be able to control my emotion. This will be a moment neither for tears nor fist-clenching. I will read three or four sentences as if I had just been the family liaison officer speaking for the family.

In time, I will speak again as a victim, but it's not right to do so on the day of the verdict, and I must show Chris Brown's family the respect and privacy they deserve. I'm sure that on the first anniversary the media will see me as fodder once again. That will be the next moment to tick off and then we will be left alone to pick up the pieces.

That is of course, assuming that I would hear the one word that meant that so many people could at least move on in our lives.

Guilty.

I am not alone in being desperate for it to end. Becky, Chris's sister, is feeling it too.

'I'll kill her… she's got my brother's name tattooed on her wrist,' she was livid.

Sam Stobbart now had a tattoo dedicated to the forgotten man in all this – someone she barely knew. Nobody had seen it before. We knew it was tasteless and were pretty confident its timing was for effect, but then what does she have to gain from doing this except inflicting more pain on everyone who was left behind in Moat's trail? She has no reason to be at the trial.

Becky wasn't alone in feeling uncomfortable, and Stobbart wasn't the only one whose presence was noted.

We had a family day at court today – not the nicest day out we've ever had but we need to go in numbers now. Kath hates it.

The sheer reminders of the impact on our lives together with the general air of criminality in the room leave a bad taste. Sitting in the same room as the scum, and then being unable to walk to the lift without hearing other riff-raff effing and blinding, make court a really negative place to be with the people who aren't quite good enough to make the underworld, sniffing and swearing away in their tracksuits and bling, oblivious to the rules of society. Kath needed it over more than anyone except me.

For Carter-Manning, defending Awan, it *was* over. He seemed to have checked out and disappeared mid-morning, kicking Awan's ego well and truly into touch. Imagine that. The guy who is defending you has buggered off back to London, or wherever it was he was based. That sends out a pretty strong message to the client, and anyone else who happens to be aware of it. It told me that he too had had enough of the bullshit and couldn't spin it out any more. He had another case to go to.

Kath felt his mind was elsewhere.

'His closing speech was all over the place compared to Sloan,' she said.

Sloan, on the other hand, gave a really polished performance, when neither of us thought he'd had much to offer from the moment Ness had initially taken the stand. His client had grunted responses and said little. It had been a minimalistic performance. Now he left me dejected with a much better argument.

'I don't think they will put Awan on the stand,' I remembered saying after seeing Ness's performance. 'It's too risky.'

And that never seemed truer.

It was jigsaw time again, and I just sensed that Sloan had worked backwards from Ness's 'Don't remember' testimony and made it all fit again. Carter-Manning may have been all over the place because Awan had been tripping himself up with loose cannon self-incriminating remarks.

To add insult to injury, Ness's performance was a distant memory. My fear was that the jury would only remember these final moments of barrister bullshit and not the pieces which went before and completed the whole picture. We were in a soundbite obsessed, low-attention-span modern era. I had to bank on the jury being better than that. They must have seen through Ness.

To me, as a policeman, he has come across as a methodical thinker, but they might think he hasn't really done or revealed that much because he has thought about the consequences of giving too much evidence.

Awan, who had less to prove, has by own his admission been a rabbit in the headlights and if he had sat there and said nothing then he would looked like he had just got roped in. If the jury see through Ness as I do, they will find him as cold and calculated as Moat. They'll ultimately convict Awan for sinking himself.

I feel more confident today. I think it is about 60–40 in our favour but these last couple of days have been agony and the Judge did me no favours either. I know he is not supposed to help me and to remain impartial, but for a man who has been a very articulate, decisive figurehead up to this point, I found him slow and monotone today and Kath felt the same. QC Smith always had rhythm and from that I took confidence; today there were so many 'erms' that it made me nervous that the tone of the guy at the top of the legal tree seemed to be offering olive branches. Or maybe that was his way after all and my nerves were simply shot to pieces. I wanted him to emphasise the points of guilt as Robert Smith had done. I couldn't understand how he could be so fair and show no bias.

Instead, he recited a scripted story dating back to 30 June when Moat was still in prison. If anything, I interpreted a lack of bias as a leaning towards Ness and Awan but that's the state I had got myself in. I couldn't believe that he spent ten minutes talking about Moat's puppies and a vet bill and that he took more time over this than he did Moat leaving prison. It was only relevant for revealing the fact that Sam Stobbart had left the pub early on 3 July because her mum and dad had had a row about the dogs which they were now looking after. I asked myself why he had included this, knowing full well that so much incriminating evidence from Ness and particularly Awan had come from their inability to recall incidental irrelevant detail. They had their big hostage story, but couldn't remember conversations, what they had bought and when, or indeed anything trivial at all.

At one point, I felt he was showing good will to Ness, but was this just me? On the day of Moat's release, Ness had claimed he had been moving furniture in Ponteland up until late in the day. Ness's mother had rung him, saying she thought he was in the company of Moat. Ness denies this.

'You can see on the CCTV that Ness appeared at 4 p.m.,' the Judge said. 'This may well point towards what he was saying about moving the furniture.'

I found it hard to swallow that he was doing his job properly. But he was. I was just picking up on everything at this stage – the good was very good, and the bad was very, very bad.

Crucially, his legal direction was crystal clear. On the duress issue, he did seem to signpost a verdict, making it very obvious that if Joe Bloggs A goes to commit a burglary, B keeps watch outside, and C is in the getaway car outside, then they are all guilty of burglary, regardless of who committed the act itself.

'They're guilty,' I said to myself. And I hope that resonated with every juror and they had all just shouted bingo.

If you read the law books, there are stated cases by which the Judge is governed. The highest court in the land would have clarified this exact point after an appeal once upon a long ago, and there would be no further doubt ever again. If C helped B and A did the crime then A, B, and C would all do the time. I couldn't help but feel that he had spelt it out in black and white. My confidence rose again.

Whether Ness replied to a text, or if he drove away without Moat, he was the assigned getaway driver and therefore was a goner. And the Judge made this quite clear. They didn't have to have pulled the trigger to be guilty.

The fact that I had them on the ANPR driving past me as Moat made the call to our control room saying he was going to shoot a policeman, combined with the fact that they admitted in the box that they all left the camp in Rothbury fully aware of Moat's intention to 'hunt cops' explains why the prosecution laboured this point at the time and why the mobile phone analysis was so important.

I had to go to bed tonight safe with that knowledge but now I was nervous that we wouldn't get a clean sweep and might struggle with the charge of possession of a firearm with intent to endanger life. *That* didn't matter if we nailed them on the rest because they would be well away on a long stretch. I so wanted them to pay for everything.

My emotions were all over place. I no longer knew my yo-yo mind.

Twice the legal teams had to correct the Judge when he got confused himself. QC Smith pointed out an error about the bag when he omitted to mention that there was nothing sticking out of it.

The defence also had to correct him on the receipts which he got confused about. There was a lot to take in, but if a man whose job it was struggled slightly, how could I have total faith that twelve people with no legal background could follow everything?

Of course, the way the British legal system works, it was the job of the prosecution to find guilt, rather than Ness and

Awan to prove their innocence. You had to pray that in the same way that Moat's image stood over me night after night as I tried to lie down to sleep, that enough of the twelve sent themselves into a deep sleep after a long day of court with Awan saying 'I know it's incriminating' running through their minds.

I have seen the final chapter of this story so many times and with so many different endings. A hundred times a day the foreman stands up and says 'not guilty' and on other occasions I see them being taken down and myself punching the court-room air. It's no different to those early nights when Moat would stand over me as I attempted to sleep. My mind was out on loan to the bad guys of this world and even if we got the result we craved and deserved, another haunting reminder would be along soon. I had to live with the fact that whatever happened, Moat's henchmen had squatter's rights on my mind from now until the day I die.

One other of these endings remains the nightmare scenario. The re-trial.

In many ways, that is the worst option because I, we, do not have the strength and energy to do this all again. If it came to that we would never know where we had gone wrong because you can't exactly have a feedback session with the jury. It is against the law to quiz them individually or collectively afterwards.

The double jeopardy law has now been changed and you *can* try a suspect a second time on further evidence but could I really be sure that the CPS would spend any more time or expense on it? They've boxed nearly every corridor off and called in over thirty suspects.

Any trail might run cold unless Lana Potts or Tara Collins had a major falling out with Ness on his release and one of them gets vindictive. *They* know the full story. Remember, the 'Burn It' letter. But for the present, it's either guilt or acquittal.

And the moment is coming ever nearer.

The press box is starting to fill up again. Seventeen media seats are already prepared for the delivering of the verdict. The Judge will pick up again in the morning from Jacqueline Wilkinson's house in Birtley. This is where Sam Stobbart returned after the pub on the Friday night when Chris was shot.

We were nearly there and I sensed the jury were close to being sent out, though Mr Justice McCombe indicated that he would need a day to sum up, meaning that he would conclude around 3.30 tomorrow afternoon.

We could be there quicker if we just lost the stuff about Moat's puppies. I was already like a dog with a bone.

WEDNESDAY 9 MARCH 2011

I feel tremendous sadness for Peter Boatman. He proves almost more than anyone that Raoul Moat was a tsunami whose waves still crash against unknown shorelines months after the first ripple and will continue to do so for years to come.

A Commons Home Affairs Select Committee had heard yesterday how he personally put in the boot of his car a batch of experimental X12 Tasers, which were still being tested by the government. He then drove them to Rothbury to assist Northumbria Police.

The problem was that the Taser was licensed for trial in one area of the country and one area only.

'We are not persuaded by this argument, and express great concern at the implications if this were to be taken as carte blanche to override legislation,' MPs had said.

Yes, and Moat's gun was licensed, wasn't it?

Boatman did what he thought was the correct thing to do as a former policeman. On 1 October last year, he was found dead at his home.

He had taken his own life.

It makes me cross because if we'd been in America, Moat would have been riddled with bullets, yet here any policeman taking that shot would probably be sidelined forever. Boatman did nothing wrong. At best, he was too keen but his intentions were honourable. He, too, had got caught up in the tidal wave of Moat's life.

Much had then been made of the Taser in the aftermath of Rothbury. I had been approached by a fellow officer to make contact with Peter Boatman's wife but was advised not to. It's very sad. I think about how Peter would have struggled to come to terms with the role he played – if any – in the termination of Moat.

Most people surely applauded him, if they even knew who he was, but he obviously felt unnecessarily that he had crossed some moral line. Not for me. Surely you cross the moral line when you make the thing in the first place, not when it is used. Licensed or unlicensed remains an irrelevance. A collective effort meant that it was over for Moat by hook or crook.

It just wasn't over for so many other people, nor would it ever be.

And it was now dragging on, and on and on.

Moat visited me again at four this morning. He has mostly kept away during the trial but he was picking up on my tension as the trial neared its conclusion.

In court yesterday I had a gorgeous vision of four puffy clouds in a beautiful blue summer sky. For a second I thought my sight was back. Then I realised it was just peace. Compare that to the havoc Moat wreaks every time he comes back to haunt me.

He was standing there in the bathroom, shaving. His head was completely bald and he was looking back at me in the reflection in the mirror. I don't know why he chose this moment. I felt he had seized on my uneasiness at the start of the week, but that he too was getting ready for the end of the trial.

Sometimes I would go looking for him, trying to picture his meathead face in my mind so I could hate him, chasing the image of when I pulled him over and not of the night of the shooting. That's the Moat I associate with. Obviously, events unravelled at speed the night he came for me whereas I controlled the pace on our first meeting, but it's that notion of unfinished business that haunts me.

If I could turn the tape back to any moment, then that would be it – the first meeting.

We have since found out about his numerous arrests. How different might things have been if he hadn't evaded the law back then, even though I thought I had done everything at the time to convict him?

And yet when I went looking for him in my mind, I couldn't always get him because in my new, dark world, all I would get when I really concentrated was blackness. Then, on other occasions he would just come to me, uninvited. And he didn't half pick his moments.

I just wish Moat wasn't such a coward and had been shaving in preparation for a real-time appearance in front of the Judge today instead of playing with me again. I wanted to see all three of them in the dock. The only dampener being that my eyes were no more of course so he still would have held some power over me.

And how would all this have played out if I hadn't made it myself and had died in the car? I hadn't even considered that.

I've done everything I can since that night to keep this case high profile and to deliver the best evidence I could. I shudder to think that with me dead, any of this would collapse and Ness and Awan could pull the wool over everybody's eyes.

These thoughts were constant, and the consequences don't bear thinking about.

‡

Today, I had to leave at 3 p.m. The last few steps to get over the line are the hardest to take, and after this roller coaster ride of the last five weeks, we were limping in slow-mo to the finish. Still, the Judge wouldn't send the jury out.

'I don't intend sending you today,' he said. 'I shall give you some routes to verdict.'

This means that the defence and prosecution have agreed on how the jury should reach the verdict – Justice McCombe would provide the jury with an aide mémoire, though I doubt

Ness and Awan knew what that was. This time there would be no need to include the words 'Burn It' on the bottom.

How the prosecution and defence can agree on a 'route to verdict' is beyond me, though that is the legal standard. Surely, in any such agreement, the defence can't protect his clients if he is helping hone the deal. Then again, the clients had already done much of the damage. Carter-Manning wasn't even there, and Sloan's body language was telling me that he thought their game was up too.

It was now just a waiting game.

My mood has improved since Monday, though you never get a moment where you are settled. Any upbeat positivity and optimism soon gets shouted down by the voices in your head. The break at the weekend had left me tense.

Starting up all the bullshit again meant we were consigned to another week of hell, but hearing the Judge signpost that he was sending the jury out was music to my ears. I knew it was nearly over.

My biggest concern today was that even though Justice McCombe had explained to the jury the principle of A, B and C committing armed robbery, they still might not understand this and therefore wouldn't find Ness guilty of murdering Chris Brown.

Sally and Becky needed that more than ever.

That bit of the verdict was for them. To be able to move on even slightly would never happen if they couldn't apportion blame to those who were still alive to face the music.

Chris hardly ever got a mention in the detail of the story whilst I had become a public figure. That was wrong.

Movingly, the Judge was very complimentary towards me, saying my evidence was 'absolutely outstanding… moving… exemplary… should be commended for his professionalism' which meant a lot because for all those moments where I could have shouted out in anguish as a victim, my evidence remained impartial and honest as a policeman, and that would surely leave its mark on the jury. I was pleased for Chris's family as well as our own that I had done a good job for all of us.

Guilty, and these two were looking at life, never likely to be released. You don't hear of would-be cop-killers ever really getting out. Even amongst the worst gangland sections of the underworld, going after policemen was pretty much overstepping the mark. Especially an unarmed one. These two would pay a hefty price, and we could all sleep a little easier at night.

I was deep in thought, satisfied with the Judge's warmth towards me, torn with anguish at the prospect of an innocent verdict. My head was all over the place, whilst still clinging on to every intonation and insinuation.

And then the Stereophonics turned up.

Chris Clarke had spent the past five weeks telling us all to make sure we had our phones turned off in court. However, he was clearly so chilled on his short golfing break to Portugal, from which he had returned last night, that he forgot his own advice.

'Maybe tomorrow...' was blasting out in the courtroom, getting louder and louder. It broke the tense spell I was under. You couldn't have picked a better song because never a truer word fitted the context.

I could feel Kath giggling under her breath and that started me off too. I knew Chris was wriggling to turn it off before the Judge finished his sentence. Half an hour later Chris was asleep, his snoring droning out the court.

I told Ali to give him a nudge in the ribs, but that wasn't the end of it.

Behind Chris, Christine from Victim Support had also dropped off, and was snoring louder than him! The public gallery was full of people having a nap. Seasoned pros who had been here a thousand times before were now feeling the strain too.

'I was jet-lagged,' Chris said.

'Don't be stupid,' I laughed back. 'You've only flown from Portugal you dickhead.'

God, if the professionals couldn't handle it, how knackered were the jury going to be?

There was some fantastic evidence too, especially the 'Burn It' letters, which totally exposed the sham that Ness and Awan had been fronting. You couldn't *not* be gripped.

'Don't tell the police,' the letters had said. 'But do keep the letters for reference for the police.'

What?

In other words, we're not really hostages, but later we'll piece it all together to fit the jigsaw and show that we were.

Awan had also written to the lad he shared the lock-up with, stating that he had gone back to the garage to remove his stuff and that his mate should do the same.

These letters began by announcing that he was being held hostage but were signed off with LOL, and 'Before I go nigger, put the kettle on'.

I'm sure you'll agree these are beautifully crafted words from a man of excellent character.

The Judge recounted the moment of their arrest in Rothbury.

'Get me mam out of the house now,' Ness had said when the police bundled him on the floor.

Except he hadn't.

Of all the police who rounded on him, nobody heard him say this.

Ness and Awan had tried to be clever, but their own story was falling apart at the seams, riddled with inaccuracies and stained by their own inability to remember the incidental detail.

And after all this, the best that the defence could object to was that they wanted it clarified that whilst Ness's letters had his and Moat's fingerprints on them, Awan's had his own and 'unidentified' marks. So, presumably Moat's but we couldn't be sure. After everything we heard and been through, this point of language was all they could quibble with. It didn't seem relevant at all.

It had taken over two and a half hours to sum up. That only meant one thing. When we returned in the morning, this would be it.

The time had come for deep breaths and sweaty palms, nervous laughter and a million thoughts racing to even more conclusions. We were nearly there, and the next twenty-four hours would determine how much looking over our shoulders the rest of our lives would consist of. The wrong verdict would mean a lingering bitterness and a fear that they will come after us; a cry of 'guilty' and we would start slowly to close that door of our lives, knowing that there was no chance we could ever slam it shut and throw away the key.

It was time to send the jury out.

THURSDAY 10 MARCH 2011

'On the charge of murdering Chris Brown, how do you find the defendant,' asked the clerk.

'Not guilty,' replied the foreman to gasps in the courtroom.

'On the charge of attempted murder of David Rathband, how do you find the defendant?'

'Not guilty.'

Ness was punching the air, beaming from ear to ear.

'Conspiracy to murder?'

'Not guilty.'

It was getting louder and louder.

'The chip shop robbery in Seaton Delaval?'

'Not guilty.'

Awan was now filling his boots; his pants a distant memory.

'Possession of a fire…?'

'Not guilty.'

The verdict had come at speed, getting faster and faster like those trains in the timeline that Sally Brown and Kath had described back on day one coming to an inevitable crash.

Bang.

On the fifth count I even interrupted the foreman, so hypnotised was I by the monotonous rhythm banging the drum of deceit.

And then we went through the whole lot again for Awan, except for the murder of Chris Brown, for which he was not charged.

The result was the same every time.

My police logic and ruthless instinct for crime had gone. That ability to be clinical and see facts as facts had been replaced by emotional turmoil. I had crossed that line again from policeman to victim.

For so much of the trial, the evidence was undeniable. In my head now, none of it sticks. The jury are twelve individuals who cannot be trusted. Amongst them are friends of Moat, Ness and Awan who have infiltrated justice, and for the others all they recall is the phrase 'reasonable doubt', 'reasonable doubt' and 'reasonable doubt'.

It is repeating in their minds over and over again. They too have replaced fact with frailty. Amongst them an aggressive foreman will emerge, already set in his mind of how this plays out. One by one, he will work the room, picking off the easy targets and turning them all until the scent of a majority is but a moment away.

'Reasonable doubt,' he will say, raising his eyebrows and getting off on the power bestowed upon him. And reasonable doubt will be a louder argument than reasonable fact – fact that is so clear cut it has barely been contested.

'But hang on a minute,' someone will say.

'What if…' another will pile in.

Then there will be an avalanche.

What if what? What if the police had doctored the images and all the time Awan was buying his chicken wrap, Moat was out of shot pointing his gun at Awan and he *was* a hostage?

No, that didn't happen.

Don't start inventing scenarios because you find yourself in a position of power. This is not *Midsomer Murders* now. Don't you start being in a movie just because Awan has showed you that was the way to go.

I was filling my pants.

These are my worst case scenarios, suddenly doubting everything and everyone, not expecting to be lucky as I never have been. My twin Darren would have got twelve returning a guilty verdict straight away. I was never that fortunate.

Later on today, or tomorrow, or heaven forbid, after yet another weekend of this, could I really face Kath being out and about, only for Ness and Awan to tool it past the house? This was going to be an agonising wait.

At 10.47 a.m., after the Judge explained the routes to verdict, the twelve members of the jury were finally sent out, thirty-six long, emotional days after we began and a whole 250 since I was shot.

That is a fair chunk of time and still it is as though it all happened yesterday. There haven't been good days during the months that have passed, only plenty of bad ones with some less bad ones.

So many days when Kath would be upset for no reason; others when I would get frustrated because I had put my clothes on the wrong way round. Plus, there was the constant medical attention from relentless tablets to newly discovered pellets.

Then came the endless media attention which I fuelled to keep the story alive for both the Blue Lamp Foundation and for justice itself.

I had acquired some sort of vague celebrity status – Carol Vorderman and Duncan Bannatyne became patrons of my charity and for a while I was a regular on the TV sofa. Millions had seen me break down on the *Pride of Britain* awards.

A band called The Strawheads even released a Christmas single in my name. I had lived a lifetime in a little over six months, and often the public front betrayed a private turmoil that cut through everything we had ever been or were dreaming of becoming. The physical scars were healing, but would never totally go away. The mental torture hadn't even run the first hundred metres yet.

But none of this mattered today. This was my *raison d'être*. The past would be paid for and the future would start here. There was nothing to do now except sit and wait.

We had been assigned a small room outside Court One on the third floor. Various well-wishers came and went.

Robin, Kath, Ash, Chris and Ali and Sav were all staying for the duration.

Chris even managed to stay awake.

We were nervous and now we just had to kill time. We had no lies and deceit to be disgusted by any more. Yes, soundbites from the trial would replay in our heads, but we were passive, just a ticking clock counting down, nowhere to go and nothing to do.

There were six other murder trials also in progress. In other private rooms, victims and witnesses were going through the same, all united by just one thing. Grief.

There had been around thirty arrests. Look at his sphere of influence if all those people had a best mate and a partner who inevitably had become aware of shifty behaviour. Suddenly, you have ninety people caught in the Moat web. Some of them might have kids too. The stain would seep from one generation to the next and the cycle would never break. What of those 300 who turned up for his funeral? Add to that, any inquiries still on-going, the time, money and emotion into my action against the police, Sue Sim's job in the balance, Paul Boatman the Taser entrepreneur who took his own life; and a million repercussions for anyone in Northumbria Police, and the North East's most famous case would be remembered for generations.

Even in death, Moat was still calling the shots.

I was less relaxed now, moving my initial sweepstake to 3.17, then on again to 3.27. There was a guess in at 4.30 and with every new time, came more self-doubt. Were my colleagues playing the sweepstake to win with the best times already taken or was this their honest reflection of how tough it was going to be? 'What's your gut feeling?' is just about the most useless, distracting question you can be asked.

And everybody did.

Then, as we sat there talking more small talk than I knew I had in me, the theories began again.

'Have you seen that member of the jury who keeps winking at Awan?' someone piped up.

'I don't know if he's winking or just has a nervous disposition,' another voice added.

There were several conversations going on around me and I couldn't isolate all the voices.

'Has he just started doing it or has this been going on all trial?'

Nobody had an answer for that.

By lunchtime Kath was so stressed that she took some fresh air for half an hour on a sandwich run but her nerves were so shot to pieces she barely brought a bun back with her. Who could eat anyway? Our stomachs were churning. Picture any neo-natal unit, any exam room, Driving Test Centre, job interview, first date or airport departure lounge and roll them all into one, then multiply that by a million, and you are probably about halfway to how we were feeling.

Ash relieved the tension for a moment.

'Here you are, has everybody seen this?' He said punching up a video on his mobile.

It was Moat's gay lover talking exclusively to *The Sun*, filling the room with laughter. We tried to remember the guy's name but nobody could, even though it had only emerged in the last couple of weeks. Today's news, tomorrow's chips.

That cheered me up no end. No disrespect or anything homophobic towards him, but I got the power back from Moat because I knew how desperate he was for his image, and this self-proclaimed steroid-ridden gangland hero would be seething at it all coming crumbling down. Not even Max Clifford could help here.

It got better and better as the lover offered his proof of the relationship. He described his locket with a picture of Moat in it. I was on the floor in hysterics.

It lifted our spirits and passed the time, and I was pretty sure that more would come out in the weeks that followed.

You never get a trial like this without some information being withheld. I had been told only yesterday that Ness's brother had just been released from prison too.

That confirmed everything I already knew about Moat's right-hand man.

By 4 p.m., there was nothing. All bets were now off. The sweepstake was dead in the water. We would be back in the morning for another go, and who knows how that night's sleep would affect the jury.

If there had been peer pressure from your classic middle-manager foreman, they would have a night to walk away from it, returning with fresh minds tomorrow. The reverse was true too that they could equally wake up bolt upright in the middle of the night when suddenly it all made sense. If they distrusted Robert Smith as a person, they could certainly see everything as 'reasonable doubt'.

It could go either way.

One thing was certain. Twelve more people with twelve more partners with twelve close friends were now in the Moat slipstream, and they too would understand later what I have felt on so many nights since last July. Moat would be joining them too in their sleep tonight.

FRIDAY 11 MARCH 2011

It was six minutes to three.

They didn't call it over the tannoy. Instead, Detective Chief Superintendent Jim Napier came for us personally and ushered us into the courtroom. We could barely take another moment in our little room, so suffocating and oppressive had it become. There wasn't any of the nervous laughter of yesterday.

We knew this was it.

It had still been an extraordinary morning waiting for this moment. How naive of us not to think that there would be another dramatic twist or a surreal turn of events.

As we sat there fidgeting waiting for the words that would send our train tracks in one of two new directions, Andrew Tweedy, the brother of Cheryl Cole, was being sent down in an adjacent courtroom for six years for his part in an armed robbery of a post office in Longbenton near Newcastle. I could see how this would end. I would be on the steps of the law courts later with Girls Aloud giving statements! Nothing more would surprise me.

But no, I wasn't the one in a movie. It was those two in the dock. The day of reckoning had come for Karl Ness and Qhuram Awan.

And there were fireworks.

First thing this morning the Judge addressed them both without the presence of the jury. The court was now full of extra security after Ness had been overheard in the back of the Group 4 van driving them in the morning.

'If we're found guilty, it's all going to kick off,' he was heard to say.

The Judge was brilliant, firm and ruthless to the pair of them. What a shame the jury *weren't* there when he told Awan he had watched him throughout the trial and had enough of his silly games.

'I've got the measure of you, and you hype it all up,' he told them straight, like a headmaster faced with naughty school children after it emerged that Ness had threatened to kill himself.

They couldn't have had their egos more battered.

'If there's any messing about in there, I won't hesitate to put you both in handcuffs,' he continued, to which the defence tamely objected.

My paranoia that the Judge had been leaning towards them was just that – fear. He wasn't messing today and this clearly put down a marker of what he expected to happen next.

Ness obviously had a high opinion of himself if he thought that his friends were going to go acka if he was sent down.

And they had all turned up this time.

The room was packed like it had never been before. I can only assume that their friends and family knew they were coming to say goodbye. Goodness, they weren't expecting to carry them on their shoulders out of the courtroom were they? Half of them hadn't been there yesterday, so despite the advice to us from the CPS that it could be as late as Monday, the defendants' mates seemed to be certain it was today. It perked me up. I read it as guilt.

'They'll come back at 2.15 this afternoon,' I had said at lunch.

That's why Jim ushered us in. Trouble was in the air.

I'd smelt it from deep in the early hours. My mind had been like a cyclone with all these objects flying around at speed. I wasn't having the 'not guilty' moment again, it was more like being bombarded with soundbites and images from the last five weeks all colliding into one.

When I got in the shower this morning I was talking to myself.

'Please, please, find them guilty,' I was almost praying – to whom I do not know.

I was that desperate.

'Kath, I can't go today,' I had said at breakfast, which I left untouched.

I was white like a ghost, sick with worry, shattered with no more than half an hour's sleep inside me.

It had all come down to this.

Ali had nailed the time spot on. When I said 2.15, she had said three, and it was now nearly that. My earlier sweepstakes had been naive.

'They won't find Awan guilty of possession of a firearm,' I predicted.

I was just talking for the sake of it.

Equally, I was now glad that the jury hadn't returned sooner, as much as it was killing me. It needed to look credible and thorough and on reflection, this was probably the correct amount of time to return a guilty verdict at the earliest possible moment.

There was a call on the intercom for the court police officer to return, and a request for security at the reception. I knew it was on a knife edge. On instinct, I wanted to go down myself to lock someone up and then I realised how useless I would be. Trouble was brewing.

'Oh, here we go,' I announced.

The tannoy made that noise it always made when someone was about to speak.

Then there was nothing.

The same thing happened for a second time.

Deathly silence.

I knew this was it.

'The verdicts are in David, it's time.'

That's when Jim Napier appeared at the door.

‡

Northumbria Police were controlling the situation, getting the right people in the room, and keeping any yob element one step behind. Two teams of Area Support Groups had been deployed to the court and were subtly positioned throughout the room. These are the heavies. The ASGs were *our* bouncers.

The moment had come.

How I longed for my sight just for this moment alone if not forever. I knew all eyes were on me.

Suddenly we were there.

What started out as a game of golf on Mia's twelfth birth-day ended here. Kath was clinging to me, shaking, tears rolling down her cheeks. My heart was beating overtime. Surrounded by my loyal friend Robin whom I had shouted at in the tension of the last few days, and my stoic son Ash who has never wavered as new responsibilities and burdens have changed the course of his life, I was amongst my own. My new-found friends Becky and Sally were nearby. I'm sure we could have made friends through better circumstances had we not met here. We were united now. Dotted throughout the courtroom were the friends of the enemy. I couldn't bear thinking that this crossroads in our life was to be shared with them too.

Everything stopped.

You could sense held breath all around you amidst a deaf-ening silence. What took a second to say lasted a lifetime. The five-second pause felt like ten minutes.

And then it came.

'Guilty,' said the foreman.

I put my head down so the press wouldn't see.

'Guilty,' he said again.

'Did I just hear that?' I asked myself.

'Guilty,' he continued, and suddenly it was a domino effect and I sat bolt upright. Ness and Awan sank to their knees, holding their heads in their hands.

'Get in!' I said to myself.

I could no longer feel my heart.

I heard the thud as Ness hit the floor. At the same time there was a huge release of air; the courtroom gasping for its lungs again after time stood still.

Kath was sobbing into my chest. I just looked down at the floor again. There were cries of yes all around us. Some of Ness's friends were in tears too.

My body went from lead to jelly. I could feel months of tension evaporating in a split second. Justice had been done.

And it had been unanimous.

The sole exception was that Awan was cleared of the fire-arms offence.

I felt so light.

This day meant so much to me. To Kath. To Mia and Ash. To Sally Brown and Becky. To Northumbria Police. To the people of Rothbury. To the NHS. To everyone connected with the Blue Lamp Foundation, and of course to all the kind souls who gave time, love and, most importantly, their thoughts to us in the days that followed 4 July and who still continue to do so.

'There have been a lot of people who have been seriously affected by this and I plan to address that next week,' Justice McCombe was spot on and spoke for all of us.

Ness and Awan's game of Jenga had just collapsed before their very eyes, and they too were unsteady on their feet as they were led away. This time, I didn't have the mental resource to send them parting words as I had done in the court after their testimony. They were about to learn a very hard lesson.

'I am not prepared to sentence you today. We'll adjourn and reconvene on Tuesday. Let me tell you now that all of these charges are extremely serious,' the Judge said.

I registered his disgust and took that as my cue to leave.

For the final time, I composed myself.

'Come on, we don't need to hear this bit,' I said to Kath.

I was desperate for Ness and Awan to see me leave.

Justice McCombe would take the weekend to read up on the guidelines on his sentencing powers. My guess is fifteen to twenty-five years for Awan, and thirty plus for Ness. They both had a long weekend to reflect that they were now just meaningless numbers as Category A prisoners and Ness would do well to register that his own mother gave evidence against him and then only irregularly returned to court. Both her sons had now been to prison. At least she had the dignity to walk away.

All my fears for the jury were unfounded. There were some good people out there after all. They hadn't been blinded by bullshit and had absorbed the salient points and overwhelming evidence, collectively arriving at the right decision in good time. My faith in humanity was restored. I had been wrong to doubt but I had done so out of fear.

Next we had to face the world.

I had prepared for this moment so many times, and I had seen so many people do this before. The press could wait. Nothing was going to interrupt the Tokyo tsunami and earthquakes anyway and my family came first.

Ash broke down in our private room. I have never known him like this. Months of pent up emotion spontaneously poured out. On instinct, I just grabbed him and kissed him. He had played his part many times over in a way my own family in Stafford could never replicate. I never got that affection from my dad and I wasn't allowing my mum back into my life just because seeing me on the news, bleeding and blinded, had awoken her after years of neglect.

'You will be with me for the rest of my life,' QC Robert Smith came by to hug me.

That meant so much that I – we – were more than just a job. I shall never forget that and I hope he enjoys the bottle of whisky that I gave him to remember me by.

At the back of my mind were the words I would say on the steps of the courtroom. They had been forming in my head all day and I knew their importance and the significance of the tone with which they were delivered. I had half of them ready. I just hoped they would come out in the right order.

I was conscious that Darren would be watching in Australia and that these images were going right round the world. This would be my last public act before I could do what we craved for so long – to shut the door tight and grieve privately.

There would be more shit ahead, of course. Awan's sister is a feisty character and is already talking of appeal. These are the usual soundbites in the aftermath and she will struggle against a unanimous verdict. I shall not let that ruin the moment that I have lived for since last year.

Today was my very own Independence Day.

Amazingly I feel like a twelve-year-old again, giddy with the result, ignoring, of course, that I am shattered, and that, as of tomorrow we face the world alone, still in dispute with the police, and with nothing bar the London Marathon to focus on and some mobility training on Monday, just to remind me of my disability.

The rest of my life is really just around the corner, and I don't know what lies beyond that turn in the road. I am liberated though, free from this sideshow that my life had become. Looking ahead, wallowing is not option, though I know I will always be David Rathband the blind cop, whom Moat shot.

Like David Blunkett, who rang to offer congratulations, I will be famous for being blind.

Equally, in the next couple of weeks Northumbria Police will, as promised, sit down with me and tell me all the crap they couldn't tell me before, and I am sure this is just the beginning.

Neil Adamson wants to talk me through the full video of the arrest.

I am proud of my colleagues, despite the initial flack that they received, and I think Neil is proud of how they got there. Part of *his* closure will be sitting down with me to tell me the whole story, much of which will go to the grave with us all.

Even today, I was still learning stuff.

A fee of £40,000 was arranged between a national newspaper and the recipient of one of Awan's letters. Neil had strong words with the reporter who had run the story. That's why during the Seven Nights in Rothbury, Northumbria Police rightly shut up shop. They couldn't make the mistake of litigating in public for the same reasons that I had never mentioned Ness and Awan in the period since the shooting.

I couldn't prejudice a trial.

Most people have only heard of Raoul Moat, but this was never going to be the Raoul Moat trial.

Yet, the reality loomed large. My claim against Northumbria Police was still pending, but whilst today has been a great day, the bigger picture was that Ness, Awan and Moat have taken away from me the job that I loved and I will never truly serve again as an officer for Northumbria Police. These could be my last moments in uniform, despite our brave words to the contrary. For £35,000, there aren't many people who would sacrifice both their eyes. I did it willingly and would still do the same tomorrow. My next hardest decision will be at what point the force and I agree to part.

Sue Sim wasn't there for the verdicts but she rang absolutely thrilled and had been updated hourly. She will now find out on 24 March about her job but, brilliant to the last, she has told the Police Authority that I am going back in April. In my soul, now I know for definite I will not be returning. That's absolutely clear to me. What to do on Monday is my next problem. After all this, a void is all that remains. I am empty, but in a good way. I still have emotion, but the heavy heart is gone. I've let the air out of my psychological balloon, and I know I will sleep tonight.

Closure?

I don't think so.

Better place? Yes, slightly.

When these two are out, I'll be in my seventies and they will be in their fifties. I can deal with that. Heaven only knows what the world will look like that then.

I couldn't care.

They will have spent twenty-three hours a day in their cell. That free hour will be for slopping out.

Bang.

That's the sound they will hear tonight as the door shuts on their life for good. By Tuesday their barrister won't even be speaking to them because he won't be getting paid. It's all over for Karl Ness and Qhuram Awan, and rightly so.

Bang.

Ness had listed on his Facebook page his philosophy as 'All police informers must fuckin rot, the horrible little kuntz.'

Bang.

That door was shutting.

Bang.

That made me happy. Visualising the key being turned set me free. There would be no more lies and no more bullshit.

Bang.

Chris Brown had kids. Moat had three. What destruction he left behind him. What a sad, terrible mess.

'I can't go back to prison,' the bastard Moat said on the night he shot himself.

Bang.

He had spent eighteen weeks inside for assaulting a minor. Who could have ever known it would end here?

Bang.

And now look at the consequences for his henchmen, let alone all of us in his slipstream.

Bang.

Night after night, they would hear that sound from within their walls. I hoped it was a metallic drumming that echoed for hours, as the warden went down the corridor shutting each of those doors one by one.

Bang. Bang. Bang.

As their cell door slammed shut, I prepared to join Sally Brown, a member of the CPS and Jim Napier on the steps of Newcastle law courts.

As we made our way down the steps of court, it was kicking off for one last time. A dozen or so lads were becoming rowdy at the bottom of the steps. Kath told me that one of them was identical to Moat. Just as we were walking into the cameras, sabotage was on the agenda.

'You couldn't make it up.'

This time it was Kath's turn to utter those words.

The police, sensing the worst, escorted them away.

It wasn't Moat's henchmen's henchmen.

It was Newcastle's finest calling card – the stag weekend, pissed out of their heads at half three in the afternoon, walking into our story – the groom looking like Raoul Moat.

'You couldn't make it up,' Kath said again.

Gazza, Mearsy and Tweedy hadn't shown up on this occasion but the comedy was still coming thick and fast. Has there ever been such a story so full of the extremes of brutality and absurdity all rolled into one?

It was time for my final role, summoning every remaining ounce of strength and courage to play it.

With my beautiful wife Katherine beside me, and my loyal son Ashley right behind me, I found the words I had been looking for.

'I have a lifetime ahead of me. They have a lifetime to reflect.'

I spoke as both a victim and as a witness.

And then I turned to Kath to wipe her tears away.

I had one last thing to say.

'It's over, Kath. It's over.'

EPILOGUE

The following Tuesday, Karl Ness and Qhuram Awan were sentenced to life imprisonment. Ness would serve a minimum of forty years and Awan twenty. There could be no appeal against the verdict.

Almost immediately, other trials connected to the Raoul Moat case began.

PC David Rathband's legal action against Northumbria Police continues and at the time of writing he has yet to return to work.

On Sunday 17 April PC David Rathband completed the London Marathon in six hours and forty-nine minutes.

The deadline for Sue Sim to be appointed Chief Constable came and went with no resolution, and then on 20 April, after a relaxation of Home Office rules previously standing in her way, she was awarded the top job.

PC David Rathband's story continues…

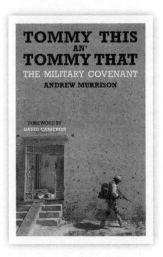

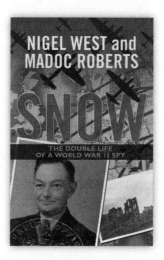